# Lawns and
# Ground Covers

*Other Publications:*

THE GOOD COOK

THE SEAFARERS

THE ENCYCLOPEDIA OF COLLECTIBLES

THE GREAT CITIES

WORLD WAR II

HOME REPAIR AND IMPROVEMENT

THE WORLD'S WILD PLACES

THE TIME-LIFE LIBRARY OF BOATING

HUMAN BEHAVIOR

THE ART OF SEWING

THE OLD WEST

THE EMERGENCE OF MAN

THE AMERICAN WILDERNESS

LIFE LIBRARY OF PHOTOGRAPHY

THIS FABULOUS CENTURY

FOODS OF THE WORLD

TIME-LIFE LIBRARY OF AMERICA

TIME-LIFE LIBRARY OF ART

GREAT AGES OF MAN

LIFE SCIENCE LIBRARY

THE LIFE HISTORY OF THE UNITED STATES

TIME READING PROGRAM

LIFE NATURE LIBRARY

LIFE WORLD LIBRARY

FAMILY LIBRARY:
  HOW THINGS WORK IN YOUR HOME
  THE TIME-LIFE BOOK OF THE FAMILY CAR
  THE TIME-LIFE FAMILY LEGAL GUIDE
  THE TIME-LIFE BOOK OF FAMILY FINANCE

# Lawns and Ground Covers

by

JAMES UNDERWOOD CROCKETT

and

the Editors of TIME-LIFE BOOKS

Watercolor Illustrations by
Allianora Rosse

TIME-LIFE BOOKS, ALEXANDRIA, VIRGINIA

Time-Life Books Inc.
is a wholly owned subsidiary of
TIME INCORPORATED

FOUNDER: Henry R. Luce 1898-1967

*Editor-in Chief:* Hedley Donovan
*Chairman of the Board:* Andrew Heiskell
*President:* James R. Shepley
*Vice Chairmen:* Roy E. Larsen, Arthur Temple
*Corporate Editors:* Ralph Graves, Henry Anatole Grunwald

TIME-LIFE BOOKS INC.

MANAGING EDITOR: Jerry Korn
*Executive Editor:* David Maness
*Assistant Managing Editors:* Dale M. Brown (planning),
George Constable, Jim Hicks (acting), Martin Mann,
John Paul Porter
*Art Director:* Tom Suzuki
*Chief of Research:* David L. Harrison
*Director of Photography:* Robert G. Mason
*Senior Text Editor:* Diana Hirsh
*Assistant Art Director:* Arnold C. Holeywell
*Assistant Chief of Research:* Carolyn L. Sackett
*Assistant Director of Photography:* Dolores A. Littles

CHAIRMAN: Joan D. Manley
*President:* John D. McSweeney
*Executive Vice Presidents:* Carl G. Jaeger,
John Steven Maxwell, David J. Walsh
*Vice Presidents:* Peter G. Barnes (Comptroller),
Nicholas Benton (Public Relations), John L. Canova (Sales),
Nicholas J. C. Ingleton (Asia), James L. Mercer
(Europe/South Pacific), Herbert Sorkin (Production),
Paul R. Stewart (Promotion)
*Personnel Director:* Beatrice T. Dobie
*Consumer Affairs Director:* Carol Flaumenhaft

THE TIME-LIFE ENCYCLOPEDIA OF GARDENING
EDITORIAL STAFF FOR LAWNS AND GROUND COVERS:
*Editor:* Robert M. Jones
*Assistant Editor:* Carlotta Kerwin
*Text Editor:* Betsy Frankel
*Picture Editor:* Adrian Allen
*Designer:* Leonard Wolfe
*Staff Writers:* Marian Gordon Goldman, Peter Wood
*Chief Researcher:* Joan Mebane
*Researchers:* Margo Dryden, Villette Harris,
Gail Hansberry, Ruth Silva, Diana Sweeney
*Design Assistant:* Mervyn Clay
*Staff Illustrator:* Vincent Lewis

EDITORIAL PRODUCTION
*Production Editor:* Douglas B. Graham
*Operations Manager:* Gennaro C. Esposito, Gordon E. Buck
(assistant)
*Assistant Production Editor:* Feliciano Madrid
*Quality Control:* Robert L. Young (director), James J. Cox
(assistant), Michael G. Wight (associate)
*Art Coordinator:* Anne B. Landry
*Copy Staff:* Susan B. Galloway (chief), Heidi Sanford,
Patricia Miller, Celia Beattie
*Picture Department:* Barbara S. Simon
*Traffic:* Jeanne Potter

CORRESPONDENTS: Elisabeth Kraemer (Bonn); Margot
Hapgood, Dorothy Bacon (London); Susan Jonas, Lucy T.
Voulgaris (New York); Maria Vincenza Aloisi, Josephine du
Brusle (Paris); Ann Natanson (Rome).
Valuable assistance was also provided by: Sue Wymelenberg
(Boston); William McK. Chapman (Charleston, S.C.);
Holland McCombs (Dallas); Jessica Silvers (Los Angeles);
Patricia Chandler (New Orleans); Carolyn T. Chubet,
Miriam Hsia (New York); Jocelyn Cox (Portland, Ore.);
Martha Green (San Francisco); Jane Estes (Seattle).

THE AUTHOR: James Underwood Crockett, a graduate of the University of Massachusetts, received an Honorary Doctor of Science degree from that University and has been cited by the American Association of Nurserymen and the American Horticultural Society. He has worked with plants in California, New York, Texas and New England. He is the author of books on greenhouse, indoor and windowsill gardening, and has written a monthly column for *Horticulture* magazine and a monthly bulletin, "Flowery Talks," for retail florists. His weekly television program, *Crockett's Victory Garden,* has been broadcast throughout the United States.

THE ILLUSTRATOR: Allianora Rosse, who provided the more than 100 delicate, precise watercolors of grasses and ground covers beginning on page 113, is a specialist in flower painting. Trained at the Art Academy of The Hague in The Netherlands, Miss Rosse worked for 16 years as staff artist for *Flower Grower* magazine. Her paintings and drawings have appeared in many gardening books.

GENERAL CONSULTANTS: Staff of the Brooklyn Botanic Garden: Louis B. Martin, Director; Robert S. Tomson, Assistant Director; Thomas R. Hofmann, Plant Propagator; George A. Kalmbacher, Plant Taxonomist; Edmond O. Moulin, Horticulturist. Raymond N. Eberhardt, County Extension Agent, Somerville, N.J. Joseph E. Howland, Professor of Horticulture, University of Nevada, Reno. Joseph J. Kern, Mentor, Ohio. Albert P. Nordheden, New York City. John Van Dam, Turf Farm Adviser, University of California Agricultural Extension Service, Los Angeles.

THE COVER: An emerald lawn near San Francisco, shown in full on pages 26-27, flows around islands of blossoming ground cover. In both color and texture, the Dalmatian bellflowers growing around the huge cypress trees contrast agreeably with the bluegrass of the lawn.

CONTENTS

# The lore of lawns 1

Whenever I ask homeowners, "What would you most want to see growing in your yard?" the answer I get is invariably the same: "A nice green lawn." It is easy to see why. The lawn is the basic element of most garden designs, linking together all the other plantings—trees, shrubs, flower beds—into a harmonious whole. More than that, a beautiful lawn has an emotional appeal that can sometimes be translated into spiritual comfort and sometimes into dollars-and-cents profit. The sight of a velvety lawn is like the sight of a mountain meadow in springtime or an oasis after a grueling drive across the desert. It offers peace and serenity, and an escape from the glare and hard surfaces of sidewalks and superhighways. And though no one can exactly measure the monetary value of a fine lawn, real estate agents know it exists—and that it usually represents an amount far above the cost of the lawn's installation.

The green of a lawn is usually grass, but not necessarily so. Lawns can be made of almost any plant that spreads fairly rapidly to cover the ground, and in certain localities ground covers other than grass are extremely popular, either as grass substitutes, or as companions for grass, to provide visual variety. Still, despite the importance of the nongrasses, grass continues to be the universal favorite. Given suitable growing conditions, it is the nearly perfect lawn-covering material—uniform in color and texture, soft and resilient, amenable to cutting and, despite the ritual grumbling about mowing the lawn, easy to take care of. Grass has remarkable recuperative powers; this is particularly true of the modern grasses that have been developed especially for lawns. Have you ever noticed how seldom you see "Keep Off the Grass" signs any more? This is because modern lawn grasses will take considerably more abuse than their predecessors could sustain. In many areas they can provide a surface more nearly maintenance-free than paving, and at a good deal less cost. They can be walked on constantly, sat on and used for every sort of outdoor activity from touch football and backyard putting practice to alfresco entertaining. Lawn fur-

*A cool green lawn of St. Augustine grass dominates the simple landscaping scheme of a Dallas, Texas, home. A curving bed of English ivy softens the brickwork of the steps and makes mowing around them easier.*

niture will not damage these improved grasses—witness the rapid growth of this special category of furniture. And even in the aftermath of a big party, bruised grass will generally recover within a matter of days.

Part of the lawn's monetary value may come from its role as a status symbol, for in many suburbs, the smoothness of the carpet of green in the front yard helps establish a man's standing in the community. The suggestion of gracious respectability conveyed by a good lawn may result from the sweeping stretches of carefully tended grass that have long been the mark of the homes of the upper classes in England. Many of the British nobility seem to reside in country mansions set in unbelievable emerald-green lawns—made perfect, according to an often repeated saying, through 300 years of tender care by armies of scythe-wielding gardeners. The English lawn had an aristocratic birth in medieval times in an orchardlike setting inside the castle walls, a place for lords and ladies to dance and dally. It was made of meadow grasses, which were kept short by beating and trampling them underfoot—a maintenance program that must have worked, for a poem often ascribed to Chaucer characterized the ideal grass as being "like unto green wool." Wild flowers crept in among the meadow grasses now and then, accounting for the references to "flowery meads," but no one seemed to mind. No doubt the flowers were very useful in garland weaving, a favorite diversion of medieval lords and ladies. Another diversion, lawn games, led in time to a lawn refinement, the "green plot," or "green," a rectangular plot of tended ground for playing at bowls or *paille maille,* a sort of croquet.

The making of a green plot could be a rather elaborate process. Here is the detailed description given by Gervase Markham in a book published in 1613, *Way to Get Wealth,* a title suggesting that, then as now, green making could be a lucrative business: "To fit a place for this manner of greene plot, it is requisite that it may be cleansed from all manner of stones and weedes, not so much as the rootes left undestroied, and for the better accomplishing hereof, there must boiling water be poured upon such endes of rootes as staying behind in the ground cannot be well pulled up, and afterwards the floor must be beaten and troden down mightily, then after this there must be cast great quantity and store of turfes of earth full of greene grasse, the bare earthe part of them being turned and laid upward, and afterward danced upon with the feete, and the beater or paving beetle lightly passing over them, in such sort that within a short time after, the grasse may begin to peepe up and put foorth small haires."

Although no one at the time seems to have questioned Markham's curious yet effective method of planting a lawn by laying sod

## THE HIGH COST OF PUTTING

*The most expensive and pampered plots of grass in the world are the putting greens of golf courses. A survey of professional greenkeepers around the U.S. shows that the cost of creating a typical lawn-sized (5,000 square feet) putting green is more than $2,500, and that the annual upkeep is around $750. The latter figure goes for the labor needed to: maintain the grass at its optimum height (which may be as low as ¼ inch and require four to seven mowings a week); water the green (daily in dry weather); roll it at least once in spring; fertilize it as often as once a week; and spray it when needed against insects, weeds and diseases.*

upside down, there was a good deal of discussion in his day of the relative merits of sod versus seeds, of grass versus nongrasses, and of the right place to look for good grass seeds. For a time many lawns were made of chamomile, a low-growing aromatic plant that can be beaten, rolled and cut just like grass. According to Shakespeare's Falstaff, chamomile grew faster the more you walked on it. It is still used occasionally today *(Chapter 5),* but other then-popular lawn coverings have long since been forgotten. Among them are Spanish clover grass; a plant called sanfoin, which was said to have "a pretty aspect" when in flower; and something named medick fodder, which sounds suspiciously like ordinary hay. One authority warned against hay. Seed from a common haystack, he said, was improper; better to look for seeds from "a clean up-land pasture."

Eventually the green plot, with its formal boundaries, was replaced by the sweeping lawns of what came to be known as the English garden. Its creators were a handful of landscape gardeners whose forte was "landscape scenery." The most fashionable of them was a man called Capability Brown, because of his habit of telling clients that their gardens possessed "great capabilities." The English garden was a romanticized version of nature, full of copses and winding streams, wandering paths, thickets and even a carefully manufactured ruin or two. It was long on sweeping vistas, especially sweeping vistas of turf. One of the best known of the landscape gardeners, Batty Langley, claimed in *New Principles of Gardening* (1728) that the formal gardens at Hampton Court, the royal residence on the Thames that was Henry VIII's favorite palace, would look much better if they were stripped of "those trifling plants of Yew, Holly, etc. . . . and made plain with grass."

## THE FAMILY OF GRASSES

Batty Langley's paving of grass for Hampton Court was presumably made from one of the few dozen lawn grasses in use today. All of them are meadow grasses, part of a far larger family, the graminae, whose members, some 5,000 strong, have made the earth habitable for mankind. Men have hunted over the grasslands, grazed their livestock on them, fenced them in, farmed them—and periodically fought over them. Genghis Khan sent his hard-riding armies across Asia and into Europe not only to conquer and rule but partly to gain new grazing lands for his nomadic people. And the range wars of the American West set cattlemen against farmers over the question of whether the frontier grasslands should be considered public or private property.

When the grasslands were tamed, they were most often planted in crops that are themselves grasses—corn, wheat, barley, oats, millet, sorghum, rice. Archeologists have found traces of these cereal grasses around the remains of Stone Age dwellings. An ancient document found in Sumer explains how to grow barley. In the Americas, the culture of corn formed the base of the civilizations of the Incas, Mayas and Aztecs.

The grasses, besides supplying man with his major source of food, have also served him in other ways, some of them grand, some humble. In the Far East the leaves of lemon grass are dried for a medicinal tea and crushed to provide a lemon-scented oil used as perfume. From another scented grass, citronella, comes the oil that has saved many a bare-armed vacationer from the bite of mosquitoes. Everywhere, all through history, the grasses have supplied the raw material for baskets, including the sweet-smelling vanilla grass baskets woven by Indians of eastern Canada. The waving plumes of pampas grass and the striped blades of ribbon grass have long been known for their ornamental value in gardens, but less well known is Job's tears, a grass native to Asia and Africa, whose porcelain-smooth, pea-sized seeds are used for beads. The king of all grasses, the towering bamboo, constitutes a building material par excellence in many parts of the world, not only because of its strength and light weight but also because the hard, shell-like coating of its seemingly varnished stem is naturally resistant to dampness.

ANATOMY FOR SURVIVAL

Bamboo's natural waterproofing is a layer of silica, which is chemically similar to sand and is part of the stems of all grasses. It is only one of several oddities in the characteristics of grass. Another is the plant's growth habit. Both leaves and stems grow from the bottom up, new growth appearing at the bases rather than at the tips. This fact explains why lawn grasses can be cut repeatedly with-

*(continued on page 15)*

# All the latest in lawn care

*"Country gentlemen will find in using my machine an amusing, useful and healthful exercise," claimed Edwin Budding of Gloucestershire when he applied to the British Patent Office in 1830 for a patent on the world's first lawn mower. While Mr. Budding may have overstated his machine's ease of operation, he did not underestimate its utility. Within a short time the mechanical mower had taken over from the scythe; its spiral cutting mechanism, borrowed in principle from a machine that sheared napped fabrics in textile mills, is essentially the same as that of reel mowers today. Many of the heavy early models had to be drawn by two men or by a horse or donkey, although manufacturers gradually developed machines light enough to be pushed by a woman or boy. With each improvement they touted their wares in advertisements like those shown here, from a garden magazine of the 1870s and 1880s. The ads were emblazoned with ringing testimonials, unconditional guarantees and the names of such royal patrons as Queen Victoria and the Russian Emperor.*

# THE "ARCHIMEDEAN"
## AMERICAN LAWN MOWER

WAS AWARDED

## HIGHEST PRIZE AT PARIS EXHIBITION, 1878;

and the Jury in their Report say :—

### "The 'Archimedean' did the best work of any Lawn Mower exhibited."

*The "Archimedean" was the only Lawn Mower used, and specially selected in preference to all other Mowers for Cutting the Grass on the most conspicuous parts of the Paris Exhibition Grounds. Also awarded*

**GRAND DIPLOMA of HONOURABLE MENTION, Vienna, 1873 | SILVER MEDAL, Vienna, 1870. | SILVER MEDAL, Hamburg, 1869.**

NOTE.—The "Archimedean" was specially selected from the Mowers exhibited at Vienna for constant use in the Exhibition Grounds, and gave great satisfaction ; and we have pleasure in calling attention to the following Testimonial, received from the Inspector of the Royal Gardens, Schönbrun, Vienna :—

"Your 'Archimedean' Lawn Mowers have been used for some time past at the Imperial Gardens, and I have great pleasure in stating that they have given perfect satisfaction. Their quick and good work prove them to be the best and most efficient machines of the kind."

### OPINIONS OF THE PRESS.

"The quickest, most simple, and most efficient Mower ever used."—*Gardeners' Chronicle.*

"Far superior to any of ours."—*The Field.*

"Remarkably easy to work."—*Gardeners' Mag.*

"We feel bound to recommend it to our readers as one of the best Mowers we have as yet made acquaintance with."—*Floral World.*

### PATRONIZED BY

HER GRACIOUS MAJESTY THE QUEEN,
HER IMPERIAL MAJESTY THE EMPRESS OF GERMANY,
THE LATE EMPEROR OF THE FRENCH,

HIS ROYAL HIGHNESS THE PRINCE OF WALES,
HIS IMPERIAL MAJESTY THE EMPEROR OF AUSTRIA,
THE VICEROY OF EGYPT,

And many of the Nobility and Gentry of Great Britain.

## CHIEF ADVANTAGES.

They are extremely LIGHT IN DRAUGHT, SIMPLE IN CONSTRUCTION, WELL MADE, and NOT LIKELY TO GET OUT OF ORDER.

They Cut LONG or SHORT, WET or DRY Grass, and do not clog.

They have no ROLLERS in FRONT of the Cutter, and therefore Cut the Grass as it GROWS, and do not miss the BENTS.

They work well on SLOPES, STEEP EMBANKMENTS, UNDER SHRUBS, and Close up to Trees, &c.

They can be USED either WITH or WITHOUT GRASS BOX, as may be desired.

## TESTIMONIALS.

From A. F. BARRON, Esq., *Royal Horticultural Society, Chiswick Gardens, W.*

"GENTLEMEN,—We have now had your 'Archimedean' Lawn Mower in use for several months, and without hesitation I can truly say it is the *best* and *most efficient* implement of the kind we have ever used."

From SHIRLEY HIBBERD, Esq., F.R.H.S., *Editor of the "Gardeners' Magazine."*

"The 'Archimedean' Lawn Mower has been in constant use in our experimental garden since Midsummer last, and has done its work remarkably well. It is a good sign when the men who have to do the work take to a thing of this sort without any persuading, and my men evidently regard it as a magical means of making mowing an amusement, for they fly through the work and enjoy the perfect shave quite as much as I who look on, and wonder we have so lately attained to real simplicity."

From the Rev. A. McALLISTER, *Plumstead Vicarage, London.*

"I have the pleasure of forwarding a cheque for the 'Archimedean' Lawn Mower which I had from you, and which does its work admirably."

## LIST OF PRICES:—

| | | |
|---|---|---|
| 6-inch, Suitable for Small Grass Plots .. .. .. .. ..£1 5 0 | 14-inch, Suitable for a Man .. .. .. .. .. .. ..£5 5 0 |
| 8 ,, ,, ,, ,, .. .. .. .. 2 2 0 | 16 ,, ,, ,, on Level Lawns.. .. .. 6 6 0 |
| 10 ,, ,, a Lady or a Boy .. .. .. .. 3 3 0 | 18 ,, ,, ,, and Boy .. .. .. 7 7 0 |
| 12 ,, ,, ,, ,, .. .. .. .. 4 4 0 | 20 ,, ,, ,, ,, .. .. .. 8 0 0 |

Grass Boxes for Collecting the Cut Grass, 5s. extra.

## DELIVERED CARRIAGE FREE AT ANY RAILWAY STATION IN THE UNITED KINGDOM.

*NO CHARGE FOR PACKING CASES, which are most convenient for storing the Machine during Winter.*

## EVERY MOWER IS WARRANTED TO GIVE AMPLE SATISFACTION,

And if not approved of may be returned within a Month, and the amount paid be refunded.

*Before purchasing a Lawn Mower send for Catalogue, containing Opinions of the Press and Testimonials from Gentlemen of high position in the Horticultural World, Noblemen, Clergymen, and others.*

**WILLIAMS & CO.** (Limited), Manufacturers and Patentees.

Selling } JOHN G. ROLLINS & CO., Old Swan Wharf, Upper Thames Street, London, E.C. } Selling
Agents } WALTER CARSON & SONS, La Belle Sauvage Yard, Ludgate Hill, E.C. ; and 21, Bachelor's Walk, Dublin. } Agents

*One of the earliest American machines, this mower took its name from the Greek who discovered the secret of the spiraling screw.*

# GREEN'S PATENT "SILENS MESSOR" AND OTHER LAWN-MOWING,
## ROLLING AND COLLECTING MACHINES FOR 1890.

*The Winners of every Highest Prize in all cases of competition, and they are the only Mowers in* **constant use**
*at all the Royal Gardens and at the Royal Horticultural Society's Gardens, South Kensington.*

**Patronised by—**
HER MOST GRACIOUS MAJESTY THE QUEEN on many occasions,
HIS ROYAL HIGHNESS THE PRINCE OF WALES,
THE KING OF THE BELGIANS.
The Late EMPEROR OF THE FRENCH.   The EMPEROR OF RUSSIA,
And most of the Nobility, Clergy, and Gentry of the United Kingdom.

**Royal Horticultural Society's Show, South Kensington, London,
June 3 to 7, 1881.** The "*Journal of Horticulture,*" of June 9, says:—
"MOWING MACHINES.—After a critical examination the Silver Medal was
granted to the old firm of world-wide fame, Messrs. T. GREEN & SON, of Leeds and
London. As the Machines are known in all lands where good lawns are cherished,
it is quite unnecessary to give any description of them."

**Upwards of 155,000 of these Machines have been Sold since they were first introduced in the year 1856,**
And thousands of unsolicited Testimonials have been received, testifying to their superiority over all others.
*They have been submitted to numerous practical tests in Public Competition, and in all cases have carried off the Highest Prize that has been given.*

**The following are their Advantages over all others:—**

1st. Simplicity of Construction—every part being easily accessible.   2nd. They are worked with much greater ease than any other.   3rd. They are the least liable to get out of order.
4th. They make little or no noise in working.   5th. They will cut either short or long Grass, wet or dry.

---

## SILENS MESSOR MOWER,
**With Improved Steel Chains and Handles.**

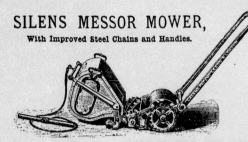

### SINGLE-HANDED LAWN MOWER.

|  |  | Price. |
|---|---|---|
| To cut 6 in., can be worked by a Lady | ... | £1 15 0 |
| To cut 8 in., do. do. | ... | 2 10 0 |
| To cut 10 in., do. by a strong youth | ... | 3 10 0 |
| To cut 12 in., do. by a man | ... | 4 10 0 |
| To cut 14 in., do. do. | ... | 5 10 0 |

### DOUBLE-HANDED LAWN MOWER.

| To cut 16 inches, can be worked by one man on even lawn ... | £6 10 0 | *To cut 22 inches, can be worked by two men | £8 10 0 |
|---|---|---|---|
| To cut 18 inches, do. man and boy... | 7 10 0 | *To cut 24 inches, do. do. ... | 9 0 0 |
| To cut 20 inches, do. do. ... | 8 0 0 | * If made stronger, suitable for Donkey, 30s. extra. | |

**These Mowers are the "Ne Plus Ultra" and "Acme" or perfection of all Lawn Mowers extant.**

Prices of Donkey, Pony, and Horse Machines, including Patent Self Delivery Box, or Side Delivery, with Cross-stay
complete, suitable for attaching to Ordinary Chaise Traces or Gig Harness :—

---

## GREEN'S PATENT GRASS EDGE CLIPPER

**Size and Price,** 7 inches
wide, 7 ins. diam., **£1 16s.**
Packing Case, 3s.

Specially designed to meet
a want which has long been
felt in cutting the overhang-
ing grass on the edges of
walks, borders, flower-beds,
&c., and do away with the
tedious operation of cutting
with shears.

☞ **A very useful and
serviceable Machine.**

---

### DONKEY and PONY MACHINES.

| To cut 26 inches | ... | ... | £14 0 0 |
|---|---|---|---|
| To cut 28 inches | ... | ... | 16 0 0 |
| To cut 30 inches | ... | ... | 18 0 0 |
| Leather Boots for Donkey | ... | ... | 1 0 0 |
| Leather Boots for Pony | ... | ... | 1 4 0 |

### HORSE MACHINES.

| To cut 30 inches | ... | ... | £22 0 0 |
|---|---|---|---|
| To cut 36 inches | ... | ... | 26 0 0 |
| To cut 42 inches | ... | ... | 30 0 0 |
| To cut 48 inches | ... | ... | 34 0 0 |
| Leather Boots for Horse | ... | ... | 1 9 0 |

The 26 and 28 inches can easily be worked by a Donkey, the 30 inches by a Pony, and the larger sizes by a Horse; and as
the Machine makes little noise in working, the most spirited animal can be employed without fear of it running away, or
in any way damaging the machine.   Packing Cases as per List, except when for export.

---

## Hurry's Daisy and Weed Extractor,
### *FOR LAWNS.*

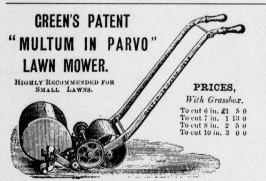

*No one possessing a Lawn should be without this wonderfully
useful little Invention.*

(See the *Gardeners' Chronicle* of August 2, 1879.)

### Directions for Use:—

The "Extractor" should be used as early in the year as
possible, in the following manner :—Place the tool over crown
of weed, and with a slight twist extract it.   The plugs so raised
discharge themselves (second pushing out first), and should be
replaced UPSIDE DOWN while still fresh.   The weed will die,
and the grass grow better where this has been done.   In using
mowing machine after "Extractor" the box should be left
off as much as possible, and the grass afterwards well rolled.
If these instructions are carried out any lawn may be effectually
freed from the obnoxious Plantain and Daisy roots which so
often offend the eye.   Lawn grass should always be kept short, to
avoid the weed seeding.

To be obtained of all Ironmongers and Florists.   Price 3s. 9d.
only.   In Polished Wood, fancy handle, 4s. 6d.

Wholesale Agent : THOMAS TILLEY, 12, Walbrook, London,
E.C.   Cambridge Agents : G. BEALES & CO. ;
*Or Carriage Free of the Inventor on receipt of P.O.O. for
4s. 3d. and 5s. 3d., payable at Cambridge or Sawston.*

**ALFRED F. O'C. HURRY,**
PATENTEE, PAMPESFORD, CAMBRIDGESHIRE.

---

## GREEN'S PATENT
## "MULTUM IN PARVO"
## LAWN MOWER.

HIGHLY RECOMMENDED FOR
SMALL LAWNS.

**PRICES,**
*With Grassbox.*

| To cut 6 in. | £1 5 0 |
|---|---|
| To cut 7 in. | 1 13 0 |
| To cut 8 in. | 2 5 0 |
| To cut 10 in. | 3 0 0 |

## GREEN'S Patent LAWN TENNIS COURT MARKER.
No. 2412.

**The Best Marker made.**
Size with 1 wheel for Ordinary
Courts, price **14s.**
Do., with 3 wheels, **17s.**

Size for Clubs and Large
Grounds, price **£1.**

Small Bag of Marking
Composition, **9d.**

---

**Delivered Carriage Free at all the principal Railway Stations and Shipping Ports in England, Scotland, and Ireland.**
*The largest stock of Mowers kept by any manufacturer is to be found at our London Establishment, SURREY WORKS, BLACKFRIARS ROAD, where Purchasers can make selection out of
several hundred Machines of Hand, Pony, and Horse Power, and have their Orders supplied the same day as they are received.*
**The above Machines are Warranted to give entire Satisfaction, otherwise they may be returned AT ONCE, Free of Cost to the Purchaser.**
N.B.—Those who have Lawn Mowers which require repairing should send them to either our Leeds or London Establishment, where they will have
prompt attention, as an Efficient Staff of Workmen is kept at both places.

GARDEN SEATS AND CHAIRS, AND HORTICULTURAL IMPLEMENTS OF EVERY DESCRIPTION, WIRE NETTING, &c., &c.

*Ads from the pages of the Gardener's Chronicle & Agricultural Gazette offer such marvels as "silent mowers," a weed extractor with*

# NEW PATENT GRASS-CUTTERS

*(PATRONISED BY THE BOARD OF WORKS).*

## W. CLARK, 232, Oxford Street, London, W.,

Begs to call public attention to a Patent Grass-Cutter he has just invented for use in the Garden and Farm, based upon the principle of the well-known "Clark's" Horse-clipping Machine, and which is, by its lightness of construction and rapidity of action, far preferable to the existing implements in use, and supplies a want long felt by every one who possesses a garden, namely, an instrument which will mow grass where inaccessible to the lawn mower, trim grass plot edges, clip Ivy and other creepers, also shrubs and trees, and keep in order Box borders and fancy Trees, &c.; all which this ingenious little instrument is capable of doing.

It is made in three sizes, to cut in breadth 8 inches, 12 inches, and 16 inches respectively; and is so easy in working, and at the same time so effective, that even ladies can work it without feeling fatigued, there being no occasion to stoop on account of the long wooden handles attached to the machine, and a greater quantity of work can be done in a given time than by any other method.

This invention is also applicable for Farm purposes—Reaping Corn and other Crops, Clover, Rye, &c., equally as well as accomplishing the objects for which it is required in the garden; and the cost being so small in proportion to the saving in time and quality of finish effected, it is placed within the reach of all, and needs but a trial to prove its superiority.

### PRICES.

| | |
|---|---|
| The 8-inch Machine, complete with Rollers and Tray | 21s. |
| Ditto, without Rollers and Tray | 18s. |
| The 12 inch Machine, complete with Rollers and Tray | 28s. |
| Ditto, without Rollers and Tray | 24s. |
| The 16-inch Machine, complete with Rollers and Tray | 38s. |
| Ditto, without Rollers and Tray | 33s. |

To be obtained of all Ironmongers, Horticultural and Agricultural Implement Manufacturers throughout the Kingdom, and of the Patentee,

## W. CLARK, 232, OXFORD STREET, LONDON, W.

---

### THE PATENT

# "EXCELSIOR."

### THE SIMPLEST AND BEST LAWN MOWER FOR ALL REQUIREMENTS.

HAS NEVER BEEN BEATEN IN OPEN COMPETITION.

### The Best and Lightest-running Hand-power Mower in the Market.

The "Excelsior" cuts the closest of any Mower, collects the grass, rolls the ground, and leaves the lawn level, with a surface like velvet.

---

## CAN BE USED WITH OR WITHOUT COLLECTING-BOX.

The "Excelsior" Horse-power Mower is well-known, and is highly successful in work. It is used on many important Estates, Cricket Grounds, and Public Parks. Its draft is lighter than that of any other Horse or Pony Mower, and is warranted to give satisfaction.

---

### Registered

# GARDEN ROLLER BARROW.

This light, elegant, and useful combination of the necessary Garden Implements, the Roller and the Barrow, for Lawns and Walks, solely supplied by

### POLLARD, JEPHSON, AND CO.
Bear Garden, New Park Street, Southwark, London, S.E.

---

# B. HIRST AND SONS, Britannia Works, Portland Street, Halifax.

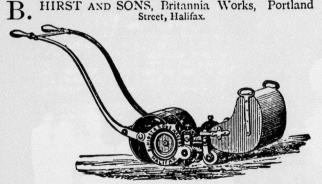

B. HIRST AND SONS call special attention to their PATENT FLEXIBLE SELF-SHARPENING and SELF-COLLECTING LAWN MOWING MACHINES, which can also be used as Garden Rollers. Intending purchasers for the present season should send for Illustrated Catalogue and Price List of these Lawn Mowing Machines. The demand for B. HIRST AND SONS' Patent Lawn Mowing Machines has already been great. These Machines are acknowledged to be the best for keeping Bowling Greens, Lawns, and Croquet Grounds in order. Shipping orders promptly attended to.

---

# HAND MACHINE.

*Every Machine is warranted to give entire satisfaction, and if not approved of can be returned unconditionally.*

## PRICES OF HAND MACHINES.

| | | | | |
|---|---|---|---|---|
| To cut 10 inches | £3 10 0 | | To cut 18 inches | £7 10 0 |
| ,, 12 inches | 4 10 0 | | ,, 20 inches | 8 0 0 |
| *Suitable for a Lady.* | | | ,, 22 inches | 8 10 0 |
| To cut 14 inches | £5 10 0 | | ,, 24 inches | 9 0 0 |
| ,, 16 inches | 6 10 0 | | | |
| *Suitable for one person.* | | | *Suitable for two persons.* | |

Packing Cases are charged at the following low rates, viz.:—For the 10 and 12 inch Machine, 3s.; 14 and 16 inch, 4s.; 18 and 20 inch, 5s.; 22 and 24 inch, 6s. Parties providing themselves with Lawn Mowers are recommended to purchase the cases in which to stow them away when not in use, to prevent them from getting damaged; if returned, two-thirds will be allowed for them.

*The above Prices include Free Delivery to all the principal Railway Stations and Shipping Ports in England, Ireland, and Scotland.*

### PRIZE MEDALS AWARDED TO GREEN'S PATENT LAWN MOWERS.

First Prize Medal at the International Exhibition, London, 1862.
First Prize Medal at the International Exhibition, Dublin, 1865.
First Prize Medal at the Namur Exhibition.
First Prize Medal at the Gand Exhibition.
First Prize Medal at the Laeken Exhibition.
First Prize Medal at the Lineene Exhibition.
First Prize Medal at the Brussels Exhibition, on two occasions.
First Prize Medal at the Hamburg Exhibition.

T. GREEN AND SON did not exhibit at the Paris Exhibition, 1867.

GREEN'S PATENT LAWN MOWERS combine all the advantages of self-sharpening, and when the cutters become blunt by running one way round, they can be reversed again and again, bringing the sharp edge of the cutters against the bottom blade, which operation can be done by any inexperienced person, owing to the peculiar adaptation of the Machine, which is possessed by no other.

*N.B. All Orders are executed on the day they are received, either from our Leeds or London Establishment.*

---

*plain or fancy handles, leather boots for donkeys to wear on the lawn and a hand grass cutter modeled on a horse-clipping machine.*

# GARDEN ROLLERS,
## SUITABLE FOR LAWNS, BOWLING GREENS, DRIVES, GRAVEL WALKS, &c.

These Rollers are made in halves, and are much easier to work than when cast in one piece. The edges are rounded off to prevent any marks being left on the Walks or Grass; a counterbalance handle is fitted to each Roller.

### PRICES.

| | | | | | | | | | |
|---|---|---|---|---|---|---|---|---|---|
| Roller, 18 Inches Diameter, | x | 20 Inches Long | .. | .. | .. | .. | .. | £3 | 0 0 |
| ,, 20 ,, ,, | x | 22 ,, | ,, | .. | .. | .. | .. | 3 | 10 0 |
| ,, 24 ,, ,, | x | 26 ,, | ,, | .. | .. | .. | .. | 4 | 10 0 |
| ,, 26 ,, ,, | x | 28 ,, | ,, | .. | .. | .. | .. | 6 | 0 0 |
| ,, 30 ,, ,, | x | 32 ,, | ,, | .. | .. | .. | .. | 7 | 10 0 |

### ROLLERS FITTED WITH SHAFTS SUITABLE FOR A HORSE OR PONY.

| | | | | | | | | | |
|---|---|---|---|---|---|---|---|---|---|
| Roller, 30 Inches Diameter, | x | 32 Inches Long | .. | .. | .. | .. | £10 | 0 0 |
| ,, 30 ,, ,, | x | 36 ,, | ,, | .. | .. | .. | 10 | 15 0 |
| ,, 30 ,, ,, | x | 42 ,, | ,, | .. | .. | .. | 11 | 15 0 |
| ,, 30 ,, ,, | x | 48 ,, | ,, | .. | .. | .. | 13 | 10 0 |
| ,, 30 ,, ,, | x | 60 ,, | ,, | .. | .. | .. | 15 | 10 0 |
| ,, 30 ,, ,, | x | 72 ,, | ,, | .. | .. | .. | 17 | 10 0 |

## COLEMAN AND MORTON'S HAND WATER-CART and GARDEN ENGINE.

For use in Gentlemen's Gardens and Grounds. The delivery valve ca be worked at the outlet when filling a watering-pot. It holds 35 gallons. The Spreader for Watering Lawns, &c., can be removed at pleasure.

Price with Spreader .. .. .. .. £5 5 0
Force Pump for Watering Trees, &c. .. 2 2 0 extra.

— COLEMAN AND MORTON, London Road Iron Works, Chelmsford.

## WILLIAMS' PATENT "ARCHIMEDEAN"
### AMERICAN LAWN MOWER

**American Lawns.**

### THE AMERICAN PATENT
### "ARCHIMEDEAN" LAWN MOWER

is admitted the best Machine ever brought out for the purpose; because it is durable, simple, and performs its work better and with LESS THAN HALF the power of other Lawn Mowers, and will do double the amount of work.

Sole Wholesale Agent for the United Kingdom,
JOHN G. ROLLINS, American Merchant, Old Swan Wharf, London.

## CARTERS'
## MAGNIFICENT LAWNS,
### Awarded the only First Prize
AT THE
### PARIS EXHIBITION.

CAUTION.—PARIS LAWNS.—The best Lawns at the Paris Exhibition (as certified by the International Jurors) were formed with Carters' Fine Lawn Grass, and were awarded the First Prize and only Gold Medal. All other competitors, English as well as Foreign, received Second and Third Prizes only.

*Lawn rollers, watering carts, gold-medal grass seed and a mower for ladies lightened the gardening chores of the 19th Century.*

out destroying the plants—mowing removes only the mature tissue that would eventually die anyway, leaving untouched the fresh young tissue that keeps the plants flourishing.

The leaves of the grass plant are different in form and behavior from those of most other plants. They grow from stem joints, first in one direction, then in another, and each leaf is divided into two distinct parts. One part is a sheath that wraps around the stem; the other is the sword-shaped upright blade—sometimes the blade is rapier thin and sometimes, as in bamboo, it is as broad as the blade of a Scottish claymore.

Many grasses flower in great clusters so heavy that they bow the stalks into arching canes. Yet the individual flowers of which the clusters are composed are rather nondescript, having neither fragrance nor bright color, because these insect-attracting characteristics are unneeded. Grasses do not rely upon bees as middlemen in their sexual life. Either they are pollinated by the wind or they are self-pollinating. Some grasses pollinate their own seeds, each plant containing within itself both the male and female organs for reproduction. And a few—notably the bluegrasses—are able to reproduce either sexually or by a kind of self-pollination; their seeds often develop without fertilization.

Grasses have developed some marvelous mechanisms for ensuring the continuity of their species. In the barren waste of the polar regions there are several tiny but tenacious grasses that hold fertilized seed until the seed sprouts, then drop it to the ground —giving each new plant a fast start in the land of short summers. Other grasses send their seed over great distances on membranous wings that keep them afloat on air currents, or on bearded extensions that behave like kites. The seeds of one of these high-flying beard grasses, Vesey grass, have been scooped up by traps in airplanes 4,000 feet above the earth.

Curiously, the most effective agent in the spread of grasses may be man himself, who has carried the seed, by chance or design, to every new place he has ventured. Bluegrass, for instance, is not a native of Kentucky, though the first English settlers who crossed the Appalachian Mountains in the middle of the 18th Century found it growing there in abundance. It is a European grass whose ancestry goes back at least to Greek and Roman times, and it probably reached Kentucky in hay brought for the cattle of the 17th Century French missionary-explorers who established trading posts in the Ohio River valley. Similarly, Bermuda grass, despite its name, is thought to be a native of Africa and has long been grown in India, where it is mentioned in the Vedas, sacred literature of the Hindus, as Preserver of Nations for its role in feeding the country's cattle. The first Bermuda grass seed to arrive in America is believed to have come in cattle fodder with Fernando de Soto's ships in 1539, and later, seeds came directly from Africa in the holds of slave ships, where the grass was used for bedding and for animal feed. (Man carried more than grass seeds; he also spread weeds. Broad-leaf plantain, the all-too-familiar garden weed, was never seen in America until the white man came; because of its shape and its source Indians called it "white man's foot.")

## BROADENING THE CHOICES

As the demand for lawn grasses grew, men began to intervene deliberately in the plants' natural distribution—and indeed in their natural breeding processes. The cultivation of existing grasses and the discovery of new ones became more and more scientific, and more and more profitable. Plant explorers went to the ends of the earth in search of new grasses, and botanists monitored the life cycle of grasses in laboratories and agricultural experiment stations to improve existing strains and create hybrids. Often the work of a single man was enough to introduce a whole new grass type. Merion bluegrass, which produces an exceptionally dense, smooth lawn, was spotted growing on the 17th green of the Merion Golf Club in Ardmore, Pennsylvania, by a sharp-eyed greenskeeper, Joe Valentine. The popular southern grasses, Zoysia and centipede grass, were brought to this country from Asia by a man named Frank Meyer, who served for many years as a plant explorer for the U.S. Department of Agriculture. In fact, the seeds of centipede grass arrived here when Meyer's luggage was brought back to the U.S. after he had been killed in an accident on China's Yangtze River.

The painstaking search for naturally produced new varieties continues. But today it is becoming more and more practical to create improved grasses in the laboratory. Man-made hybrids of bluegrass, for example, would have been impossible until recently, for a key fact about this species' life was unknown. The bluegrasses belong to that group of grasses that multiply by a type of asexual reproduction; more than 90 per cent of the time they produce viable seeds without normal fertilization. Consequently the only way of crossing one strain with another is to catch a plant just as its flowers open, before the seeds start developing by themselves, and at that moment to fertilize it with pollen from another plant. But, until the mid-1960s no one had ever devised a practical method of making hybrids. At that time a team of plant geneticists at Rutgers University in New Jersey decided to get to the bottom of the matter and put a round-the-clock watch on bluegrass. One of the team, a young Korean scientist named Sang Joo Han, had the nighttime tour of duty, and he noted that bluegrass flowers customarily opened between 1 and 3 o'clock in the morning. Once the plant had been caught in the act, it was relatively simple to fertilize it with

## THE BOOMING LAWN BUSINESS

*To plant and care for some 40 million residential lawns covering more than five million acres in the U.S., Americans spent over a billion dollars in 1970. More than $55 million went for grass seed, almost $285 million for lawn mowers, over $200 million for fertilizers, $130 million for chemical soil conditioners and pesticides, and $350 million for such items as hoses, sprinklers, spreaders, edgers, wheelbarrows, hoes, rakes and shears.*

the pollen of another strain. The Rutgers team has since produced some 7,000 new strains of bluegrass. The hybrids grow side by side in patches on an enormous checkerboard test field, where they are being observed in the hope of finding some that are superior to known bluegrass strains.

The search for new varieties has led to lawn grasses that are far better than those of even a generation ago. Once fine-bladed grasses were considered exceptionally fragile; now many such grasses will take treatment almost as rough as the kind their coarser relatives will endure. And there are currently so many strains and mixtures of lawn grasses, each of which has its own merits and drawbacks, that you must make a careful choice, whether your intention is to nurture the lawn you already have, replant a small section or start an entirely new lawn. The characteristics and culture of the 13 most important types (and of many of their varieties) are described in the encyclopedia of lawn grasses in Chapter 5.

The choice of a lawn grass is governed by a variety of things, and the first of these is climate. In North America lawn grasses are grouped into three major climate categories: warm-climate grasses, cool-climate grasses and dry-land grasses. Cool-climate grasses prevail north of the wavy line that runs east-west on the map on page 150; warm-climate grasses predominate in the regions south of this line. Members of the third category, the dry-land grasses, are used primarily in certain areas of the West where the lack of moisture makes it difficult or impossible to grow other strains. Within these three broad categories, many individual species of grass have special preferences as to fertilizer and soil acidity or alkalinity; these factors are indicated under each grass's separate listing in the encyclopedia section.

THE ROLE OF CLIMATE

The territorial imperatives of the grasses are greatly influenced by elevation. In the eastern part of the country, for instance, the Appalachian Mountains carry the range of cool-climate grasses down into northern Alabama and Georgia. In the West the Rockies extend the range of these same grasses into the high country of Arizona and New Mexico. Of course the demarcation lines are not lines at all, but transitional zones—and rather fuzzy ones at that. Locally, they can be affected by such things as exposure—that is, by whether a slope faces north or south—or by the amount of sunlight or shade the site receives. Cool-climate grasses sometimes do beautifully on southern lawns, for example, when the direct rays of the sun are filtered by the leaves of trees.

While both cool-climate and warm-climate grasses can provide fine lawns, the dry-land grasses are coarse in texture and generally gray green in color. They are, curiously enough, the only indigenous American lawn grasses—such kinds as buffalo grass and grama grass blanketed the virgin prairie, and the tough turf of buffalo grass supplied the sod for the pioneers' sod huts. These native types are still prized for their sturdiness in some localities (particularly in Area D on the map) where rainfall is sparse and regular watering impractical. But where moisture can be supplied regularly, most gardeners choose grasses of other types.

Cool-climate grasses survive the rigors of northern winters, languish in the heat of summer, but retain some trace of green during most of the year. There is a seemingly endless number of varieties but three major kinds are those most often grown—bluegrasses, fescues and bent grasses. Bent grass is the aristocrat of the group. Fine as silk, soft as velvet, it is the grass often associated with the traditional English lawn, and in fact it does superbly well in the gentle, drizzly British climate. On American lawns bent grass needs a great deal of care, the kind that usually is provided only by professional gardeners. Regular watering and fertilizing are essential, and so is attention to the control of disease; bent grass is host to almost every known fungus that attacks lawn grass. Except on golf courses, where bent grass's affinity for close cropping suits it ideally to the requirements of putting greens, and in the Pacific Northwest, which has a climate closely resembling that of England,

## HOW A GRASS PLANT GROWS

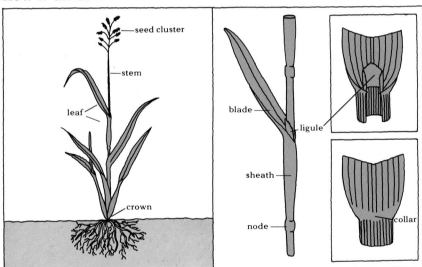

*A grass plant is shown at left, with a close-up section of its stem in center and details of a leaf at right. The stem grows from the base, or crown, and ends in a seed cluster. Joints, or nodes (middle drawing), divide*

*the stem. From each node springs a leaf, which starts as a sheath around the stem, then flares outward. At the point of flare is a curved section, or collar (lower right), with its ligule (upper right), which grips the stem.*

this type is, understandably, seldom used on American lawns.

Most cool-climate lawns are planted in fescue and bluegrass. Fescues are sturdy grasses that demand a well-sharpened lawn mower. On the other hand, a fescue lawn does not have to be watched over. Fescues tolerate sun or shade (provided the shade is not too deep); they can be grown in poor sandy soil, under drought conditions and with very little fertilizer. Bluegrass is generally considered to be the best all-purpose lawn grass because it combines both beauty and practicality. Its color is a clear, rich green (the "blue" is a reference to the bluish cast of a field of unmown plants while they are flowering), and it produces a thick, soft turf that is both pleasant to walk on and very sturdy—some types of bluegrass are standard choices for the turf of football fields.

GRASS MIXTURES

Sometimes a single strain of grass is used alone, but more often several types of grass are combined. The reasons are very practical. Although a lawn of one kind yields a superbly uniform turf, unvarying in color and habit of growth, and may be exceptionally resistant to certain kinds of lawn damage, it suffers serious drawbacks. For one thing, it may be more demanding. Merion bluegrass, for instance, requires more fertilizer than do other bluegrasses. Also, a pure stand of grass makes a much more vulnerable lawn. Though it may resist one disease or one kind of lawn trouble, its susceptibility to another leaves the lawn open to catastrophe. If the single grass fails, the lawn is wiped out. And no single type of grass is likely to suit every part of a lawn. Most lawns, even relatively small ones, contain some areas that are shadier than others, or wetter than others or more susceptible to drying out. If you plant a mixture of lawn grasses, you are in effect planting different grasses in each area. By a process of natural selection the seedlings that are most suitable to shade will take over in the shady places, while those that prefer sun will predominate in sunny locations.

Because mixtures offer so many advantages, I prefer them. But you must consider their components carefully before buying one. Some are formulated to give undue weight to what I call the impatience factor. Soon after a new lawn is seeded, most neophyte lawn owners begin to look for results. Seedsmen realize this and so they include in their mixtures "nurse" grasses, quick-sprouting, fast-growing types that provide a temporary cover of green until the slow-growing, more permanent and more desirable grasses can develop. One species commonly used for this purpose is rye grass. It comes in two forms, annual and perennial, and both have been frowned upon by most turf experts. For one thing, rye grass is cheap and its seeds are large and bulky, so that a mixture provides less grass per pound than finer seeds do. For another, many experts feel that in the role of nurse grass, rye grass steals moisture and fertilizer from the more valued grasses and should properly be called a robber grass. And finally, the common forms of rye grass are coarse-bladed and unattractive. New improved strains, however, have more or less removed this last objection. Among them is the variety called Manhattan rye grass, which has been developed from rye grasses that were found growing in New York City's Central Park. Sown in a mixture, it may still rob other grasses of some food and moisture, but it has shiny dark leaves and a fine texture, and it is longer lived than the older rye grasses.

The problems of selecting seeds and seed mixtures are mainly a concern for northern gardeners, for most southern lawns are not started from seeds but from pieces of living plants. The reason is botanical; many of the finer varieties of warm-climate grasses are hybrids. They may provide seeds, but some of their seeds are sterile, and in any case, the seeds of hybrids seldom produce new plants that resemble their parents. Most of the warm-climate grasses spread by sending out lateral stems from which new plants take root and grow at intervals. Bits or clumps of these stems, which are called rhizomes if they grow below the ground and stolons if they creep along the surface, are simply placed in the ground to spread and grow together, forming a lawn.

Because a warm-climate lawn is generally developed from the spread of a relatively few living plants, such a lawn is most often of a single species of grass. The four most popular Southern grasses are Bermuda grass, Zoysia, St. Augustine grass and centipede grass. Of these Bermuda grass is most widely used. It spreads very rapidly —the stolons will run 5 or 6 feet in a year.

Zoysia, although it is classified as a warm-climate grass, will survive winter weather as far north as Boston—at least some Zoysias will do so, in certain protected situations. The Zoysias are formidably vigorous grasses; they grow so thick they keep out crab grass—a capacity that accounts for the popularity of Zoysia lawns in areas where crab grass is a severe problem. And their resistance to damage from salty sea spray makes them a frequent choice for oceanside lawns even in the North.

St. Augustine grass and centipede grass are used mainly in the Deep South and along the Gulf Coast. Neither tolerates much cold and neither produces an ideal lawn—each has its virtues. St. Augustine grass, brought to the American mainland from the West Indies, is blue green and coarse, but its natural habitat is the seashore and it is tolerant of salt air and ocean spray; it is widely used on lawns in Florida. Centipede grass is often called "poor man's grass" because it gets by on so little food and moisture—in fact it actually seems to resent too much fertilizer.

All these warm-climate grasses thrive in hot weather and are killed by prolonged exposure to freezing temperatures. Most of them survive mild frost, but when the weather gets cool in fall they become dormant and turn brown. Zoysia, in particular, loses its green color at the first touch of autumn frost and stays brown until after the last frost of spring. Many southern gardeners simply accept a brown lawn for the winter season. Some, distressed by the brown expanses around their houses, spray the dormant lawn with green dye. But most people who want a green lawn in winter use a technique known as overseeding. In fall they spread over the existing turf seeds of a cool-climate grass, usually an annual such as rye. The cool-climate grass quickly germinates and grows well, its green hiding the dormant brown, until warm weather returns and the permanent grass of the lawn takes over once more.

Although there are a great many cultivation techniques and grass varieties, the choice of fundamentally different grass types is nonetheless limited. Every grass belongs to the same botanical family and within that family only a few botanically distinct genera are used for lawns—the 13 listed in Chapter 5 include all the important lawn grasses. But if you decide to cover some of your ground not with grass but with the plants that are loosely categorized as ground covers, the choice dramatically broadens. Chapter 5 lists 88 different kinds and within these are numerous varieties, many of which are distinctly different from one another in appearance and habit. Ground covers often do what grasses do and are often thought of as grass substitutes—a sort of second-class citizenship they do not deserve, for in some respects they are better than grass. I am thinking, for instance, of dichondra, a ground cover commonly used for lawns in the desert areas of California and the Southwest. It is often admired by visiting easterners who would be delighted to give it lawn room back home, except for the fact that dichondra cannot stand cold weather. A very tiny evergreen vine with round cup-shaped leaves, it creates a smooth, even turf sturdy enough to walk on. It does require regular watering but it gets by acceptably on a once-a-month mowing.

Most ground covers, however, do not resemble lawn plants at all. That is precisely why so many gardeners prize them. They may be rough or fine, smooth or billowy, green, bronze, gray or flashed with bright color. They grow in the places where grass will grow and in other places where grass will not—deep shade, rocky or excessively moist soil, steep, rainwashed slopes. They, combined with the grasses, provide the variety that enables you to make your grounds enjoyable, useful and admirable—without the services of a small army of scythe-wielding gardeners deployed for 300 years.

USING GROUND COVERS

# Coverings to enhance the garden floor

No one can say when the term "ground cover" was first coined to distinguish between the most popular ground cover —grass—and all the other low-growing plants that can also enhance the home and garden. Originally the distinction was unnecessary. Ernest H. Wilson, the noted botanist, describes nature's own ground cover this way: "The depths of the tropical forests are carpeted with a wondrous miscellany of plants, the open treeless areas of the world with grasses and herbs in great variety, the alpine regions with herbs and low shrubs, endless in species, which usually bear richly colored flowers, the boreal regions . . . with low, trailing, stem-rooting plants, many of which are evergreen in character." Gathered from all over the world by men like Wilson, cultivated and hybridized for domestic use, these are the ground covers of today's gardens. Too few enjoy the popularity they deserve.

The favored ground cover is, of course, mowed grass, and its popularity comes from those magnificent lawns surrounding the stately homes of England. England has a good natural climate for grass—cool and moist—and once upon a time there were sheep to graze on it and armies of gardeners to scythe and roll it. The English bowled and played croquet and even lawn tennis on it. And then, about 1830, Mr. Edwin Budding invented the mechanical lawn mower.

Now every homeowner could be a country squire even if all he had was an eighth of an acre. Along with the motorcar, a fine lawn eventually became a Western status symbol, and so pervasive was its influence on suburban landscaping that other ground covers were virtually never considered. Finally, however, a better proportion is being achieved. No other ground cover is as durable underfoot as a grass lawn, or produces as satisfying a sense of orderliness. But with all of nature's vines and creepers, tufted grasses and dwarf bushes to choose from—as well as a multitude of hybrids that plant breeders have developed over the years—the gardener who restricts himself to a lawn alone is missing the chance to add a fascinating, varied and personal dimension to his garden floor.

*With harmonizing shades and textures, native chaparral in Southern California complements a Kentucky bluegrass lawn.*

# Blending lawns with ground covers

"Nothing is more pleasing to the eye than green grass kept finely shorn," wrote Sir Francis Bacon. The famous 17th Century philosopher and essayist added, however, that the lawn—or green, as he called it—ought to be accompanied by a heath: "some thickets made only of sweetbrier and honeysuckle, and some wild vine amongst; and the ground set with violets, strawberries, and primroses . . . wild thyme, pinks, germander . . . periwinkle, roses, juniper, holly, barberries . . . kept with cutting, that they grow not out of course."

The heath that Sir Francis described was made up largely of what is now called ground cover, and although the landscape he conceived "ought not well to be under thirty acres," the principles he outlined apply equally to a suburban lot of today. A good lawn is far more pleasing when it is skillfully blended into the landscape. And its appearance is even more enhanced when some harmonious ground covers are blended in with the lawn itself. The possible variations are almost endless, limited only by the availability of ivy and vines, juniper and bellflower, and all the other ground covers that can be interspersed with and contrasted with the even carpets of lawn. Lawns that slavishly follow the straight lines projected on some land developer's drafting board, or those that simply carpet the entire outdoor space, will inevitably lack interest. As some of the possible combinations shown on these and the next two pages illustrate, the proper use of ground covers adds an entirely new dimension to the lawn.

*The contrasting textures of Algerian ivy and a dichondra lawn magnify the air of order and neatness around a home in Pacific Palisades, California. Dichondra, a tough and drought-resistant plant, is technically a ground cover, but because of its small, dense leaves it is often used as a lawn in California and the Southwest.*

The owners of this Southern California home have achieved a harmony of textures, colors and lines with a red brick walk curving through a green expanse of dichondra and past a long white fence. The walk is accented by beds of "needlepoint," a kind of English ivy whose coarse texture contrasts with the dichondra lawn.

A well-balanced job of landscaping a Los Angeles home contrasts a satiny lawn on one side of the driveway with a billowy mass of tamarix juniper on the other. The choice of tamarix juniper, a low-growing bush, permits a driver to have a clear view of the street when backing out. Japanese boxwood accents a wall at the entrance.

*A stand of gnarled cypress trees rises out of beds of dainty blue-blossomed Dalmatian bellflowers on a blended bluegrass lawn in Hillsborough, California. In addition to framing the trees in an attractive manner, the bellflower makes it an easier chore to mow the grass around the trunks.*

# Ground covers for decoration

A major advantage of many ground covers over grass is that they are so colorful and decorative. These three examples are from the same New Bedford, Massachusetts, nursery and were photographed in early fall. The varied ornamental qualities of ground covers offer pleasing contrasts in texture and color. And they have the added advantage of lasting longer than flowers. Evergreen ground covers are not only ornamental in areas where a lawn has turned brown for the winter, but their bright berries add color at the time it is most welcome.

*A mixture of pachysandra and a small-leaved variety of English ivy provides a calm green border at the base of an autumn-red euonymus bush. The dwarf spruce in the foreground adds a touch of blue, and the hosta at top left, with its heart-shaped leaves, gives diversity to this colorful backdrop for the lawn glimpsed at left.*

*A bed of pygmy barberry (foreground), turned a rich purple by the cold October nights, complements the feathery red leaves of a Japanese maple. Underneath the maple are two other ground covers, dwarf gray-blue Japanese cypress and evergreen bearberry. The stone wall is overlapped by a sprig of dusty miller.*

*A pale mass of dusty miller, which keeps its silvery sparkle late into the fall, flows over a brick wall and contrasts with the already-turning leaves of native woodbine, overrunning a piece of garden statuary at right. In the background the light green new growth of a bed of pheasant-foot ivy decorates the border of a garden path.*

A geometrically planted bed of blue fescue, an unusual grass that grows in globular tufts, adds a formal touch to the entrance of a home in Southern California. Not an ideal ground cover because considerable weeding is required between the clumps, the fescue compensates for the extra work with striking appearance.

# Colorful accents for borders

A good rule from the point of view of landscape design is: put a border beside each path. And when instead of grass the border is planted in periwinkle, say, as in the first picture at right, how much more practical and pleasing the effect becomes. It is practical in this instance, because periwinkle, whether it is the annual variety shown here or the less bushy perennial species, tolerates the shade of the boxwood hedge far better than most grass would. Annual periwinkle, which has rose, pink or white blossoms, is often preferred for its longer blooming season. It begins to flower soon after being set out in spring and continues to blossom until it is killed by autumn frost. Perennial periwinkle, on the other hand, blooms for less than a month in mid-spring.

Practical as well as esthetic considerations help in the selection and matching of ground covers. Boxwood and periwinkle, for example, blend naturally and have been used together for centuries. The choice of dichondra, which can flourish in rocky crevices, is perfect for the stone terrace in the middle picture, as is the use of drought-resistant leadwort for a low driveway border in the dry desert climate of New Mexico in the third photograph.

Sometimes contrasting ground covers are more effective than complementing ones, especially when the aim is to create borders upon borders, as in the case of the differing textures and appearances of the zigzag pattern shown on the next two pages.

*Between imposing walls of boxwood, on an estate in Oyster Bay, Long Island, a flagstone walk is bordered by annual periwinkle in blossom. Set out in spring, the glossy leaves of this plant provide dense foliage that is a beautiful foil for the flowers when they begin to bloom in early summer.*

A touch of green is added to a flagstone terrace in New Mexico by planting the interstices with dichondra, which is tough enough to stand up under heavy traffic. A tendril of grapevine climbs over the terrace wall at right, and a field of ordinary cotton spreads off toward the horizon beyond the rosebushes in the background.

A ground-cover border made up of blue-flowered leadwort interwoven with ajuga defines the driveway (right) of another New Mexico home. Crushed red scoria, a local rock, covers the drive and the ground fronting the house, making a colorful base for assorted evergreen plants, including a feathery-blossomed red yucca (left).

*Shown close up, a ground cover becomes almost an architectural adjunct to a brick walk in a formal Texas garden. The dwarf yaupon, a holly that is easily controlled by clipping, follows the zigzag pattern of the walk and an edging strip of white stones. For textural contrast the yaupon is backed by a bed of loose-growing mondo grass.*

# The right plant in the right place

Nothing prospers so little—or looks so sad and out of place—as a patch of ground cover planted without regard to how much sun or shade evolution has fitted it for. Plants need conditions like those they enjoy in the wild, and the ground covers that will grow best in your garden are those that naturally grow in a similar habitat. If the area you wish to cover lies under a heavy roof of conifers, you will do best to use such typical forest ground covers as ferns or mosses. But if the area receives full sun and is unprotected from the wind, look to the plants that grow naturally on open fields or moors —the many varieties of heather, for instance, or bearberry or cotoneaster.

Although nature provides ground covers for nearly all imaginable conditions of climate, illumination, soil and moisture, these plants are usually categorized by their light requirements. Those growing on the forest floor and those growing in the wide open spaces even look different. As a general rule the forest dwellers, as exemplified by the three shown at the right, have leaves of an exceptionally dark green, indicating the added chlorophyll they contain to make the most of dim light for photosynthesis. Plants that grow in full sun, illustrated on the following pages, vary from the dark green of the cotoneaster to the red and yellow of sedum.

*Few shade-loving ground covers do better under difficult conditions than pachysandra. Overcoming competition from neighboring shrubs, it grows whorls of spoon-shaped leaves on trailing stems to make a rich evergreen carpet, even in the dense shade of maple trees. The variegated type shown has white-tipped leaves.*

*Favorite ground covers for the shade—easy to grow, resistant to cold and most pests— are the many varieties of ivy, such as the English ivy (pictured below). The waxy luster of its leaves and the difference in hue between new and old leaves give a bed of this ground cover a lively, vibrant and attractive quality.*

*Hairy cap moss, plump and lush when grown with an abundance of moisture in ample shade, as here, but also able to survive in open fields, makes a closely woven 4- to 6-inch mat of white stars set in a textured bed of green. Tall for a moss, hairy cap moss is quick growing and has proven itself to be exceedingly hardy.*

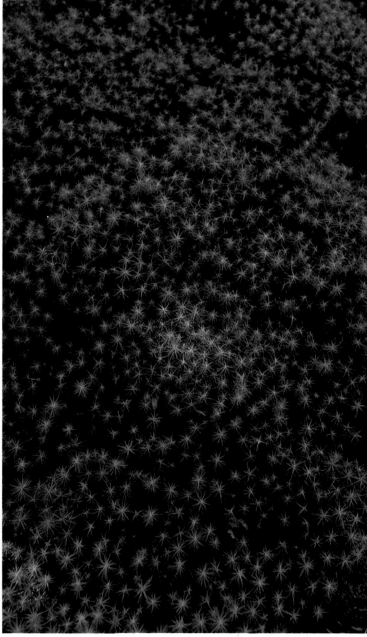

The soft feathery look of blue-gray needles, the silvery berries and the rich brown of rough-textured branches make Wilton carpet juniper an exceedingly handsome ground cover for sunny places. Requiring little care, it grows 4 inches high but spreads up to 8 feet across, which makes it especially suitable for large areas.

In areas that are largely frost free, dichondra is a good choice for sunny locations. Seen from a few inches away, its leaves look like tiny lily pads on a pond. When viewed from a distance, however, dichondra appears almost as uniform as a grass lawn; the more it is mowed and walked on, the smaller and denser its leaves become.

Looking like a sea of jelly beans, the leaves of a succulent species of sedum called pork and beans turn a bronze red in the sun. Growing on sprawling, leaning stems from 6 to 8 inches tall, these unusual plants make a good choice for rock gardens—or wherever an open, sunny spot calls for a splash of color to delight the eye.

Capable of growing anywhere in the U.S., even in poor soil and sub-zero temperatures, cotoneaster makes a bright display of its large red-orange berries, which appear in the fall and may last through the winter. This ground cover is actually a tiny evergreen shrub, only 6 to 12 inches tall, and looks best when unpruned.

Both utility and the eye are served when two or more ground covers are used, as here, to carpet an area that lies partly in sun and partly in shade. The fine, purple-tinted ajuga does well in sun and in partial shade, while the East Texas wood fern, which makes a striking contrast of texture, needs moist, shady nooks in order to be at its best.

# How to take care of your lawn  2

Everyone knows what a perfect lawn looks like—it is a thick, uniform carpet of green that holds its color for most of the year. But not everyone is equipped to achieve it. Some people are unwilling to do more than "mow what comes up," and along the New England coast there is a familiar phrase among yachtsmen who tend to their lawns after their boats: "The height of the weeds is proportionate to the height of the mast." At the other extreme is an English gardener who literally takes his lawn in during the winter; sod by sod, he carries it into his greenhouse, where he picks out the weeds, nourishes the soil and probably even combs it before setting it back in the ground in the spring. In Denver some statisticians estimated that as many as 86 million man-hours were being devoted to lawn care during the five-month season; calculating the labor at $1.60 an hour, they concluded that lawn tending was the largest single industry in the area.

The average homeowner, however, lies between the extremes; he is not satisfied with a lawn taken over by weeds, but he does not have apoplexy if an occasional dandelion pokes its golden head through the grass. He is, in short, willing to work on his lawn but unwilling to become a slave to it. And he does not have to. For if he understands the basics of nurturing, watering, weeding and mowing a lawn—and knows a few tricks that ease the job—he can have a fine lawn and enjoy his golf game too.

Behind every principle of good lawn care lies the fact that grass plants, unlike the plants in a flower garden, grow under intense competition with their neighbors for food, moisture and sunlight. Often as many as 100 plants occupy one square foot of lawn. They are the survivors of hundreds of plants that sprouted when the lawn was first seeded, and now they are crowded so closely together that the soil beneath them cannot be seen. Complicating their struggle is the unnatural condition under which they are forced to grow. The close-cropped lawn is an invention of man. The normal height of nearly all the grasses used for lawns is 18 inches

*A rotary sprinkler, starting work in the long shadows of early morning light, gives a lawn of Kentucky bluegrass and fine fescues the deep weekly soaking it needs to survive the heat of a St. Louis, Missouri, summer.*

to 3 feet; the demand that they never be allowed to grow more than 2 or 3 inches tall imposes a great hardship on them because it deprives them of the foliage they would otherwise use to build strength in their roots and stems, exposing them to injury from drought and competition from weeds. Most lawn care consists of replacing artificially what has been denied the grasses by cutting them so short: food, water and protection from the weeds that compete with them for sunlight and the available supply of nutrients.

TESTING THE SOIL

The first requirement—food—is generally supplied in the form of fertilizer, but before any fertilizer can be effective the ground must be in the right chemical condition to receive it. In a soil that is too acid or too alkaline the fertilizer will remain insoluble and its usefulness will be limited. Consequently the first step in lawn care is to determine the degree of the soil's acidity or alkalinity. Generally speaking, this condition is closely related to rainfall. In sections of the country where rain is abundant, such as the East Coast and the Pacific Northwest, the soil tends to be acid, or sour, because the chemicals that sweeten it, calcium and magnesium, are dissolved by rain water and carried away. Where the rainfall is less, the acidity is less, and in dry parts of the country, where the scant rainfall does not wash away minerals, the soil tends to be alkaline. Almost everywhere the chemical balance is off one way or the other, and correcting it has a seemingly miraculous effect. The grass shoots up bright green, as if the corrective treatment were a fertilizer. It is not, of course; it simply enables the plants to use foods that were already in the soil.

Either acidity or alkalinity can be determined by using an inexpensive home soil-test kit or by sending a sample of soil to a testing laboratory. Usually the local agricultural extension agency provides such a service. In either case the sample should be taken from 2 to 4 inches below the surface of the lawn *(opposite)*, the level at which most of the grass roots grow. It is also a good idea to take samples from several different spots because conditions may vary a good deal within a fairly small area. In interpreting the results of these tests, indicated on the pH scale of numbers from 0 to 14, all you have to remember is that 7, which is the center of the scale, is neutral, while lower numbers denote acidity and higher ones denote alkalinity. (The scale is based on logarithms, so the increments are in multiples of 10; thus a pH reading of 6.0 is 10 times more acid than one of 7.0 and a reading of 5.0 is 100 times more acid than 7.0.)

All grasses do not require the same soil pH. Centipede grass (so called because its double rows of roots suggest a centipede's legs) thrives in acid soil, with a pH of 4.0 to 6.0, whereas the west-

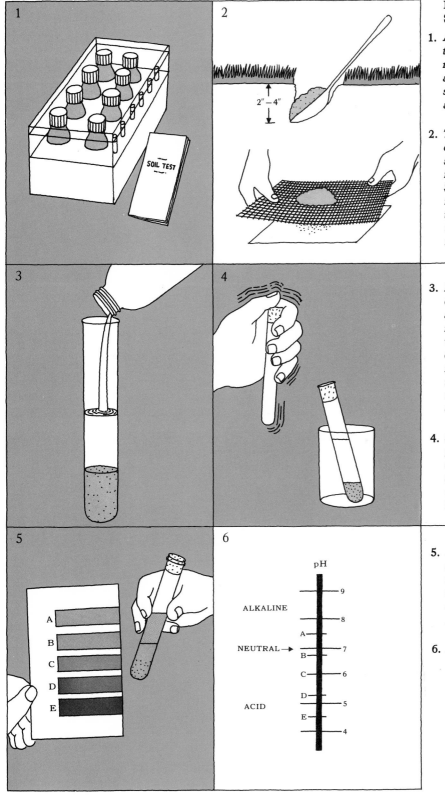

## HOW TO MAKE YOUR OWN SOIL ANALYSIS

1. *An inexpensive test kit contains the chemicals and test tubes necessary for determining the acid-alkali balance of your soil and the nitrogen, phosphorus and potassium it may lack.*

2. *Test for the pH factor first (the other tests follow the same steps). Take a spoonful of earth from the top 2 to 4 inches of soil. Strain it through coarse wire mesh onto a piece of plain paper to remove any debris. Do not touch the earth with your hands or you may affect its chemical make-up.*

3. *Fill a test tube one quarter full of the dry soil and add an equal amount of liquid from the bottle marked "lime." Close the tube with a cork. In many kits the corks are color coded so that in future tests you can be sure to use the same test tube and cork for the same chemical, thus avoiding errors caused by contamination.*

4. *Shake the tube thoroughly, then give the soil time to settle completely before proceeding. Some types of soils settle rapidly while others may take several hours or as long as overnight.*

5. *Match up the color of the liquid above the sediment with one of the colors in the coded chart in the kit. If your solution color falls between two of the chart colors you must interpolate the results.*

6. *A chart keying color to pH factors enables you to approximate the pH of your soil. Compare this figure with the optimum for the grass or ground cover you are using (Chapter 5) to see how much, if at all, the soil pH needs to be altered. Then correct any imbalance by applying lime or sulfur to the soil (see text).*

ern dry-land grasses—buffalo grass, crested wheat grass and grama grass—survive even in soils that are as alkaline as pH 8.5. Nevertheless, most of the widely grown lawn grasses flourish in soils that are mildly acid, 6.0 to 7.0. (For the individual acidity requirements of 23 species of lawn grasses, see Chapter 5.) Under these mildly acid soil conditions there is a great deal of bacterial action, which causes the decay of organic material, releasing the nutrients that are needed to encourage strong, vigorously growing plants.

## CORRECTING THE CHEMISTRY

Correcting the acidity or alkalinity of a soil simply consists of adding lime for the one and sulfur for the other. There are two kinds of lime suited for sweetening lawn soil; both are natural limestone rock untreated except for being ground into a fine powder. One is calcite, which is crystallized calcium carbonate; the other is dolomite, which is calcium magnesium carbonate. Of the two, dolomite is somewhat better because it has a greater neutralizing capacity and also contains magnesium, an element essential to photosynthesis. (There is a third lime, called slaked or hydrated lime, but it should be handled only by professional gardeners who know how to use it without burning the grass.)

The amount of lime to apply depends on the pH reading, on the pH preferences of the particular grass, and on the physical characteristics of the soil itself. If you have a heavy clay soil, for instance, you will need approximately twice as much lime to accomplish the same pH change as you would if your soil were sandy, since the heavier soils are composed of many more particles, which, though tiny, have in aggregate much more surface area to be neutralized by the lime.

All the lime should not be applied at once; too much lime at one time can upset the soil's chemical balance. I would never put more than 50 pounds of lime per 1,000 square feet on a lawn in one application. If more is needed to correct the acidity, an additional application can be made after six months. Where cool-climate grass is grown, the lime can be applied in late fall or very early spring while the ground is still frozen, and it can work its way down into the soil gradually through the crevices caused by alternate thawing and freezing. For warm-climate grass, the best time to apply lime is late fall; then it can work its way into the soil before the spring growing season. Once the correct pH reading has been reached, it can usually be maintained at that level by an application of about 35 pounds of lime per 1,000 square feet at three-year intervals.

In arid and semiarid parts of the country, where the lack of rainfall allows minerals to accumulate in the soil, the problem is not acidity but alkalinity. Soil pH readings may range from 7.5 to

## THE VERSATILE DANDELION

*Though most lawn owners look on the dandelion as an enemy, this ubiquitous plant has long enjoyed a loyal following among those who have used it to make a variety of foods, drinks and medicines. As far back as the 17th Century, it was valued as a prime ingredient in many tinctures, tonics and salves recommended for every malaise from gallstones to dropsy. Even today young dandelion leaves, with their tart but not unpleasant taste, are often put into sandwiches, soups and salads, or boiled to make a spinachlike vegetable. The dried leaves are used to produce beer in parts of England and Canada; the flowers can be fermented into wine and the dried, roasted roots are ground into a powder to make dandelion coffee.*

as high as 9.0—well above the pH range of most lawn grasses. Many alkaline soils contain excessive amounts of the chemical element sodium, trapped in such a way that it hinders the flow of water and air through the soil. The alkalinity can be corrected and the harmful effects of sodium eliminated by applying sulfur, either pure in the form of a yellow powder, or in a compound such as ferrous sulfate. Whichever is used, the application should be followed immediately by a thorough watering. About 20 pounds of sulfur per 1,000 square feet should be sufficient to reduce the soil's pH reading by one point and dispose of the excess sodium.

These additions to the lawn—or, as the professional gardeners call them, "soil amendments"—perform another important function in soils with a high clay content. They alter the actual physical structure of the soil, breaking up the stickiness that binds the particles of soil together, thus enabling roots to move through the soil more easily in search of nutrients and moisture.

## CHOOSING A FERTILIZER

A lawn may or may not need one of these chemicals, depending upon the results of the soil test. But it will almost unquestionably need fertilizer because of the artificial conditions under which grass is forced to grow. Cropped close and crowded together, the plants starve unless artificially fed.

Most lawn fertilizers contain the three major nutritive elements most apt to be lacking: nitrogen, phosphorus and potassium (in the form of various compounds). Labels on bags specify in numbers the percentage of each of these elements in the order given above. A popular formulation is 10-6-4: 10 per cent nitrogen, 6 per cent phosphorus compounds and 4 per cent potassium compounds. But in most types you will notice that the percentage of nitrogen is far larger than that of phosphorus or potassium. This is partly because nitrogen washes out of the soil quickly, but mainly because nitrogen is the most important part of lawn fertilizers, the element that promotes lush green growth. Lawn fertilizers are unlike those used for flowers, vegetables and fruit, for the primary goal is vegetation rather than fruit or flowers.

Phosphorus, the ingredient indicated by the second number on fertilizer labels, moves very slowly through the soil. For that reason smaller amounts of it are needed, but on a regular basis, since without phosphorus roots do not grow fully, leaves are stunted and plants fail to mature properly. Lawn fertilizers sold in different parts of the country may vary considerably in their percentage of phosphorus content to allow for local variations in soils. Coastal areas along the Gulf of Mexico and the South Atlantic states, for instance, are notably deficient in phosphorus, and fertilizers prepared for use there are relatively high in it.

Potassium, the third essential element in fertilizers, helps build strong root systems, aids in disease resistance, increases the rigidity of grass stems and improves the ability of the plants to withstand cold weather and drought. As a rule, soils in the eastern part of the country are in greater need of potassium than are those in the West, where, because of light rainfall, chemicals are less rapidly washed away.

While all three of these major elements are contained in most of the fertilizers sold for general use on lawns, not all fertilizers act alike. There are three types: inorganic, organic and synthetic organic. The differences among them affect the way the fertilizers influence grass growth and how they should be used.

Inorganic fertilizers contain chemical salts mixed with large quantities of vermiculite or other inert substances. Many of these salts are immediately soluble in water; they are quickly available to plants, but they also wash away swiftly. They may be used very early in the spring to encourage immediate growth, but whenever they are used great care must be taken that the salts do not burn the foliage. To forestall burning, apply inorganic fertilizers only when the foliage is completely dry, and water thoroughly to be sure that none remains on the grass leaves. Caution is also necessary when grass is suffering from drought. Foliage already wilted from lack of moisture may be harmed by further drying when dusted with inorganic fertilizer. Inorganic fertilizers are also sold as liquids, to be sprinkled on the lawn with a hose attachment. The liquid form may hasten results, but even distribution is difficult to attain with this method.

Organic fertilizers are made from natural organic materials such as cottonseed meal, fish scraps, soybean meal, animal manures and processed sewage. They seldom burn grass because they release their nutrients slowly, and only when the weather is warm and humid enough to encourage decay. This means they cannot be counted on for quick effect; not too much should be expected of organic fertilizers when they are applied in the early spring while the weather is still cool. Sometimes the gardener, impatient at little sign of change, applies a second coat, whereupon the grass becomes overstimulated with the first warm weather and has to be mowed every few days. And because the new growth is so succulent, the grass is more susceptible to disease. To guard against this common miscalculation, manufacturers of organic fertilizers often add a small amount of quick-acting inorganic fertilizer to their mixtures, to make the grass "green up" earlier in the spring.

A third variety of fertilizer is the so-called synthetic organic. It is made of urea, rich in nitrogen, and formaldehyde. But like organic fertilizers, the synthetics release their nutrients slowly. With

GETTING OUT GRASS STAINS

*The best way to remove grass stains from white fabrics, according to the American Institute of Laundering, is by a thorough washing with detergent and an ordinary household bleach. For colored fabric or wool, use denatured or rubbing alcohol. Place the stain face down on a paper towel or clean rag, pour the alcohol through the fabric and tamp it with the fingers. Then move the stained area to a clean spot on the absorbent material and repeat the process until the stain has disappeared.*

synthetic organics a gardener can keep his lawn well supplied with nitrogen with only two applications a year as opposed to the four or five applications needed for quick-acting inorganics. And since they are highly concentrated materials, far fewer pounds are needed than when using organic fertilizers—you handle less weight and have a much less arduous application job.

HOW MUCH TO FERTILIZE

Too little fertilizer is one of the commonest causes of a scrawny lawn. But too much can encourage disease, and there is also the possibility of causing chemical burning. To avoid such errors, regulate fertilizer application by gauging how much nitrogen is being supplied. The average lawn requires about 3 or 4 pounds of nitrogen per 1,000 square feet over the course of a year. This amount may have to be increased if the lawn is shaded by trees, because tree roots compete with grass roots for nourishment and, being more vigorous, often take the lion's share. In fact, one of the best ways to help grass survive under trees is to double the standard allotment of fertilizer.

Since lawn fertilizers are not cheap, it is wise to check the relative costs of fertilizers and their nutritional value. Read the label on the bag before you spend your money, and find out how much each pound of nitrogen costs. Do not be confused by the statement that a bag will cover 5,000 or 10,000 square feet. After all, coverage is not the vital statistic; it is the nitrogen present that matters.

For example, suppose a fertilizer is labeled 20-8-5. That means 20 per cent, or 20 pounds out of each 100 pounds, is nitrogen. To provide 4 pounds of nitrogen per 1,000 square feet per year, you need 20 pounds of that mixture per 1,000 square feet per year. But if you use a 10-6-4 mixture, 10 per cent of whose contents is nitrogen, the amount you need to buy jumps to 40 pounds.

I recently checked garden supply centers and found that the cost of fertilizer—figured on the basis of nitrogen content—varied as much as 100 per cent. The fertilizer at the lowest price per bag often had a very low nitrogen content, so that the total cost of using it correctly was considerably higher than that of using a high-nitrogen fertilizer. In addition, the bargain fertilizers represent more weight and bulk, which requires hard work to distribute.

APPLYING LAWN FERTILIZERS

In deciding when and how often to feed lawns, consider the type of fertilizer. If fast-release inorganic materials are used, much of the nutrient content will wash away under heavy rain or irrigation, and applications will have to be made more often. The picture-book quality seen on some golf greens comes from quick-acting inorganic fertilizers applied once a month and sometimes more often. Very small amounts are put on and watered in so as to maintain the optimum amount of fertilizer in the soil at all times. Such careful and regular care is out of the question for most home gardeners, and it is for this very reason that slow-release fertilizers have become so popular. The following suggestions on applying fertilizer are based on the use of such slow-release fertilizers—whether they be inorganics, organics or synthetic organics.

The best time to fertilize a lawn comes just before the grass begins its most active season of growth. There are two such seasons for cool-climate grasses, one in the spring and another in early fall when the weather turns cool and rainy. But warm-climate grasses reach their peak growth only once a year, during the hottest months of summer. The spring feeding for cool-climate grasses should be applied as soon as the ground begins to thaw and before it becomes muddy; the second feeding should go on in late summer. And this later application should be watered in well, since the soil tends to be dry then; if it is left on the surface, the fertilizer would only dry the grass further and could do it permanent injury. Sometimes an additional feeding is called for just as summer is approaching, if the grass slackens in its rate of growth and seems to lose its bright green color. This early-summer application should be made two or three months after the initial spring feeding. Again, it should be watered in thoroughly.

For warm-climate grasses the feeding schedule also begins in the spring when the grasses begin to green up, and is followed by a second feeding in midsummer when the growing cycle is approaching its peak. Depending on the grass, a second summer feeding or a third or even a fourth one may be necessary—Bermuda grasses, for instance, require more fertilizer than Zoysias. But in no case should warm-climate grasses be fed in the fall, when they are entering their period of dormancy. Fertilizing encourages weeds.

HOW TO APPLY FERTILIZER    The simplest, surest way to get fertilizer onto a lawn in the right amount is to use a fertilizer spreader. There are two versions of this useful device—which can also double or triple its usefulness by serving as a distributor for seeds, lime, sulfur or other chemicals. Both versions are two-wheeled carts, but one is trough-shaped and distributes its contents through adjustable holes in the bottom of the trough, while the other broadcasts its contents from a spinning disk that operates on much the same principle as the road-sanding machines used on highways in the winter. The trough spreader distributes the fertilizer in swaths 18 to 36 inches wide, while the broadcast spreaders can cover a swath 4 to 8 feet wide depending partly on the heaviness of the material and partly on the operator's walking speed (the spinning disk, connected to the wheels, throws harder when the wheels go fast). A broadcast spreader's coverage

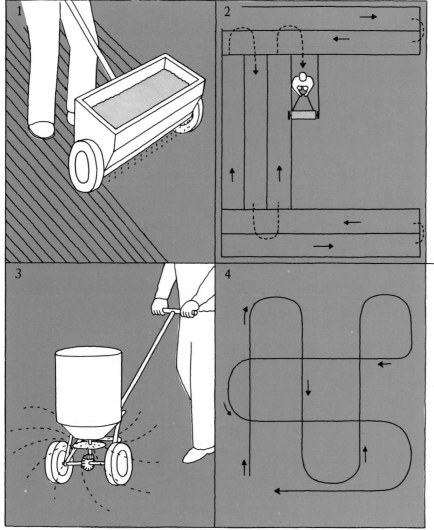

1. *In a trough spreader, fertilizer, stirred by a mixing bar connected to the wheels, drops through a row of holes at the bottom. A lever adjusts and shuts off the flow.*

2. *To distribute fertilizer evenly with a trough spreader, first lay down two rows at either end of the area to be covered. Then go back and forth across the lawn, making all your turns in the previously covered end zones with the spreader shut off; this avoids dumping excess fertilizer as you slow down to make your turn.*

3. *A broadcast or spinning type of spreader drops fertilizer through a single adjustable hole onto a spinning disk, which sprays the fertilizer ahead of the machine in an arc up to 8 feet across.*

4. *When using a broadcast spreader, simply push the machine back and forth across the area so that the swaths of fertilizer overlap slightly; then repeat the process, crossing at right angles to the original pattern. Both types of spreader can also be used to distribute lime, sulfur, seeds and granular weed-killing chemicals.*

is less uniform than that of a trough spreader, but the result is less evident than the streaks that can appear if the paths followed by a trough spreader are not carefully overlapped *(above)*. The broadcast spreader rarely causes streaks since the fertilizer is "feathering" as it falls; i.e., the application is thicker nearest the spreader and thinner as it fans out.

Spreaders should be emptied, washed and thoroughly dried after use, for many fertilizers are highly caustic and will corrode the metal parts. And if yours was a bargain-basement spreader—or a fairly expensive one that has seen better days—it may not distribute its contents at the rate indicated on the machine. The easy way to check the distribution rate is to see how far a 20-pound bag will go. If your calculations indicate 20 pounds are needed for 2,000 square feet, stake off a rectangular lawn area 40 by 50 feet wide, ad-

## FITTING THE SPRINKLER TO THE LAWN

1. *A soil sample helps tell how long to water turf so that moisture reaches grass roots. Use a trowel or a hollow earth auger with a cutaway "window" to take some samples during a trial watering. The rate of water penetration depends upon the soil: an inch of water, for example, will reach 4 inches down in clay but 12 inches in sandy ground (diagrams).*

2. *A three-conduit sprinkler hose releases fine soaking mist through pinprick holes; it can be snaked to sprinkle an oddly shaped area.*

3. *An oscillating sprinkler sprays a fan of parallel jets through holes in a slowly moving crossbar; it covers rectangular areas (diagrams) typical of most lawns. For smaller areas, it can be made to spray a partial pattern (center) or one side only (right).*

4. *A traveling sprinkler distributes a circular spray pattern from its whirling nozzles while moving slowly along a track made by its own outstretched hose, which can be laid out to cover areas of different shapes. The type shown winds up its hose on a reel.*

5. *A pulsating sprinkler moves slowly back and forth, shooting long, rapid-fire jets of water or shorter bursts of fine spray, covering narrow wedge shapes to full circles (diagrams) depending on the adjustment. It allows water to be absorbed in one spot before returning to deliver some more.*

6. *A turret sprinkler has multiple heads with many holes that send out a steady spray, giving a maximum soaking in minimum time. The turret can be turned to sprinkle patterns ranging from a square to long, narrow rectangles.*

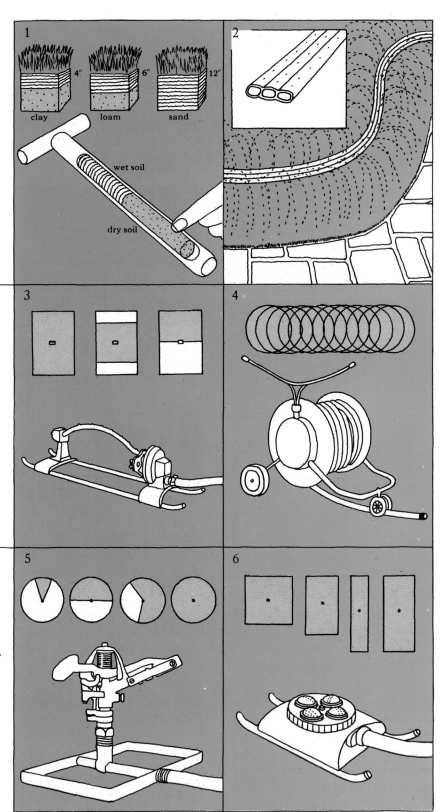

just the spreader gauge to the setting specified for this coverage and use up the bag. If you do not come out even, recalibrate the gauge, slightly up or down to make up for any discrepancy.

While you won't have to fertilize your lawn more than two or three times a year, you will find that watering will probably be a regular part of your lawn maintenance, especially during hot weather. Indeed in some areas of the country, where all gardening is done under irrigation, lawn watering is so much a fact of life that most lawns are provided with built-in irrigation systems, even though such a system is quite expensive. (The procedure for installing such a system is shown in the drawing on pages 54-55.) A lawn needs water because water makes up about 85 per cent of a grass plant's bulk. And water is rightly—if, in a technical sense, inexactly—called "the cheapest fertilizer." Give your lawn adequate water and it will flourish; let it get too dry and its green will start turning to brown.

Sometimes, however, the lawn dries out through no fault of your own. In areas where normal rainfall is usually adequate for lawns, a drought can sometimes be so severe that homeowners will be forbidden to use their sprinklers. In such cases it is better not to water at all than to tease your lawn with brief sprinklings. Not all lawn experts agree on this subject; some will tell you that a little water is better than none, just to "keep the lawn alive." I do not agree. In my opinion a lawn that cannot be watered abundantly should not be watered at all. The grass will not die; it will merely turn dormant and will quickly revive with the next drenching rain. But the lawn that gets only a light sprinkling does not receive enough moisture to grow, while the weeds do. Better a brownish lawn for even a few weeks than a weed-choked lawn for the remainder of the season.

What constitutes a drenching rain or a thorough job of watering depends on so many things that it is folly to set down rules for how often a lawn should be watered. Some grasses —bent grasses and Bermuda grasses, for instance—require more water than others. Soil also makes a difference. Water penetrates sandy soils quickly, and is as quick to leave them. Loam soils hold water twice as well, and clay four times more so. Perhaps the easiest way to check how much water your lawn needs is to sprinkle it for an hour or two and then dig a small hole 6 to 8 inches deep. If the hole is wet at the bottom, give your lawn about that much water the next week. If the bottom of the hole is dry, you have not watered the lawn enough; give it more water. Of course one of the clearest indications that the soil is parched is the condition of the grass itself. Grass suffering from lack of moisture, particularly in hot, windy weather, turns bluish in color, the in-

# LAYING AN UNDERGROUND SPRINKLER SYSTEM

1. *Before an underground sprinkler system can be installed, exact planning is essential. Draw a plan of your house and grounds, at a scale of 1 inch to 10 feet. Locate all buildings, walks, drives, drains, trees and shrubs.*

2. *The best sprinkler heads pop up, as shown, when the water is on and drop when not in use. To choose among the many pop-up heads, ask your water company or city engineer what your water pressure is, then consult a garden or plumbing supply dealer.*

3. *To locate and estimate the number of heads needed, place a piece of tracing paper over your plan and use a compass to plot the spray pattern. Overlap the circles by at least a quarter of the diameter, since the spray from each head lessens with the distance from the center. Half-circle sprays go on the edges, quarter-circle sprays at corners.*

4. *On a second overlay, sketch in a piping diagram showing main lines and spurs. Here, three main lines are needed to supply enough water to each of the heads.*

5. *Each line (three in this case) is connected to the house water supply and equipped with an on-off valve combined with a vacuum breaker so that water cannot syphon back into the main supply.*

6. *Semirigid polyvinyl chloride, called PVC, makes the most satisfactory piping material for underground sprinkler systems. Plumbing supply outlets sell it in 20-foot lengths (above). The fittings below are also of plastic The adapter is used to connect tubing of differing diameters and the end cap terminates lines.*

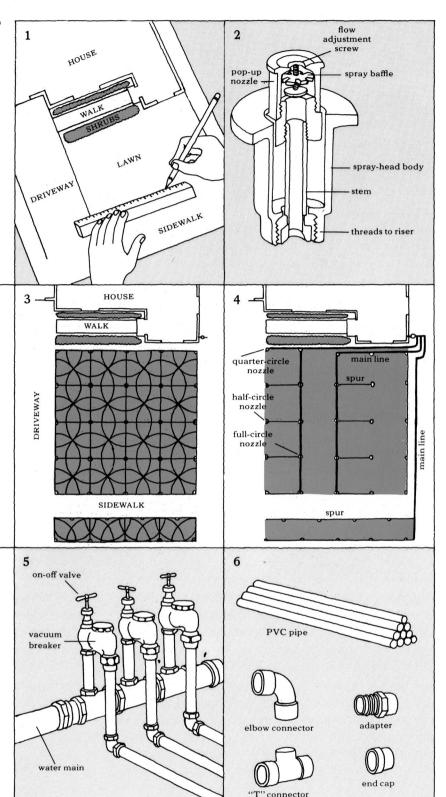

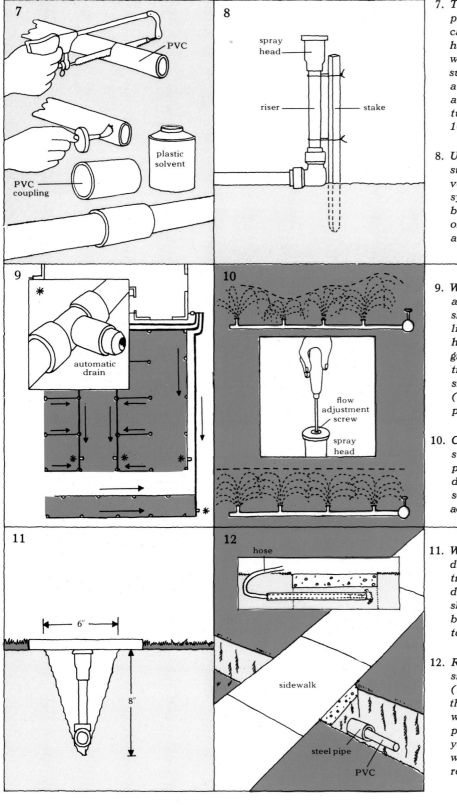

7. To make connections with PVC pipe, measure each length carefully. Cut the pipe with a hack saw. Wipe the joints clean with PVC primer and brush all surfaces that are to be joined with a plastic solvent. Join them with a connector and give a quarter turn to ensure a bond. Hold for 10 seconds for the joint to set.

8. Using stakes and string to support each sprinkler head in a vertical position, assemble the system atop your lawn to test it before trenching. Follow your original piping plan, using pipe of a smaller diameter on spur lines.

9. Where there is danger of freezing, automatic drains (asterisks) should be installed on each major line. These should protrude horizontally (inset) into a bed of gravel for drainage. On flat lawns, trenches should be dug to pitch slightly toward the drains (arrows). On sloping ground, place drains at all low points.

10. Connect the system to the water supply and turn it on; if the pattern it makes is irregular (top drawing), adjust the heads with a screwdriver (center) until you achieve an even pattern (bottom).

11. When the system is adjusted, disconnect it and then begin trenching. Dig a "V" to an average depth of 8 inches, allowing a slight pitch for drainage. Use a board across the top of the trench to fix the height of each head.

12. Rather than slice through a sidewalk, make a water drill (top) with a steel pipe (wider than your PVC pipe) threaded with a garden hose; the water pressure softens the ground so you can drive the pipe beneath the walk. Then remove the hose and replace it with a length of PVC.

dividual blades roll into cylinders and the grass itself loses its springiness and does not bounce back when stepped on.

The best kind of lawn sprinkler is one that provides a *slow,* uniform spray that soaks into the soil. Clay soil requires a very fine spray so that water can penetrate. To allow time for moisture to seep into clay soils I suggest you run the sprinkler for 10 or 15 minutes, then move it away for half an hour to other sections of the lawn before bringing it back for another 10 or 15 minutes; repeat this cycle until your test boring indicates that the soil is sufficiently watered.

Sprinklers come in a wide variety of styles *(drawing, page 52).* And they vary just as widely in their performance. The old-fashioned whirling-arm types are not very satisfactory because they sprinkle unevenly over a circular area and miss the corners. A garden hose with an ordinary nozzle is almost useless. I have found several types of sprinklers that work effectively. One popular device has an oscillating arm that waves a fan of fine spray back and forth, completely covering a rectangular area. Even simpler is a sprinkler hose, a flat, triple-tubed plastic hose that is perforated with many tiny holes to cast a gentle rainlike spray; it can be snaked out to cover a plot of almost any shape.

GETTING RID OF WEEDS    So much has been written about crab grass and dandelions and how to control them that I would like to begin this section on weeds with one simple statement: in a lawn where the grasses are healthy and thriving, weeds are not likely to be much of a problem. Most lawn weeds need light to germinate, and a thick dense turf—the product of good lawn care—automatically excludes them. To deter weeds during the height of their growing season, set the mower blades high, so that less sun reaches the surface of the soil. Although many people are convinced that the weeds in their lawn blew there as seeds from their neighbor's weedy lawn, in fact they were probably there all along, buried beneath the surface. Some weed seeds can remain dormant for 75 years, only to sprout when exposed to the sun. So let sleeping seeds slumber on.

Getting rid of weeds after they have sprouted is usually not a problem these days, if the lawn is a normally healthy one. When I was a boy the common way to deal with dandelions was to combine a boy and a prong-ended asparagus knife, and let him cut out the plants one by one. It didn't always work; dandelions have long taproots that will grow again if part of the root is left behind. Nowadays there are chemicals that are much more efficient, but it is vital to understand them before undertaking their use. Chemical control of weeds should be considered analagous to the use of wonder drugs in human health. When they are needed for emergency treatment, use them, but do not rely on them as a regular medicine. (For a listing of common weeds and methods of controlling each, see the chart on pages 70-73.) There are two main kinds of weed killers, designed to deal with the two main weed categories—broad-leaved weeds and grassy weeds (technically the two categories are designated dicotyledons and monocotyledons). Broad-leaf killers are used to control such common troublemakers as dandelions and plantain, but they will also of course attack any broad-leaved plant—which includes most flowers and ornamental shrubs. So do not use them indiscriminately. Similarly the chemicals that control weedy grasses may also damage the permanent grasses if they are not used with caution.

The most familiar of the broad-leaf killers is 2, 4-D, a hormone compound that destroys plants by speeding growth so much that they wear themselves out and die. A related compound, 2, 4, 5-TP, or silvex, is effective against ground ivy, mouse-ear chickweed and oxalis. Such chemicals are so potent that minute amounts of them are sufficient to do the job, and for this reason alone I would use them for spot treatment rather than overall distribution. To broadcast them, unless the lawn is excessively weedy, seems like shooting flies with an elephant gun. But there is another reason to use these compounds sparingly. Not all grasses are equally tolerant of them. Bent grasses, for instance, are apt to be injured by 2, 4-D and 2, 4, 5-TP, but it is safe to use a weed killer called mecoprop, and on St. Augustine grass, use atrazine.

Among the weedy grasses the chief offender is crab grass, a prolific annual that comes in two versions, smooth and hairy, and plagues homeowners everywhere there are hot humid summers. Consequently most of the controls for weedy grasses are aimed specifically at crab grass—although other noxious grasses may succumb to them too. Crab grass controls are of two kinds: pre-emergent and postemergent. The former attack the seedlings before they appear above ground; generally only one application each year is needed. The latter attack the young plants, and repeated applications may be required. Both varieties are available in a number of complex chemical formulations that can be sprayed on an infested area or broadcast in dry form. Some of these compounds do well on one kind of lawn, some on another, and lawns that are unharmed by one sort of chemical may be stunted or discolored by another. DCPA, for instance, should never be applied to lawns containing dichondra, and both centipede grass and St. Augustine grass may be injured by the postemergent control known as MSMA and DSMA. Each compound also has its own particular peripheral benefits. MSMA will control dallis grass, a problem grass in southern lawns, for instance, and DSMA will control dallis

## GRASS: THE STAFF OF LIFE

*Since men first learned to cook their meals, the cereal or grain grasses—corn, wheat, rice, oats, barley, rye, millet—have been staples in their diets. Only the seeds of these grasses are eaten; the stalks and leaves are indigestible by or unpalatable to humans and are used for animal fodder. The main exceptions are sugar cane, grown for the high sugar content of its pulp, and sorghum, another canelike grass, whose juice makes a syrup, familiar to Southerners, poured on cornbread or hoecakes.*

## WEED KILLERS FOR
## SPOT AND AREA CONTROL

1. *An easy-to-handle device for eradicating occasional weeds —particularly those that resist being uprooted—is a foam aerosol applicator. Good for small-sized lawns, it shoots a liquid jet of weed-killing chemical foam directly onto the offending weed.*

2. *Another device for spot control of weeds is the wand, which can be used without bending over. The wand's hollow shaft is filled with a solution of weed killer that squirts out when the tip of the wand is pressed against the weed.*

3. *A wax bar or roller impregnated with a weed-killing chemical is useful for destroying weeds close to a hedge or other plants that could be damaged by drifting spray. Drag the bar or roller slowly across the ground right after the grass has been mowed.*

4. *Most effective for deweeding large areas of lawn is a tank sprayer mounted on wheels. The tank, filled with chemicals and water, has a hand pump mounted on top to build up pressure. The spray from the hand-held nozzle is applied to each weedy area.*

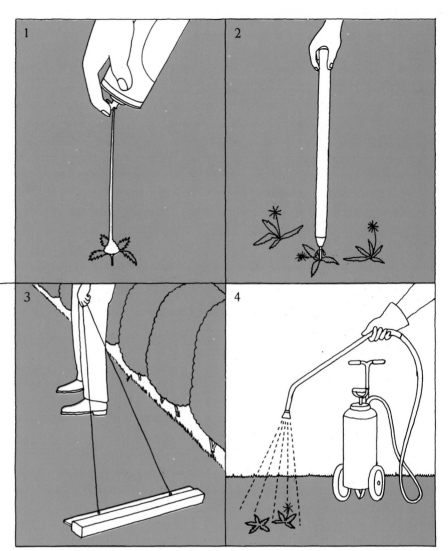

grass, goose grass, foxtail and nut grass along with crab grass.

Weed killers come as granules, powders and liquids, and sometimes they come mixed in with fertilizer. Because the combinations distribute herbicide all over the lawn, not just on the weeds, they should be used with caution. One of the weed killers commonly used in combination with fertilizer is a broad-spectrum material called dicamba—and dicamba's side effects can be damaging. The U.S. Department of Agriculture warns that dicamba should not be used around the root zone of trees and ornamental shrubs, and that it may injure lawns of bent grass, St. Augustine grass, carpet grass, clover and dichondra. If for convenience's sake you elect to use one of these fertilizer and weed-killer combinations, by all means check the contents on the label and proceed accordingly. And whatever the contents, never use those materials except when the air is still. Even the slightest breeze can cause them to drift onto plants they may damage. Worse yet, they may drift across property lines to kill or maim your neighbor's plants.

I have the same reservations about the wholesale use of weed killers alone. Not only is it potentially damaging to other plants, but the overkill is ridiculous. I much prefer to spot-treat the individual plants. The idea of course is to hit each weed dead center—an innocent form of target practice that may be done with a choice of "weapons" (opposite). One good weapon is foam aerosol, which looks like a spray can but ejects a blob of herbicide-laden foam that will not drift away from the target the way spray does. Just move in close and touch the push-button release lightly—the chemicals are so potent that only a small amount of foam is necessary. If all that bending is hard on your back, try my favorite weapon: a hollow wand into which you put a small amount of weed killer plus water. I go from weed to weed, pressing the wand against each one—an action that releases a small squirt of the contents. The same effect can be achieved by tying a small sponge to the end of a stick and saturating the sponge with a mixture of weed killer and water; one soaking of the sponge is enough to treat a good many weeds. Another weed-killing weapon, carried by garden supply stores, is a wax bar or roller impregnated with chemicals; it is pulled by rope across the surface of the lawn. Various types of sprayers can also be used, but the simpler devices described above are usually sufficient to take care of the average weed infestation of a home lawn.

Weeds, unfortunately, are not the only pests that invade a lawn. Grasses are also vulnerable to attack by a number of insects and diseases. Detailed descriptions of the symptoms of the most common of these ailments and prescriptions for treatment are given in the chart on pages 66-69.

Two main kinds of insects damage lawns. Cutworms and similar pests gnaw away at the stems and leaves aboveground. Below ground, beetle grubs, billbug grubs and others of their type go after the roots. Both aboveground and below-ground pests can be controlled by common insecticides such as carbaryl, diazinon or chlordane. But the application methods are different. For aboveground insects, water the lawn, apply insecticide and then do not water again for several days. For below-ground insects, apply the insecticide first, then water heavily to soak the chemicals into the ground. If your lawn is infested by both, attack the aboveground insects, and after a few days water heavily to get the ones below.

Disease control can be more complicated because lawn grasses are susceptible to attack by many kinds of fungi, and the cure

INSECT AND DISEASE CONTROL

should be matched to the fungus. Both undernourished and overnourished lawns are vulnerable, particularly during hot, humid summer weather. If such attacks are a problem in your lawn, they can be prevented by applying a fungicide in advance of the season —early in spring is usually the best time.

## MOWING THE LAWN

Though weeding, feeding and watering are essential for a good lawn, the one overriding job of lawn care is of course lawn mowing. Lurking in the back of every man's mind as he wheels his mower into the garage after this routine chore is the thought that there ought to be some way to keep grass from growing so rapidly. The thought has occurred to scientists too, and some of them have been working on it. A research project called Shrinkaplant at The Ontario Agricultural College found a chemical that, when applied to the lawn, stops growth at any desired height. It has a serious drawback: It turns the grass purple. More promising is the development of grasses that grow very slowly. But for the time being the lawn mower seems in no danger of being replaced.

The frequency with which grass should be mowed depends on how fast the grass grows. Ideally, grass should be cut often enough so that only a quarter to a third of the total grass height is removed at one time. When grass grows too long, the clippings look unsightly and, if wet or too thick, they can smother the grass beneath. As for the actual height of the lawn, that depends on many things —the species of grass of which the lawn is composed, your own personal preferences, the use to which the lawn is put, the time of year. Normal mowing heights for each species of grass are given in the encyclopedia section, pages 114-119, but generally speaking, the higher you keep your grass, particularly in the summer months, the stronger it is likely to be and the better able to survive drought. As an overall rule, it is a good idea to cut grass somewhat higher in midsummer, to discourage germination of weed seeds and to insulate the soil against drying heat.

Of course to some extent the height of a lawn is determined by the kind of lawn mower used to cut it. The two commonly used mowers, reel-type and rotary-type, have different cutting actions and produce different results. A reel mower can be adjusted to cut much closer than a rotary mower. Indeed, reel mowers are universally used on golf greens, where they are sometimes set to cut at an incredibly low 1/8 inch. But most people prefer rotary mowers, which are simpler and much easier to care for.

The mowing action of a rotary mower is supplied by a revolving blade, or blades, set parallel to the ground and driven by a motor. Whirling at high speeds, the blade cuts with a whiplike, scything action in swaths up to 48 inches wide, depending on the

### A PATTERN FOR MOWING

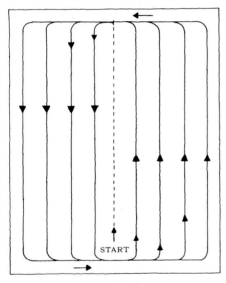

START

*A mowing technique that lightens the chore and produces an attractive result is diagramed above. Start cutting down the center of the lawn, then describe a counterclockwise path of wider and wider ellipses working out toward the sides. The turns at the ends are gradual and easy to manage; each half of the lawn is mowed in only one direction, eliminating the striped effect of back-and-forth cutting. To prevent the grass from being bent constantly in one direction, a problem particularly with reel mowers, the next time you mow start at one side of the lawn or at the other end.*

size of the machine, and in heights that normally adjust from about an inch to about 3½ inches high. Rotary mowers are powered by gasoline engines, batteries or household electric current. In simpler models all this power is directed to the blade, but more elaborate models have power-driven wheels as well.

Because the blades whirl so fast, even a dull rotary mower will cut grass—but it is a bruising cut, and potentially bad for the lawn. The injured tissue at the end of each blade of grass will die, the surface of the lawn will take on a brownish tinge and the lawn will become increasingly disease prone. Sharpening a rotary blade can be done easily with a file or sharpening stone (before detaching the blade to sharpen it, be sure the motor is disconnected so that the machine cannot start up accidentally).

Although rotary mowers do a perfectly adequate job for most lawns—and offer the added attraction of being less expensive and somewhat easier to use than comparable reel mowers—in fact, a reel mower is generally conceded to be a superior lawn-cutting mechanism. The cutting action of a reel mower does not depend on the speed of the blades; it operates just as effectively at low speeds as it does at high. The spiraling blades, mounted cylindrically, rotate across a stationary metal plate or "bed knife," to shear the grass, scissors-fashion. Most standard reel mowers intended for

## THREE SPECIAL KINDS OF MOWERS

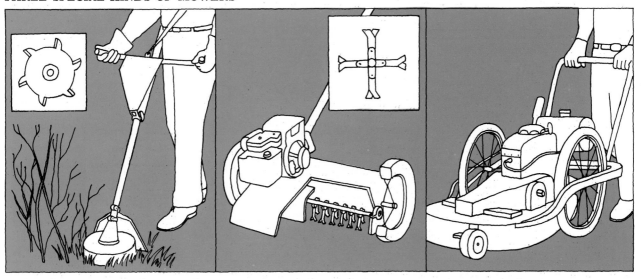

*A brush cutter will go where a mower on wheels cannot—into rough woods, for instance. Slung from a shoulder harness, it has a gas engine at one end of a long drive shaft and a rotary cutting blade at the other (inset).*

*The unusual Y-shaped knife blades of a flail mower (visible in the cutaway drawing above) permit its use in rocky or rubbish-laden areas without fear of hurling dangerous projectiles or damaging the machine.*

*A rotary mower with bicycle wheels is especially well suited to irregular terrain. The oversized wheels roll with ease over bumps and can be used as pivots to raise the cutting blades to clear any large obstacles.*

## MAINTAINING TIDY EDGES ON A LAWN

1. *To keep lawns neatly edged along plant beds and paths, set a strip of plastic or thin metal edging (top) into the ground with about an inch of the strip protruding, or build a "mowing strip" of stones or bricks laid flush with the soil surface (bottom); a regular mower is run with one wheel on the strip, reducing the necessity for hand trimming along the edge.*

2. *When you do have to trim off shoots that spread over an edge, use a pair of long-handled grass shears to help eliminate stooping.*

3. *A hand-operated rotary edger neatly clips off spreading grass as it is pushed along. A spoked disk rotates as the tool moves, bringing each sharp spoke against a stationary blade in a shearing action, snipping off the grass.*

4. *An electric power edger, which works like a small rotary mower set on edge, is especially useful for edging large lawns. Inside its casing is a single blade with cutting edges at both ends (inset); the blade rotates at high speed and slices off any blades of grass in its cutting line.*

home use have at least five blades, and some have seven. The more blades the mower has and the faster the reel spins, the more frequent the cutting interval, and the smoother the lawn. Mowers with fewer than five blades or with slow-turning blades may produce an ugly ridged or "washboard" effect.

Most reel mowers adjust downward from 2½ inches to ½ inch and they cut in swaths 16 to 24 inches wide. There are also some narrow reel mowers designed especially for trimming. Like the rotary mowers, many reel mowers are now powered by gas engines or electricity.

But the simplest and best reel mower for cool-climate grasses may well be a nonpowered model. The clumsy cast-iron models remembered by many middle-aged men from their youth have been superseded by lightweight machines that are much easier to operate and offer in addition a mild form of exercise. Besides being virtually noiseless—a boon to the neighbors—they do not pollute the air with exhaust fumes and they are ready to use at a moment's notice. There is no balky motor to fuss with, no gasoline to store. And most of them are less expensive as well. However, they are very difficult to use on the tough, wiry grasses that are usually grown in the warm climates.

Many lawn mowers, reel and rotary, powered and unpowered, come with optional grass-catching attachments. Probably they are the simplest of all solutions to the job of keeping the lawn free of the grass clippings that mar a smooth appearance. It used to be thought that the clippings would sift in among the live grasses and make an excellent mulch—and they may if they are fine enough. But it has been learned that such mulches, particularly if composed of fairly large particles, often harbor diseases.

Two other occasional tasks complete the routine care of a lawn. One is rolling, which should be done with discretion; the other is edging. Many a gardener thinks that his lawn should automatically be rolled every spring, to get rid of the surface irregularities caused by frost. This is not only unnecessary but it can be downright detrimental. One of the greatest enemies of a lawn is compact soil, and a roller creates just that. The roller should be confined to its use in starting a new lawn from seed *(page 93)*. Edging, the finishing touch in lawn maintenance, need not be done with every mowing and is done purely for appearance. Mechanical lawn edgers, either powered or hand operated, make short work of what was once a tiresome job done on the hands and knees with lawn shears. The chore can be greatly simplified if you install mowing strips, built as shown in the drawing *(opposite)*, around the edges of flower beds and the bases of trees.

ROLLING AND EDGING

After all the testing, feeding, watering and mowing, you may still have to combat attacks on your lawn from unexpected sources. One lady I know complained to a local lawn expert about the damage done by her neighbor's 89 cats; the lawn expert's answer to the problem was: get a dog.

Sour soil, drought, crab grass, animals—no wonder that the man who overcomes all these obstacles and achieves a rich green lawn feels not only an immense sense of satisfaction but also a tender concern for his enormous investment. A friend of mine was recently seen by his wife mowing his new lawn in his Sunday-go-to-meeting suit. When she asked what he was doing, he explained that after all his tribulation and the money and time he had spent on getting that lawn to grow properly, he felt it was only fitting to dress up for its first cutting.

# Lawn problems

Patches of dead or dying grass are a sure sign of lawn trouble, but isolating the cause of the trouble is not always a simple matter. Lawns are attacked by a variety of pests, some of which do their work invisibly below ground, and by an array of fungus diseases whose effects on the lawn tend to look very much alike. To complicate the diagnosis, a number of lawn injuries caused neither by pests nor by disease resemble the damage done by such enemies. The chart on this page covers these miscellaneous ills, many of which are cured by such simple remedies as extra watering or a change in mowing height. On the following pages are charts explaining how to recognize and eradicate or prevent pests, lawn diseases and weeds. The best defense against such agents of destruction is vigorous health: a well-fertilized, well-watered lawn with a thick turf kept free of decaying vegetation and debris will be safer from attack, and better able to fight it off if it comes, than a neglected lawn. When pests, diseases, and weeds gain a foothold—or, in the case of fungus diseases, even threaten—chemical treatment generally is required.

Because chemical controls work in various ways, the manner and timing of their application may be critical. Fungicides, for instance, are more effective as preventives than as cures. They coat the stems and leaves of plants with a protective film that makes the plant a less attractive host to disease-bearing spores, thus discouraging the spores from germinating. A fungicide should therefore be applied in advance of an expected infection, and the application should be repeated at regular intervals as long as the danger exists. Under normal conditions the interval is 10 to 14 days, but if the weather is humid, a condition favoring fungus attack, and if the lawn is vulnerable because showers have washed away earlier applications, the interval can be shortened to as little as once every four to seven days.

Insecticides are seldom applied until after the pest strikes, but frequent observation will help you catch an infestation in its early stages. Most lawn in-

| PROBLEMS | SYMPTOMS | CONTROLS |
|---|---|---|
| ALGAE, GREEN SCUM | A green or blackish scum, which cracks and peels back when dry, may form in low, wet or shaded areas, especially if soil is compacted. | Improve drainage and aerate soil (page 86). Copper sulfate and mancozeb are effective chemical controls. |
| BURIED DEBRIS | Patches of grass turn pale green and dry out because root growth is inhibited by buried scraps of leftover lumber, plaster or metal. | Dig out debris; if necessary, replace soil and reseed or lay sod. |
| CHLOROSIS | Grass turns yellow when a deficiency of such elements as iron or magnesium interferes with the normal metabolism of the plants. | Correction of soil pH may allow a needed element, already in the soil in indigestible form, to become available. If a soil test shows an iron deficiency, apply 2 to 3 ounces of iron sulfate dissolved in 5 to 10 gallons of water per 1,000 square feet of lawn; water well. If magnesium is lacking, use magnesium sulfate—½ pound to 5 gallons of water per 1,000 square feet. |
| COMPACTED SOIL | Lawns develop hard, bare spots or areas of knotweed or crab grass. | Use a turf aerator (page 86) on large areas, or dig up smaller spots to a depth of 5 to 6 inches with a spading fork, incorporating peat moss and fertilizer, or reseed or resod. If the section is one that must be walked on frequently, replace the grass with paving. |
| DOG URINE | Dead areas in the lawn, roughly circular, like injury by brown patch, snow mold or fairy ring, show a rich green circumference. | Dig up and reseed as above. |
| FERTILIZER BURN | Grass browns, especially in hot weather, because inorganic fertilizers have been spread unevenly and/or too heavily and not watered in. | Always water lawns thoroughly after applying inorganic fertilizers. If damage occurs, drench the lawn, especially in injured areas, to leach excess fertilizer deep into the soil and away from the grass roots. Avoid using inorganic fertilizers during hot weather. |

secticides are formulated to kill either by contact (with a penetrating poison for sucking insects) or by ingestion (with a stomach poison for chewing insects). Insecticide application techniques also vary with the eating habits of the pest. To kill those that operate aboveground, by chewing or sucking on stems and leaves, you should avoid washing insecticide off the plants. Supply the lawn's moisture needs by a thorough soaking before applying the insecticide and then do not water at all for several days. To kill pests that operate underground by feeding on the roots, apply the insecticide to the lawn and then water thoroughly to wash the poison down into the root zone.

Pesticides come in various forms—as granules for use in spreaders, as liquid concentrates and wettable powders that are used in spraying equipment, and as ready-to-use dusts and liquids in convenient squeeze-plastic or aerosol containers. Many of them are mixtures, designed to take care of several lawn problems at once; check the label to make sure it contains the particular chemical you want. Read the label too for directions about amounts and application procedures, and follow them scrupulously. If the instructions say one tablespoon per gallon, do not conclude that two tablespoons per gallon will do the job more quickly or thoroughly; often the extra-strength mixture will simply damage the lawn. Also, heed the manufacturer's precautions. Many of these chemicals are toxic or will burn the skin, and in addition may be harmful to birds, household pets and beneficial insects like honeybees if not used correctly. Never spray or dust on a windy day, never use insecticides, herbicides or fungicides while you are smoking, and never spray or dust around foodstuffs. Do not dump out leftover chemicals in puddles or piles where children, birds or household pets might get into them. Wash out sprayers and spreaders after use, and thoroughly wash your face and hands. Never use a sprayer of weed-killing chemicals for any other purpose. Store all chemicals in a safe place that is well out of the reach of children.

| PROBLEMS | SYMPTOMS | CONTROLS |
|---|---|---|
| IMPROPER MOWING | Lawns cut too closely weaken, turn yellowish and often look diseased. Cutting with a dull mower frays leaf tips, which then turn brown. | Set mower to the recommended height for your type of grass (Chapter 5). Mow often enough so that you remove no more than one third of the grass height at one time. Keep mower blades sharp. |
| IMPROPER WATERING | Light sprinkling encourages shallow roots and weakened, stunted grass that dries out too quickly; overwatering encourages lawn diseases. | Water only during dry spells, when the grass begins to wilt, soaking the soil to a depth of at least 6 inches. Water early in the day so the grass will dry before nightfall; grass that remains damp overnight is especially susceptible to fungus diseases. |
| MOLES | Long, rounded ridges, soft when stepped on, indicate mole tunnels close to the surface of the ground. | Mole baits and mole traps are effective. Since moles eat grubs, make sure you control grubs with proper chemicals (pages 66-67). |
| MOSS | Moss may grow in patches or take over entire areas of lawn. It thrives in shady, moist conditions and in acid or compacted soil. | Prune or remove trees to lighten shade. Improve the drainage and correct soil acidity. In heavily shaded or naturally moist areas it may be easier to grow shade- and acid-tolerant plants—moss itself is one choice—than to develop the conditions needed to grow grass. |
| SLIME MOLD | A bluish gray, black or yellow slimy beaded mass that dries to a powder on grass foliage. It usually appears in warm, wet weather. | Sweep off the mold with a rake or broom, then wash down the foliage with water. Avoid overwatering of lawns, especially in warm, humid weather. |
| THATCH | An accumulation of mowed grass stems and dead or dying roots that blocks water, air and nutrients. It leaves lawns dry and ailing. | Use a dethatching machine as illustrated on page 88. |

| PESTS | DESCRIPTION |
|---|---|
| ANTS <br> 1  2  3 | Ants most troublesome to lawns are the cornfield ant (1), the pavement ant (2), which often nests at the edge of paving, and the Argentine ant (3). All are ⅛ inch long or less. |
| ARMY WORMS | Army worms, the larvae of night-flying moths, are so called because they travel in densely packed groups, devouring grasses along their route. Especially troublesome is the fall army worm, a ½-inch-long tropical insect, tan, green, or black with stripes down its back, that attacks southern lawns in summer and migrates to plague northern lawns in the fall. |
| BILLBUGS | The adult billbug, a ¼- to ¾-inch-long reddish brown or black beetle with a long snout, lays eggs that hatch into white, chunky, legless larvae about ½ inch long. |
| CHINCH BUGS | Chinch bugs rapidly develop from brick-red nymphs of microscopic size to 1/16-inch-long adults that have black bodies with white wings and red legs. |
| CUTWORMS | Smooth brownish or grayish caterpillars that grow up to 2 inches in length, cutworms hide in the soil or under pieces of trash during the daytime and come out at night to do their feeding. They are a threat to lawn grasses from spring until late summer. |
| FIERY SKIPPERS | The orange butterflies called fiery skippers fly over the lawn during the day and lay eggs that hatch into brownish yellow caterpillars that are ½ to 1 inch long. |
| GRUBS <br> 1  2 <br> 3  4 | Thick, whitish U-shaped worms ¾ inch to 1½ inches long, grubs are the larvae of beetles, including Japanese (1), Asiatic garden (2), June (3) and rose chafer (4) beetles. |
| LEAF HOPPERS | Leaf hoppers are slender, wedge-shaped insects, yellow, green or brown in color and less than ½ inch long. They hop away quickly when they are disturbed. Several species cause damage to lawn grasses, particularly along the East and West Coasts. |
| MITES <br> 1  2 | Two species of these tiny spiderlike creatures cause the most trouble on lawns: pale green, microscopic Bermuda-grass mites (1) attack Western and Gulf Coast lawns, while clover mites (2), dark red and about as big as specks of pepper, attack lawns throughout the U.S. (and also get inside houses where they lay eggs and multiply). |
| MOLE CRICKETS | Relatives of grasshoppers, these 1½-inch-long, brownish insects live in the soil during the day and come out at night to feed. They are especially harmful to lawns in the South. |
| NEMATODES | Tiny, often microscopic animals, nematodes are virtually colorless; they are transparent wormlike animals whose bodies have a slight whitish or yellowish tint. |
| SOD WEBWORMS | These ¾-inch-long, light brown or gray wormlike larvae come from eggs laid in the grass at dusk by hovering, tan-colored lawn moths. Sod webworms do their greatest damage from spring to midsummer, especially to bluegrasses and bent grasses. |

| SIGNS OF INFESTATION | CHEMICAL CONTROLS | OTHER CONTROL METHODS |
|---|---|---|
| These insects form small mounds around the entrances to their nests, making the lawn surface unsightly and smothering the grass beneath. | carbaryl | |
| Army worms mar a lawn with dead spots or streaks several inches wide as they eat through grass foliage, starting at soil level and working up. | carbaryl<br>diazinon | |
| Adult billbugs chew holes in grass blades, then deposit eggs in them. The larvae tunnel inside grass stems, eating their way down through the roots and killing the grass in sharply defined patches. Bluegrass is especially vulnerable. | carbaryl<br>diazinon<br>(both only partially<br>effective because larvae are<br>inside stems) | |
| Throughout their lives, chinch bugs attack grasses, leaving brown, dead patches. As nymphs they begin sucking juices from grass in spring and continue until fall, mainly on dry, sunny sections of lawns. A second brood feeds in midsummer. | Aspon<br>carbaryl<br>diazinon<br>(propoxur on<br>St. Augustine grass) | For a small area, soak the soil with warm water and cover it with a white cloth. Fifteen minutes later, pick the bugs off the cloth and destroy them. |
| These pests eat away grass stems near the surface of the soil, causing dead spots 1 to 2 inches wide. | carbaryl<br>chlordane<br>commercial poison baits<br>diazinon | |
| The caterpillars tie grass stems together for their nests, feeding inside this covering and killing the shoots as they eat. Damage appears first in circular spots, from 1 to 2 inches in diameter, then the affected areas gradually expand to larger sizes. | carbaryl<br>diazinon | |
| In spring and fall, grubs eat away the roots of grass, creating brownish dead patches that are slightly soggy and can be lifted out of the lawn. | carbaryl<br>chlordane<br>diazinon | Pull up dead grass and pick the grubs from the underside. A preparation of milky disease spores, which kill grubs, can be applied in severe cases. |
| These insects suck the juices from grass blades, causing them first to become strippled white, then yellow and finally brown. Leaf hoppers also carry several virus diseases harmful to plants. | diazinon<br>pyrethrum | |
| Mites suck juices from grass blades, causing them to wilt, turn yellow and die. Severely damaged lawns become so thin that weeds take over. Mites are especially attracted to lawns that are lush and green from heavy fertilizing. | chlordane<br>diazinon<br>malathion | Since the clover mite migrates from grass to house interiors, maintaining a grass-free border around the house will help reduce indoor infestation. |
| These creatures tunnel through the upper 2 inches of soil to sever underground roots and stems during the day and aboveground stems at night, leaving patches of grass that appear to have been closely clipped off with shears. | chlordane | |
| Nematodes feed mostly on roots, but also on stems and leaves, stunting the plants. Often the lawn takes on a bleached-out appearance. The damaged plants are weakened and become especially vulnerable to bacteria and fungus disease. | DBCP<br>VC-13 Nemacide<br>(both applied two to three<br>weeks before or just after seed<br>is planted) | Use of an organic fertilizer made from processed sewage sludge suppresses nematodes, presumably by encouraging the nematodes' predators. |
| Larvae eat their way through the grass, causing irregularly shaped, brownish spots. If damage goes unchecked, spots may run together to form large areas of browned-out turf. | carbaryl<br>chlordane<br>diazinon<br>propoxur | |

| DISEASES | SIGNS OF INFECTION | GRASSES ATTACKED |
|---|---|---|
| BROWN PATCH | Irregularly shaped brown spots 1 inch to several feet in diameter usually appear in warm, humid weather giving a "smoke ring" effect. At first leaves are dark brown and look water-soaked; then they wilt and become light brown. Roots and stems of grasses may rot. | All grasses are susceptible, but bent grasses and St. Augustine grass are most seriously affected. |
| COPPER SPOT | Straw-colored spots with dark rims form on the grass leaves, then copper-colored dead areas 1 to 3 inches in diameter appear in the turf. This disease, frequently found in humid coastal areas where soils are acid, may kill the grass affected. | Bent grasses and redtop. |
| DOLLAR SPOT (SMALL BROWN PATCH) | Brown patches soon develop into bleached or straw-colored spots about the size of a silver dollar (thus the name). Spots may run together to make irregular blotches. This fungus usually appears during warm wet weather on lawns low in nitrogen. Affected grass is killed. | Bent grasses are most susceptible, but Bermuda, fescues, Kentucky bluegrass, St. Augustine and Zoysia may also be affected. |
| FAIRY RINGS | Fairy rings are circles of mushrooms that appear during wet weather in spring and fall, leaving areas of dead grass as they spread. Grass close to the mushrooms grows vigorously. The grass inside the rings dies as nutrients and moisture are exhausted by the mushrooms. | These fungi do not attack grass directly, but deprive the roots of essential nutrients and moisture. |
| FUSARIUM BLIGHT | Small tan or straw-colored spots appear in early summer and may merge to cover large areas. Most prevalent in the Northeast and Central states on sunny lawns, Fusarium blight is encouraged by frequent light watering and by heavy thatch buildup (page 86). | Bent grasses, red fescue and Kentucky bluegrass are most susceptible to this disease. |
| GRAY LEAF SPOT | Tiny brown spots appear on grass leaves, then spread to become elongated lesions with gray centers and brown or purple waterlogged edges, causing the grass to appear scorched. This fungus spreads rapidly in hot, humid, rainy weather. | St. Augustine grass. |
| GREASE SPOT | A white cottony film develops on the surface of the turf, soon followed by roundish, reddish brown spots several inches in diameter with greasy looking, nearly black borders. The grass eventually dies. Grease spot is most prevalent in hot, humid weather on poorly drained soils. | Bent grasses, Bermuda grass, fescues, Kentucky bluegrass, rye and St. Augustine grass. |
| LEAF SPOTS AND BLIGHTS | Round or oval lesions appear on leaves as brown, purplish black or gray spots and may spread to kill both foliage and roots. Leaf spots occur from midspring until late fall, mostly in wet weather. | Almost all grasses are susceptible but bent grasses, Kentucky bluegrass, Bermuda grass and fescues are particularly vulnerable. |
| OPHIOBOLUS PATCH | Irregularly round light reddish brown patches 2 inches to 2 feet in diameter appear and eventually turn gray or yellowish tan as both foliage and roots die. This disease is prevalent in the Pacific Northwest and appears occasionally in the Northeast. | Bent grasses, bluegrasses, fescues and rye. |
| POWDERY MILDEW | White, grayish white or brown mold forms on foliage, especially in shade or where air circulation is poor or soil is not well drained. Mildew occurs most often when days are warm and humid and nights are cool. Grass may wither and die, especially when newly planted. | Bluegrasses (especially Merion) and fescues. |
| RED THREAD (PINK PATCH) | Grass blades become stuck together with red threadlike growths. This fungus thrives in cool, damp weather in spring and fall, spreading to form irregular pink patches 2 to 6 inches in diameter. Grass roots may be killed. This disease is prevalent along northern coastal regions. | Bent grasses, bluegrasses, fescues and rye. |
| RUST | Yellow-orange, orange, reddish brown or black blisters form on grass leaves and can cause plants to wither and die. When blisters burst, infection can be easily spread. Heavy dew in late summer and fall encourages development of rust. | Bermuda grass, bluegrasses (especially Merion), rye, St. Augustine grass and Zoysia. |
| SNOW MOLD | Pinkish or tan patches ranging from 6 inches to several feet in diameter usually appear as snow melts in the spring. Shaded, wet areas of lawn where snow lingers are especially susceptible to this fungus. Severe infections will kill grass roots. | All grasses in areas where snow lies on the ground for extended periods. |
| SMUT | Leaves develop gray or black stripes, which rupture to discharge powdery black spores that infect other plants. Diseased leaves become shredded and curled before dying. Infected plants are usually stunted and yellowish green. | Bent grasses and bluegrasses (especially Windsor and Merion). |

Do not apply too much quick-release high-nitrogen fertilizer in hot weather. Apply lime if soil pH is below the optimum. Mow often and remove clippings. Do not water late in the day. When establishing a new lawn, provide good drainage.

Keep grasses well fed in spring and fall. Remove clippings after mowing. It may help to lime the soil if the pH is below the optimum recommended.

Keep grasses well fed in spring and fall. Remove clippings after mowing.

Complete eradication may involve replacing the entire lawn. However, forcing great quantities of water 10 to 24 inches into the soil through a metal root feeder attached to a garden hose close to the fairy ring will keep the grass roots alive.

Water lawn during dry spells, giving it a thorough soaking so the soil is wet to a depth of 6 or 8 inches. Remove thatch at regular intervals. Lime should be applied if the soil pH is below the recommended level.

Avoid excessive use of quick-release high-nitrogen fertilizers.

Water grass only when necessary and do so early in the day so it will dry before nightfall. When establishing a new lawn, provide good drainage. Sow seeds only when the weather is cool and dry.

Water grass only when it is necessary. Avoid applying excessive amounts of quick-release high-nitrogen fertilizers during the summer. Mow regularly and always remove grass clippings. Remove thatch regularly.

Maintain proper soil pH and avoid using excessive amounts of quick-release high-nitrogen fertilizers. Supply nitrogen by applying an acid-forming ammonium sulfate fertilizer.

Avoid overfertilizing and overwatering during hot, humid weather. Remove grass clippings after mowing.

Keep grasses well fed in spring and fall.

Feed and water grass regularly to promote good growth. Mow frequently to remove infected blades and stems. Remove clippings after mowing.

Mow grass very short in late fall and remove clippings.

Since varieties of bluegrass differ in their susceptibility to this disease, plant either a mixture of varieties or a single one known to be resistant to smut.

## CHEMICAL CONTROLS

Many fungus diseases that attack lawn grasses are hard to identify; even experts have trouble telling some apart. For this reason, manufacturers of garden chemicals have formulated multipurpose fungicides. These are sold under a variety of trade names and each is designed to control several specific diseases. There are also some single-purpose fungicides. In selecting a fungicide, keep in mind that while one type may do the job in an area where conditions favor a light infection, a differently formulated fungicide may work better in an area that is usually subject to severe infections.

The best way to be sure of the results you will get is to choose a fungicide that has been tested in your area and has been found to be effective against locally prevalent fungi. How do you find out? You can seek advice from a garden supply dealer in whom you have confidence. But if you need more specific information, your local agricultural extension agent is the person to call. He will know about local tests and—equally important —he will have current information about which chemicals have been restricted in their use.

Be sure to read the label of any fungicide before you buy it. The label or accompanying leaflet will list precisely the fungus or fungi the formulation has been designed to control. And it will give you detailed instructions on how to use the product.

Grass fungicides are generally available as wettable powders or liquid concentrates that are mixed with water and sprayed on the infected area of the lawn. Since the active chemical ingredients may be washed off the grass by rain or removed as the grass is cut, repeat applications may be necessary.

# What to do about weeds

Despite its bad name, a weed can be an attractive plant, as the paintings below indicate; actually a weed is nothing more than a plant that is out of place. The lawn, of course, is no place for weeds. There are two kinds that appear in lawns, grassy weeds and broad-leaved weeds, and each requires its own type of chemical control. Grassy weeds—crab grass is the most troublesome—can be stopped even before they are visible by "pre-emergent" killers, which destroy the germinating seed. When such weeds do appear, they can be destroyed by chemicals that poison the grow-ing plant. Broad-leaved weeds, such as chickweed and dandelion, are killed by chemicals that upset their hormone balance, causing the plants to speed up their processes and literally grow themselves to death.

Whatever the weed, it is best dealt with individually. Use one of the spot-treatment devices discussed in Chapter 2 unless you face such a heavy infestation that you must spray. Spray with care and only on a windless day. This caution applies especially to broad-leaved weed killers, which can harm any broad-leaved plant, including valued trees and shrubs.

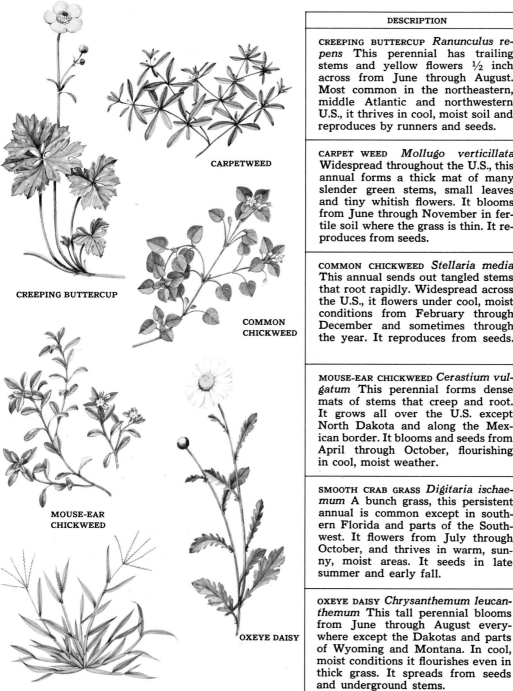

CARPETWEED

CREEPING BUTTERCUP

COMMON CHICKWEED

MOUSE-EAR CHICKWEED

SMOOTH CRAB GRASS

OXEYE DAISY

| DESCRIPTION | TREATMENT |
|---|---|
| CREEPING BUTTERCUP *Ranunculus repens* This perennial has trailing stems and yellow flowers ½ inch across from June through August. Most common in the northeastern, middle Atlantic and northwestern U.S., it thrives in cool, moist soil and reproduces by runners and seeds. | Apply silvex, dicamba, mecoprop or 2,4-D in the spring. |
| CARPET WEED *Mollugo verticillata* Widespread throughout the U.S., this annual forms a thick mat of many slender green stems, small leaves and tiny whitish flowers. It blooms from June through November in fertile soil where the grass is thin. It reproduces from seeds. | Apply 2,4-D in the spring and repeat applications if the weed persists. Thicken the turf *(Chapter 2)*. |
| COMMON CHICKWEED *Stellaria media* This annual sends out tangled stems that root rapidly. Widespread across the U.S., it flowers under cool, moist conditions from February through December and sometimes through the year. It reproduces from seeds. | Control with dicamba, silvex, or mecoprop in the spring or fall. Or you can pull this weed easily by hand. |
| MOUSE-EAR CHICKWEED *Cerastium vulgatum* This perennial forms dense mats of stems that creep and root. It grows all over the U.S. except North Dakota and along the Mexican border. It blooms and seeds from April through October, flourishing in cool, moist weather. | This weed is hard to pull out because it becomes entangled in the grass, so it is best controlled by applying dicamba, mecoprop or silvex either in spring or in fall. |
| SMOOTH CRAB GRASS *Digitaria ischaemum* A bunch grass, this persistent annual is common except in southern Florida and parts of the Southwest. It flowers from July through October, and thrives in warm, sunny, moist areas. It seeds in late summer and early fall. | Mow the grass high. In early spring, apply siduron, DCPA, terbutol or bensulide. In summer, make two or three applications of DSMA or MSMA every seven to 10 days. |
| OXEYE DAISY *Chrysanthemum leucanthemum* This tall perennial blooms from June through August everywhere except the Dakotas and parts of Wyoming and Montana. In cool, moist conditions it flourishes even in thick grass. It spreads from seeds and underground stems. | Remove the plants by hand with a knife or trowel. This daisy is hard to eliminate and silvex may have to be applied to individual plants in stronger-than-usual concentrations. |

| DESCRIPTION | TREATMENT |
|---|---|
| DALLIS GRASS *Paspalum dilatatum* This perennial may reach 5 feet in height. It thrives from May to fall in moist, warm regions, in the South and parts of the Southwest, on the East Coast as far north as New Jersey, and in coastal Oregon. It spreads by underground stems and seeds. | If few plants are present, remove by hand. Apply DSMA or AMA in early spring or summer when growth begins; usually two to four treatments a week apart are necessary. |
| DANDELION *Taraxacum officinale* A nuisance except in southernmost Florida and Texas and southwestern Arizona, the perennial dandelion thrives under almost any soil and weather conditions. In warm areas, it flowers and seeds all year, and elsewhere from March to frost. | Dig plants with a knife or other tool (they will grow back unless the entire taproot is removed). Apply 2,4-D in spring or fall. |
| CURLY DOCK *Rumex crispus* A perennial, curly dock has a husky taproot that may go 2 feet deep, and one or more stems that may grow as high as 3 feet. Prevalent throughout the U.S., it flowers from June through September and reproduces itself from seeds. | Remove the plants by hand, making sure to pull up the entire root. Or apply 2,4-D, dicamba or silvex in fall or spring; direct the chemical spray onto individual root crowns. |
| GREEN FOXTAIL *Setaria viridis* A widespread annual, this weed may grow 3 feet tall. It is found throughout the U.S. and is most prevalent in new lawns or in old lawns where the grass has become thin. Green foxtail flowers from June through September, reproducing from seeds. | Apply DCPA in early spring. |
| WILD GARLIC *Allium vineale* (also called wild onion) A perennial, wild garlic is found on the East and Northwest Coasts, all over the South, and in many central states. It flourishes in wet, fertile clay, flowers from May through July and spreads by producing bulbs as well as seeds. | Mow frequently. Control major infestations with repeated applications of dicamba and 2,4-D in late fall and early spring. |
| DISSECTED GERANIUM *Geranium dissectum* This annual grows up to 2 feet tall; it is particularly common on the U.S. West Coast and is found occasionally in the East. It flowers from February through June and thrives in dry, sandy soil. It reproduces from seeds. | Pull weeds when the ground is moist. Apply 2,4-D if they persist. |
| GOOSE GRASS *Eleusine indica* (also called silver crab grass) An annual that grows in tufts, goose grass has stems as tall as 2 feet. It is found everywhere except the Northeast on warm, damp lawns. It blooms from June through October, seeds from July through October. | If there are few plants, remove them by hand. Apply DCPA, bandane or bensulide before the seeds germinate. After the weed appears, treat it with DSMA or AMA at 10-day intervals. |
| GROUND IVY *Glechoma hederacea* A perennial, ground ivy has four-sided stems and blue or purple flowers. It is found in fertile, damp, shaded areas throughout the eastern half of the U.S., except Florida. It flowers from April through June and spreads by rooted stems as well as seeds. | Apply silvex or dicamba in the spring or fall when active growth of the weed is underway. |

DALLIS GRASS

DANDELION

GREEN FOXTAIL

CURLY DOCK

DISSECTED GERANIUM

WILD GARLIC

GROUND IVY

GOOSE GRASS

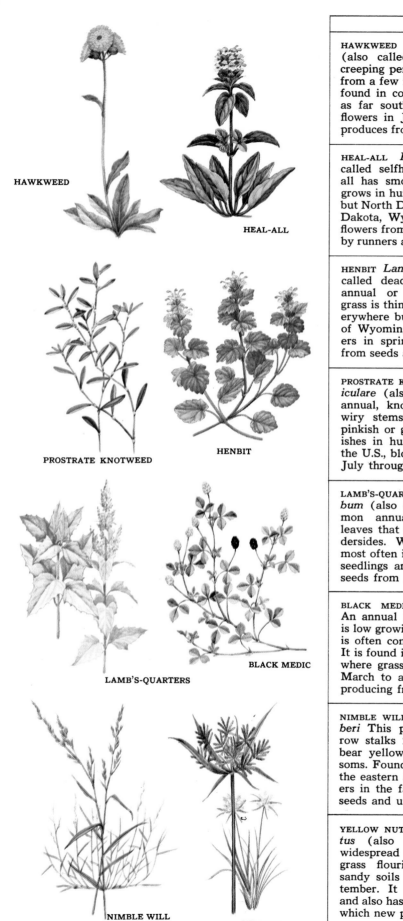

HAWKWEED

HEAL-ALL

PROSTRATE KNOTWEED

HENBIT

LAMB'S-QUARTERS

BLACK MEDIC

NIMBLE WILL

YELLOW NUT GRASS

| DESCRIPTION | TREATMENT |
|---|---|
| HAWKWEED *Hieracium aurantiacum* (also called devil's-paintbrush) A creeping perennial, hawkweed grows from a few inches to 2 feet tall. It is found in cool, moist soil sometimes as far south as North Carolina. It flowers in July and August and reproduces from seeds. | Apply either 2,4-D or dicamba in the spring or fall when hawkweed is growing actively. |
| HEAL-ALL *Prunella vulgaris* (also called selfheal) A perennial, heal-all has smooth or hairy leaves. It grows in humid, rich soil everywhere but North Dakota and parts of South Dakota, Wyoming and Montana. It flowers from May to fall and spreads by runners as well as seeds. | Apply 2,4-D or dicamba in the spring or fall during periods of active growth. |
| HENBIT *Lamium amplexicaule* (also called dead nettle) Henbit is an annual or biennial, found where grass is thin in humid, fertile soil everywhere but the Dakotas and parts of Wyoming and Montana. It flowers in spring and fall, reproducing from seeds and spreading roots. | Use dicamba or silvex on established turf, but remove weeds by hand from new lawns. |
| PROSTRATE KNOTWEED *Polygonum aviculare* (also called wire grass) An annual, knotweed forms a mat of wiry stems and bears clusters of pinkish or greenish flowers. It flourishes in humid, cool areas all over the U.S., blooming and seeding from July through November. | Apply dicamba; 2,4-D or silvex may be effective if applied when plants are young. Old woody plants are hard to kill and usually must be pulled by hand. |
| LAMB'S-QUARTERS *Chenopodium album* (also called pigweed) A common annual, lamb's-quarters has leaves that appear white on the undersides. Widespread, it is found most often in new lawns where grass seedlings are sparse. It flowers and seeds from June through October. | Mow closely, and pull up the weeds by hand. If the infestation is severe, apply 2,4-D anytime during the active period of growth. |
| BLACK MEDIC *Medicago lupulina* An annual or biennial, black medic is low growing, with hairy stems, and is often confused with white clover. It is found in dry, less fertile regions where grass is thin. It flowers from March to as late as December, reproducing from seeds. | Use dicamba or silvex in early spring when the plant is growing actively, and again in fall. |
| NIMBLE WILL *Muhlenbergia schreberi* This perennial has long, narrow stalks 2 to 6 inches high that bear yellowish or light green blossoms. Found in moist soil chiefly in the eastern and central U.S., it flowers in the fall and reproduces from seeds and underground runners. | Hand pull weeds during the growing season, or spot treat with dalapon, being careful not to damage the surrounding grass. Reseed if necessary in fall. |
| YELLOW NUT GRASS *Cyperus esculentus* (also called nut sedge) A widespread perennial, yellow nut grass flourishes in moist, fertile, sandy soils from July through September. It reproduces from seeds and also has food-storing tubers from which new plants can sprout. | Spray on DSMA or AMA in two to three applications at seven to 10-day intervals, for two or more consecutive years, mainly in early summer. |

| DESCRIPTION | TREATMENT |
|---|---|
| PENNYWORT *Hydrocotyle rotundifolia* A creeping perennial, pennywort thrives in moist, shady areas from Massachusetts to Florida, west to Indiana and Texas and in southern California. It blooms from July to October, reproducing from seeds and underground stems. | Apply either mecoprop or silvex. |
| BROAD-LEAF PLANTAIN *Plantago major* A perennial and sometimes an annual, broad-leaf plantain has 3- to 6-inch leaves that cluster on the ground. It is widespread, in soil of moderate to good fertility. It blooms from June through October and reproduces from seeds. | Dig up the individual plants if there are not too many. Spray with 2,4-D in the spring and again in fall. Use spot treatments during September and October. |
| BUCKHORN PLANTAIN *Plantago lanceolata* (also known as narrow-leaf plantain) An annual, narrow-leaf plantain has lance-shaped leaves 3 to 12 inches long. Widespread, it blooms in areas of low to moderate fertility, from May to fall, reproducing from seeds. | Dig out the individual plants with a knife. Apply 2,4-D in the spring and again in the fall. |
| QUACK GRASS *Agropyron repens* (also known as couch grass) A perennial, quack grass may exceed 3 feet in height. Common, except in the Deep South and parts of the Southwest, it flowers from late May to fall, spreading by seeds and by very long underground stems. | Treat the affected area with dalapon and wait three weeks before reseeding. Moisten the area weekly during this period. |
| RED SORREL *Rumex acetosella* (also known as sheep sorrel) A perennial that may grow 18 inches tall, red sorrel is found all over the U.S., usually in the early summer, in lawns with poor soil and poor drainage. It reproduces with creeping underground stems and from seeds. | Use dicamba in early spring or in early fall when the plant is actively growing. |
| CANADA THISTLE *Cirsium arvense* A perennial, Canada thistle has branching stalks that may grow as high as 4 feet. It is found throughout the northern half of the U.S. in rich clay soil and flowers from July through October. It reproduces from seeds and from underground roots. | Cut off isolated plants just below the root crown with a knife. Apply 2,4-D or dicamba in spring or fall. |
| YELLOW WOOD SORREL *Oxalis stricta* A perennial, yellow wood sorrel has hairy stems that may grow 18 inches tall. It thrives in dry, open places throughout the U.S. and blooms from May through October. Mature seed pods explode if touched, disseminating tiny seeds. | Treat plants with silvex or with several applications of mecoprop. |
| YARROW *Achillea millefolium* (also called milfoil) A perennial, yarrow may exceed 3 feet in height. Often grown in gardens for its flowers, it is considered a weed in lawns. It thrives in poor soil everywhere, except the Southwest. It spreads by seeds and underground stems. | Dig the yarrow out when it first appears. Later, control it with 2,4-D or dicamba, repeating applications as necessary. |

PENNYWORT

BROAD-LEAF PLANTAIN

BUCKHORN PLANTAIN

QUACK GRASS

RED SORREL

YELLOW WOOD SORREL

CANADA THISTLE

YARROW

# An ant's-eye view of lawn grasses

Not to see the forest for the trees is a common failing of perspective. But with lawns, if there is an oversight it is usually the other way around. The gardener, lost in contemplation of an expanse of green, too often overlooks the nature of the individual plants that comprise the turf. And yet, as the close-up photographs on these and the following pages demonstrate, it takes what might be called an ant's-eye view to reveal best how one kind of lawn grass differs from another, to explain why those differences influence growth habits, and to document the harm caused by disease or improper maintenance.

The anatomy of lawn grasses clearly influences the way they spread to form a thick lawn. Under close scrutiny, two basic growth patterns emerge. There are the creepers, whose stems grow horizontally, like a tangled mop. And there are the upright grasses, whose stems form upright clusters, like the bristles of a broom. Then there are a few, most notably the famous Kentucky bluegrass, that grow both ways. Kentucky bluegrass appears to grow as an upright plant, spreading as it multiplies its vertical stems around a central core. But when the earth is removed, as in the photograph at right, the creeping nature of Kentucky bluegrass is revealed. The four distinct sets of upright stems and leaves, each sprouting a cluster of fibrous roots and each resembling a separate upright plant, are seen to be connected by horizontal underground stems called rhizomes. These rhizomes have spread from the mother plant, the cluster at center. However, that cluster has also spread on its own, the way upright grasses do, sprouting several stems from what was originally a single stem. So long as sufficient moisture and nourishment are present, both spreading patterns will continue through the growing season, keeping the sod thick and firm, one reason for the special favor Kentucky bluegrass enjoys as a lawn material.

Not many other varieties of lawn grasses share the schizophrenic growing habits of Kentucky bluegrass. But all reveal, in the fine details that are visible only from close up, how they can serve in your lawn and react to your care.

*A parent clump (center) and its three satellite shoots show how Kentucky bluegrass spreads laterally underground.*

# Grasses that creep

Nearly all the grasses used in southern lawns (Areas B, C and E on the climate map, page 150) are creepers—and as a general rule the warmer it gets the faster they creep. As the summer thermometer climbs, the grass grows thicker and thicker, creating smooth greens like the one at left at a time when northern lawns lose their spring freshness.

The ability to thrive in heat is shared by many creepers. But the three most useful of the southern creeping grasses —Bermuda, Zoysia, and St. Augustine —are prized because they are also very attractive. All three spread rapidly, producing not only the underground stems called rhizomes but also aboveground lateral stems, or stolons. The stolons and rhizomes reach out in all directions, sending green shoots up and roots down at points called nodes. Stolons, however, can start a new plant only where a node comes in contact with a bit of moist earth. The result of this process, clearly visible in the picture of St. Augustine grass on the opposite page, is another new and semi-independent grass plant.

As the vinelike stolons proliferate and intertwine, they produce a tightly woven layer of stems that, when kept closely mowed, sprouts a dense mat of green leaves. However, if the southern creepers are not kept mowed to the recommended height, the leaves tend to lie down, creating a disheveled appearance.

*A lawn of St. Augustine grass*

*Its fine, closely packed green leaves make Bermuda grass a popular one for southern lawns. In the photograph above, a sturdy underground rhizome shoots off to the left while above it can be seen one surface stem, a stolon, sprouting leaves.*

*Sprigs of Zoysia grass rise at evenly spaced intervals all along a rhizome. This specimen lacks visible stolons, distinguishable from the white rhizomes by their green color.*

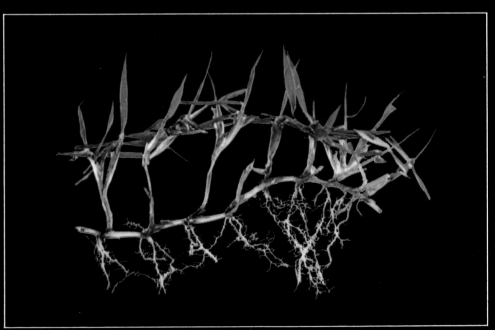

*Bahia grass makes a virtue of its coarseness. It grows from lumpy, thick rhizomes that sprout robust roots, which enables it to withstand shade, some drought and rough use, discouraging to finer southern grasses.*

*This green stolon of St. Augustine grass has sent down roots wherever its knuckly nodes have touched moist soil. From this point spring its lush green leaves. Rhizomes will develop as the grass becomes thicker.*

*Unlike other creeping lawn grasses, centipede grass does not produce rhizomes but spreads aboveground by long stolons. The sprig below is growing to the left. Roots have formed and new white shoots are just beginning to become visible.*

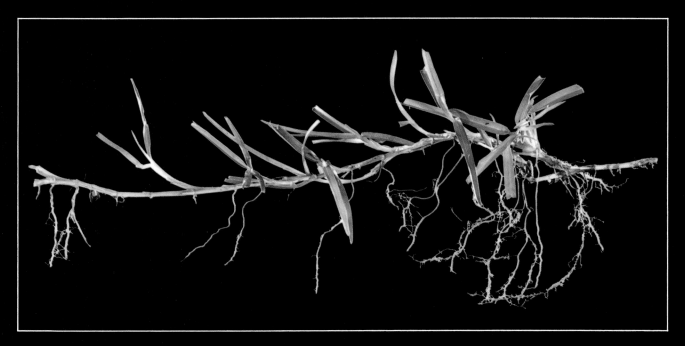

*When grown as tight turf, Colonial bent grass
sends its stems almost straight up, rather than
out and then upward in the characteristic
pattern that gives the bent grasses their name.*

# Grasses that grow straight up

A lawn of upright grasses resembles a velvet carpet, countless individual plants each sending thin stems and leaves almost straight up in much the way the carpet fibers project upward. If the individual plants are packed closely enough together, such a lawn (right) will have a velvet carpet's resilience. Upright grass species are seldom grown in the South except as a temporary winter lawn—the summer heat kills them—but they are widely used in the northern half of the U.S. (Areas A, D and F on the climate map, page 150).

Most upright grasses are similar to those pictured here: individual plants having bunchy fibrous roots that support tight clusters of vertical stems. They produce no more than rudimentary rhizomes and possess no stolons at all. They spread by expanding the size of each cluster as new stems spring up around the base of the cluster. These new stems are called tillers. The growth process, known as tillering, is encouraged by frequent mowing, which thickens the lawn. But mowing too closely harms most upright grasses. The food-manufacturing parts of the plant are vertical, and if you cut too much of them away, the whole plant suffers from lack of nourishment. That is why frequent fertilizing and intensive care must be lavished on the closely cropped patch of Colonial bent pictured above to keep it so richly green and thick.

*A section of Colonial bent grass*

*The tough, wiry leaves of red fescue (above) call for a sharp mower. That same toughness enables the fescues to thrive where most lawn grasses fail—in shade, poor soil and drought.*

*An improved strain of perennial rye grass, grown at Rutgers University, boasts finer leaves than its forebears, although they are still coarser than those of the fescue shown above.*

to see clearly the harm caused to any individual grass plant by mistreatment —the bruising and weakening caused by improper mowing *(right)*, the choking by unremoved thatch *(far right)*, the stunting that comes from chemically unbalanced soil *(below and left)*.

Failure to keep the soil nearly neutral —neither too acid nor too alkaline—is one of the commonest causes of a scrawny lawn. The reason, oddly enough, depends partly on bacteria. They operate most efficiently when their systems are chemically near neutral. And it is soil bacteria that, through a complex series of chemical transformations, make nitrogen—the single most important nutrient for leaf growth—available to plants. The nitrogen compounds in many fertilizers are of no direct benefit to a plant; they must be converted into other compounds that the plant can use for nourishment, and this essential job is performed by bacterial enzyme systems. But the enzyme systems are deactivated by acid, so that grass plants may go hungry although abundantly fertilized. The fertilizer itself may even produce reactions that increase acidity. A well-fertilized lawn should be tested periodically to see if lime is needed to reduce its acidity to a level closer to neutral *(Chapter 2)*.

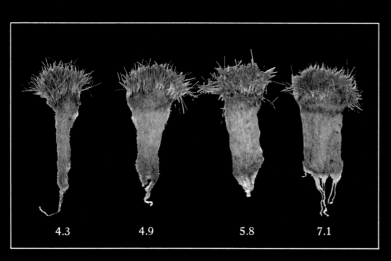

4.3          4.9          5.8          7.1

*The three-month-old plants above demonstrate how Kentucky bluegrass, like most grasses, gains in vigor as ground limestone is added to an acid soil, shifting the acid-alkali balance (indicated beneath each of the samples) toward a neutral pH reading of 7.0. Nitrogen, essential for leaf growth, becomes available in greater quantities in a nearly neutral soil.*

*Bare dirt and lawn coexist in a demonstration plot in New Jersey. The same seeds and fertilizer were used on both sides of the white stake. The difference was the addition of 225 pounds of lime per 1,000 square feet to the area in the background, mixed in to a depth of 6 inches, to correct an unusually acid soil.*

A close look at the sheared ends of two pieces
of grass (right) shows what a dull rotary
mower may do to a healthy lawn. The near leaf
was cut by a poorly maintained machine,
the other by a sharp one. Dull blades tear the
leaves, giving a brown, dry cast to the lawn.

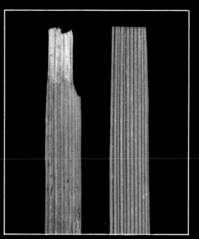 

A cross section of bluegrass turf (far right)
shows the stunting of roots that results
from accumulated thatch—a matted tangle of
rhizomes, old roots and dead leaves at the bases
of the plants. Acid soil encourages thatch
because it slows the decay of dead plant matter.

Two bluegrass samples demonstrate some
of the advantages and disadvantages of
close mowing. The clump above, cut under
3/4 inch, is thickened by dense tillering; it
would produce a thick but weak lawn. The
right clump, cut to 2 inches, is the sturdier
plant, as its robust root growth indicates.

*A healthy sprig of St. Augustine grass, unmarred by the diseases that afflict the plants shown on the opposite page, shows only the ordinary wear and tear that lawn grass undergoes. It will quickly repair its minor blotches and broken leaves, caused by mowing, trampling and natural decay.*

If a brown patch suddenly appears in your lawn do not rush for the spray can. The chances are that disease is not the culprit. More likely is some incidental cause—the neighbor's dog, a too-heavy application of fertilizer or an overturned charcoal grill that you forgot about. But if the condition persists, or grows worse, your lawn may have become infected by one or more of a multitude of microscopic parasitic fungi that prey on lawn grasses, particularly when the weather is unusually wet. In periods of heavier-than-normal rain, in fact, prudent gardeners will sometimes spray their lawns with multipurpose fungicides even before any symptoms appear. To select other remedies, see the chart on pages 68-69, which lists the methods used to control 14 of the most common lawn diseases.

Identifying the disease infecting your lawn can be difficult outside the laboratory, for the symptoms seldom present themselves in textbook form. Nevertheless, some grass diseases are more easily recognized than others. Three of the most obvious are pictured at the right. But before you start examining your lawn with a magnifying glass and diagnosing every blemish and bruise as brown patch or leaf spot, remember that even the healthiest piece of grass, as exemplified by the sprig of St. Augustine grass shown at the left, will reveal at close range the inescapable scars of everyday life.

# Signs of disease

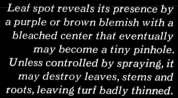

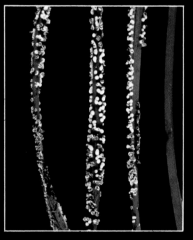 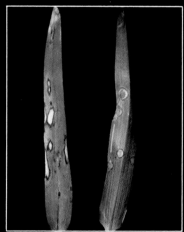

*Leaf spot reveals its presence by a purple or brown blemish with a bleached center that eventually may become a tiny pinhole. Unless controlled by spraying, it may destroy leaves, stems and roots, leaving turf badly thinned.*

*Slime mold is a fungus capable of amoebalike movement. On a lawn, it may look from a distance like a dusting of cigarette ash. A thorough raking, or sweeping with a stiff broom, is all that is needed to remove it.*

*Brown patch turns individual grass blades a dark brown color, as it has begun to do to this specimen of St. Augustine grass. It may appear in a lawn as an expanding irregular ring, with the dead, dry grass in the center.*

# Repairing old lawns and building new ones 3

In the annals of man's struggles with grass, there are countless stories about people who have "tried everything" and finally given up. I know of one man who, angry because his manicured bent grass would not grow in the shade, cut down his best trees. There is also the story of the TV fan who spent so many Sunday afternoons indoors envying the new synthetic carpeting of the football stadiums that, at great expense, he installed the same green plastic turf in his own yard—only to find it did not really look like grass from up close and was considerably hotter underfoot. I even heard of a prominent scientist who actually did what so many people talk about and paved over his whole yard in concrete tinted green.

Most people will do a reasonable amount of work to avoid such extreme measures and hold onto real grass, not to mention real trees. But even with reasonable care, a lawn every now and then becomes sickly or develops bare spots or patches of weeds and needs some kind of overhauling. If things have gone too far, the lawn must be rebuilt almost as if a new lawn were being started from scratch. I call these two levels of lawn treatment minor and major surgery; like their medical counterparts, one is an extension of day-to-day care while the other is a serious undertaking. Before you totally rebuild a lawn, you must remove the lawn that is already there, and this can involve some heavy work indeed. So before you embark on such a course, try diagnosis and minor surgery.

It is not always easy to determine what ails an ailing lawn. Some lawns do not thrive because they are planted in the wrong grasses—for example, if the man who cut down his trees had used a shade-tolerant grass instead of insisting on a sun-loving, close-cropped bent-grass lawn, he might have saved both his lawn *and* his trees. If other lawn-plagued homeowners had watered a little less, or a little more, or had paid slightly closer attention to the chemicals they were using, they might never have come to grief.

In many cases the trouble with a lawn is that it is simply undernourished, regardless of whether it is being fertilized or not. In

*A power-driven aerator, similar to ones available for home use, riddles a golf green with 3-inch-deep holes to bring air, water and nutrients to compacted soil. The cores it removes are left in rows to be raked up.*

fact this is so often true that I would begin any program of lawn repair with a test to determine the soil's level of acidity or alkalinity, which determines how easily grass can get nutrients from the soil. Perhaps you need a long-overdue application of lime or sulfur. In addition, I recommend two equally simple corrective steps: raise the cutting height of the mower half an inch to an inch, and give the lawn an extra application of fertilizer. Often these three measures result in dramatic improvement.

If they do not, you may have to look deeper for the trouble. The problem may be poor drainage or tightly compacted soil. Or the lawn may have built up a condition known as "thatching," a term applied to the tangled mat of dead or dying plant material —clippings, stems, runners—that accumulates on the soil's surface. All three conditions interfere with root development by cutting off the roots' supply of moisture and air, and all three are correctable.

AERATING A LAWN   The best way to open up compacted soil is with an aerator (drawings below), a drum-shaped device fitted with hollow tines that make holes in the soil by extracting fingerlike plugs of dirt. The holes refill themselves and soon grow over; but the permeability of the lawn is permanently improved. Aerators are a comparatively new development in lawn-care machines, but more and more gar-

## AERATING A COMPACTED LAWN

*To open up compacted soil, drench the ground a day in advance to soften it, then punch holes in it with an aerator. The machine's tubes, attached to a rotating drum, remove 2- to 4-inch soil cores and eject them.*

*Crumble the scattered cores by dragging a piece of chain-link fence back and forth over them; this soil helps make a good top-dressing when pulverized. Rake to remove small stones and unsightly pieces of root.*

*After spreading a ½-inch layer of peat moss and loam over the surface, use the back of the rake to force the mixture down into the holes left by the turf aerator. Apply fertilizer (page 49) and water thoroughly.*

den supply shops now have them for hire. Another tool, the spiking machine, simply has spikes on a roller and punches holes in the soil; it is useful but much less efficient.

There is also a machine for dealing with thatch; it is called, logically enough, a dethatcher *(drawing, page 88),* and it too is available for hire at garden centers. Thatching used to be a problem mainly for Southern gardeners because it was associated primarily with warm-climate creeping grasses like Zoysia and Bermuda grass, and referred specifically to the mat of dead stems and clippings that collected along the surface of such lawns. Nowadays the term "thatch" also includes the dense layer of undecomposed stems and leaves that builds up on any modern lawn that has been subjected to an intensive program of lawn care. Heavy watering and fertilizing make some of the new vigorous-growing grasses produce such thick turf that, particularly if clippings are not raked up, thatch develops. As a result, dethatching has become increasingly necessary on many lawns, north and south; it has in fact become a rather in thing to do in some suburban communities, and doubtlessly lawns are being dethatched that have no need of it.

HOW TO DETHATCH

It is perfectly normal, even beneficial, for a lawn to have a shallow layer of dead plant material around the base of the grass plants. This layer acts as a mulch to retain moisture and keep soil temperatures cool; it discourages germination of weed seeds; and its decay adds nutrients to the soil. But when the layer becomes more than ¾ of an inch thick, it acts like a thatched roof; air, water, soil additives and fertilizers cannot pass. The signs of excessive thatch are dry and dead patches of grass and an unusual springiness underfoot, as if you were walking on wire sponge or steel wool. A dethatcher's vertical blades slice through this dense mass and drag it in clumps to the surface, opening channels for water, air and nutrients to get through.

Grasses revitalized in this way should soon grow to fill in any small bare spots on the lawn. If the spots are larger than 8 to 12 inches across, however, you will have to put new grass in them. Sodding, if you can get a proper match with your existing grasses, is a reliable way to cover the spots immediately. Most people are put off by the high price of sod and use sprigs, plugs or seed. Any of these methods work well—if you follow the right procedure. First of all, clear the spot of dead grass and remove any sickly plants along the spot's perimeter. Spread a 2- to 3-inch layer of moistened peat moss over the spot, add a dusting of fertilizer, and dig both into the ground thoroughly to a depth of about 5 or 6 inches.

At this stage the spot will be higher than the surrounding

RESTORING BARE SPOTS

## CURING A LAWN CHOKED BY THATCH

1. *If your lawn develops dead or dry spots, examine it for thatch, an accumulation of clippings and dead or dying grass. The layer should not exceed ¾ of an inch.*

2. *The best way to remove thatch is with a dethatching machine. Its vertical blades slice through the lawn at high speed, cutting through the thatch and pulling it to the surface. A dethatching rake (inset) also can be used to slice and lift thatch but it has to be pulled by hand and is more likely to uproot the grass in the process.*

3. *The dethatching machine leaves behind parallel slits about an inch deep and between them narrow ridges of piled-up thatch. Remove the dead thatch by raking it up (it will make good compost for your garden); then mow to trim away straggly loose ends of stems.*

4. *After removing the excess thatch, spread a dressing of fertilizer over the lawn. It will sift down into the newly opened turf and stimulate the healthy grass. Water the fertilizer in and water regularly thereafter; the lawn should soon grow over with new green shoots.*

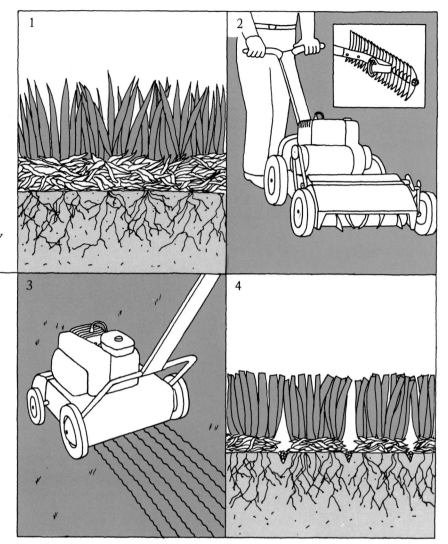

lawn. To level it, firm it down with your foot or the back of the spading fork until a footprint sinks in no more than a half inch. Then, if the spot is still not even with the surrounding soil, remove some of the mixed soil. (After a little practice, you will find that you can save a step on subsequent bare spots by gauging the amount of soil to be removed before adding the peat moss and fertilizer.) When the soil is the right height, sprinkle the grass seeds over it (*drawings, next page*) or set in sprigs or plugs (*drawings, pages 98-99*). Be careful when watering—use a fine mist and apply just enough to keep the soil moist until the new grass is well established.

REBUILDING FROM SCRATCH When minor surgery fails to cure an ailing lawn, the temptation is strong to give up and start all over. It has often been said that a lawn that is 50 per cent weeds is not worth reclaiming. In some

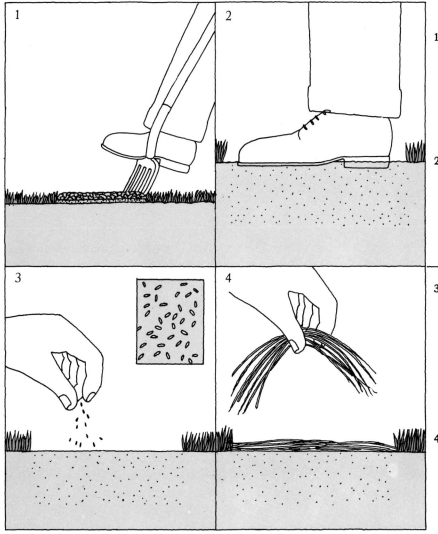

## PATCHING BARE SPOTS WITH SEED

1. *Prepare bare spots for reseeding with a spading fork, digging 2 to 3 inches of moist peat moss and a light dusting of lawn fertilizer into the top 5 or 6 inches of soil. Turn the soil over two or three times to be sure soil, peat moss and fertilizer are well mixed in.*

2. *Make the soil mixture even with the surrounding soil by tramping it firmly down with your foot until your footprint sinks in no more than half an inch; if the level is still too high, remove the requisite amount of excess soil.*

3. *Sprinkle grass seed evenly over the spot by dropping it in a fine stream from between thumb and forefinger. Space seeds as shown in the inset; heavy seeding will give too great a concentration of shoots competing for nutrients. Rake the seeds carefully into the top 1/8 inch of soil and tamp the area with the back of a hoe.*

4. *To help retain moisture, cover the reseeded spots with a layer of straw thin enough so that half the soil shows through. Water lightly and keep dampened until the new grass is established.*

cases this may be true, yet renovating a half-lost lawn, however arduous, is nothing compared to the task of rebuilding a whole one. Rebuilding may be more complex, in fact, than building a brand-new lawn on the bare ground of a just-completed home. An old lawn, no matter how bad its appearance, still consists of a dense mat of dead and living plants. When dug up, this turf becomes a mass of root-filled clods that will not disintegrate and cannot be raked smooth. So if you decide to rebuild the lawn, you must first strip off this turf with a sod cutter, or chop it up into small pieces with a rotary tilling machine. Both machines are rentable in most areas, and each has its advantages.

The sod cutter slices off the top inch or so of lawn, taking with it the heaviest part of the root growth, and thus practically eliminates the material that forms clods. On the other hand, sod is not easy to dispose of; even the amount taken from a very small lawn can be staggeringly heavy to handle. Also, there is a follow-up to sod removal: the soil underneath must be tilled.

These drawbacks of the sod cutter lead many professional lawn builders to prefer the rotary tiller (*drawings, page 93*). It does two jobs at once—chops up the turf and tills the soil. If a heavy-duty tiller is run back and forth across a lawn, with the blades set to cut only an inch or two into the ground, the machine reduces the turf to finely cut, useful organic matter. Then when the tiller is used to turn over the soil and mix in fertilizer and additional materials preparatory to replanting with grass, the chopped-up turf will simply be incorporated into the soil along with the other ingredients. Inevitably some clods are not completely chopped up. When tilling is all finished, these remaining pieces must be raked to the surface, then picked up by hand and carted off; if you try to rake them up, they will only catch in the tines of the rake.

From this point onward the task of preparing the ground is practically the same for rebuilding an old lawn as for starting a new one. The contours of the land should be checked to make sure they allow for proper drainage and, if necessary, be altered by regrading. Then the soil needs to be loosened and the topsoil treated to make it the best possible medium for growing grass.

### GRADING A NEW LAWN

The foundation of a good, trouble-free lawn is land that has been graded to give proper drainage. The ground should slope gently and evenly so that rain water is carried steadily away from the house, not toward it; there should be no low spots in the lawn to collect and hold water. Most land has a general slope in one direction, and a well-planned house is placed to take advantage of it. In the instances when natural drainage will not take excess rain water off the yard quickly, an underground drainage system will be needed; this may turn out to be an elaborate network of tiles or pipes, and its installation is usually a job for experts.

Grading is generally the responsibility of the contractor who builds a house, and if you are planning to put in your own lawn after buying a new home you will avoid disappointment if you make sure this essential preliminary is properly accomplished. It is ordinarily done in three stages. Before house building begins, the valuable topsoil is bulldozed into a corner of the lot, out of harm's way. (Unscrupulous builders have been known to truck away the topsoil and sell it, leaving the hapless homeowner with infertile subsoil for his lawn and garden.) After the house is up, the bare subsoil is rough graded; that is, the ground is shaped to the contours that provide proper drainage. Finally the topsoil is spread evenly back over the land.

A good job of rough grading eliminates steep slopes (over 25°); they are hard to grow grass on and dangerously tricky to cut —more than one foot has slipped into mower blades on a slippery bank. Where the land must pitch abruptly from one level to another, use a retaining wall of rough stones or timbers, leaving relatively level ground for lawn above and below it. But in leveling the land this way, be careful not to alter the existing grade close around trees. The majority of tree roots lie in the top 12 inches of soil in a circular area that stretches from the trunk out beyond the ends of the farthest branches. If soil is scraped away, the roots may be damaged, they will be exposed to too much air and they will suffer from drought. Burying the roots also causes harm; if they are covered with more than 3 or 4 inches of soil, they will smother from lack of air. Where the level of the lawn must be changed, maintain the grade around the tree for at least the spread of the branches and, if necessary, put in a retaining wall or "tree well" at least 4 feet in diameter to accommodate the step in grade.

## LOOSENING THE SOIL

But rough grading, as vital as it is, may cause its own problem because the weight of the bulldozer severely compacts the subsoil. Loosening of the subsoil is necessary, especially in the vicinity of the house because the builder's heavy trucks will have packed the soil so hard that nothing less than a pickax will penetrate it. Obviously neither water nor roots can pass such a barrier. Thus, after the rough grading is done, but before the topsoil is replaced, I recommend that the entire area be tilled with a rotary tiller to a depth of 4 to 6 inches. This one extra step can add measurably to the health of the lawn subsequently planted in the area.

## CONDITIONING THE SOIL

When rough grading is completed and topsoil put back, the second major step in lawn building begins: soil conditioning. It is required for the rebuilding of old lawns as well as the start of brand-new ones. All soils intended for lawns, regardless of their composition, benefit from the addition of organic matter—compost, peat moss, ground corncobs, sawdust, whatever is most easily available. Organic matter is the single most important contribution you can make to your lawn to get it off to a good start. In heavy clay soils such organic matter opens the soil's structure, improving drainage and allowing air and water easier access to the root zone; in light, sandy soils it acts as a sponge, soaking up and holding moisture and nutrients. Indeed, I would even go so far as to say that organic matter, plus fertilizer, can convert ordinary subsoil into a satisfactory growing medium for grass, making it unnecessary to go out and buy the expensive topsoil that your property might otherwise need.

My rule of thumb is that the top 6 inches of soil intended for a lawn should consist of one third organic matter; this means adding a layer of organic material about 2 or 3 inches thick and thoroughly mixing it into the existing topsoil with a rotary tiller.

ADDING NUTRIENTS    But the added organic material creates a problem of its own. As it decomposes it uses up the soil's nitrogen, the very element most needed for plant growth. The easiest way to compensate for this loss of nitrogen is to mix in with the organic matter double the usual amount of fertilizer: if you would ordinarily use 1 or 1½ pounds of nitrogen per 1,000 square feet of lawn, use 2 to 3 pounds. (For a detailed discussion of lawn fertilizers and how to gauge their nitrogen content, see Chapter 2.)

In addition to the temporary deficiency in nitrogen that may be caused by the addition of organic matter, many soils chronically lack other nutrients. Southwestern soils are often low in iron, an important ingredient in the manufacture of chlorophyll, the green substance that makes grass grow. In the East, soils tend to be low in potassium and phosphorus, two elements essential to plant life. And everywhere the acid-alkaline balance may require redressing with lime or sulfur. Standard soil tests *(page 45)* disclose the deficiencies that may be a problem where you live.

Iron is commonly added to soils in the form of iron sulfate or chelated iron. The usual dosage for iron sulfate is 5 pounds per 1,000 square feet; chelated iron comes in various strengths, so it is best to follow the manufacturer's directions for rates of application. (Be careful not to spill iron sulfate on paved terraces or patios; it causes rust spots.)

Since potassium and phosphorus, along with nitrogen, are standard ingredients in all lawn fertilizer mixtures, chances are that a soil being treated for nitrogen deficiency will also be receiving adequate amounts of the other two chemicals. If not, or if you want to do as professional turf-builders do and supply the lawn's needs of potassium and phosphorus for many years to come, add an extra dressing of 0-20-20, a high-potency potassium-phosphorus fertilizer. The amount to use ranges from 40 to 60 pounds per 1,000 square feet, depending on the soil's existing resources. If 0-20-20 is unavailable, a combination of superphosphate and muriate of potash (potassium chloride), both of which are available from plant nurseries and garden supply centers, will produce the same results; use 50 to 60 pounds of 20 per cent superphosphate and 10 to 15 pounds of muriate of potash per 1,000 square feet.

PREPARING THE BED    The simplest way to get these soil supplements into the ground is to till them in all in one operation. First spread them on the topsoil. Then, with a rotary tiller, go over the soil in a crisscross pattern

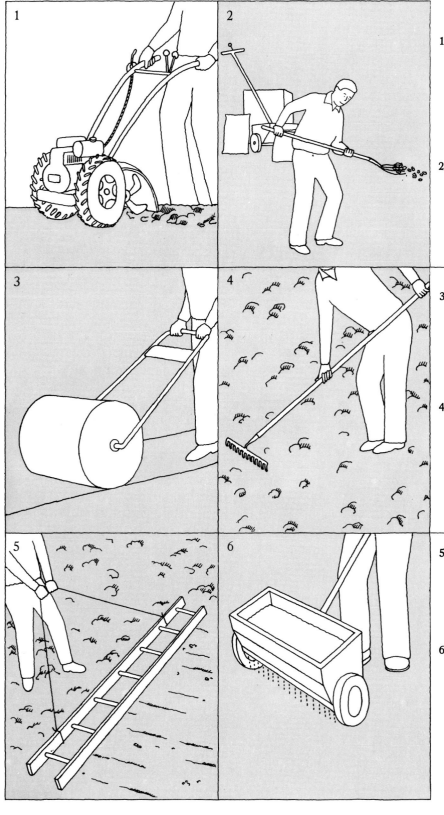

## HOW TO PREPARE SOIL FOR PLANTING A NEW LAWN

1. *To make the ground ready for building a new lawn, use a rotary power tiller with rear-mounted blades. Go over the area in one direction, then again at right angles, churning the soil 4 or 5 inches deep. Rake out big stones, root clods or other debris.*

2. *Using a pitchfork, spread 1 to 2 inches of peat moss on top of a dressing of fertilizer and any lime or sulfur that soil tests indicate may be required. Go over the area again with the rotary tiller to mix all these elements into the soil.*

3. *If the soil is so loose that your feet sink in 2 or 3 inches, firm it by going over the area once with a light roller (one emptied of the water that weights it). Push the roller ahead of you to make the surface easier to walk on.*

4. *Use an iron rake to smooth the tilled soil and remove small stones and bits of roots. To avoid gouging holes, hold the rake low, at a 20° to 30° angle, with one hand halfway down the handle. Work the rake back and forth with a smooth push-pull motion.*

5. *Level off bumps and hollows with a drag made by attaching a rope to a ladder. Pull it sideways over the surface. The sod, plugs or sprigs can now be planted; if you use seed, rake the soil lightly first.*

6. *Sow the seed evenly with a trough spreader, following the pattern shown for spreading fertilizer on page 51. Then drag a flexible leaf rake lightly over the surface to work the seeds into the top ⅛ inch of soil. Mulch with a light covering of straw, water with a fine spray and keep the soil moist until the seeds germinate.*

until the added materials and existing soil are well blended to a depth of 5 or 6 inches. The texture of the resulting soil mixture will be light and fluffy, so soft you may sink to your ankles walking across it. This is too soft to be a proper base for a lawn. To firm the soil, use a light roller—one whose cylindrical tank has been emptied of the water that gives it weight; roll the ground gently, again in a crisscross pattern, until a footprint leaves an indentation that is barely visible; if the surface is too fluffy to permit a roller to be pushed easily, water the ground until the soil settles.

After the surface dries out again, it should be raked with a garden rake to remove stray roots and stones. This job is one that many gardeners find tiresome and frustrating, mainly because they do not handle the rake properly. The tines should not dig into the ground but should rest lightly on it; if they dig in, the rake bounces up and down, making high and low spots instead of smoothing the surface. The trick is to balance the rake so that most of its weight rests in the hands rather than on the tines; push and pull it almost parallel to the ground, holding the handle at an angle of 20° to 30°. In raking a slope you may be tempted to stand at the bottom and rake downward. This is a mistake; too much of the soil is pulled from the top, where it is most needed. Even though it may be a little harder to do, stand uphill and rake up from the bottom.

Raking, no matter how carefully it is done, often leaves small irregularities in the soil's surface. The best way to level out these high and low spots is to use a homemade drag—a ladder, preferably a heavy wooden one, laid flat and pulled across the ground by ropes tied to the ends. This final smoothing completes soil preparation if sprigs, plugs or sod are to be planted *(pages 98, 99, 101)*. But if seed is to be sown, the entire surface should be given another very light raking, just enough to loosen the top ¼ inch. The texture of the top of the soil need not be very fine; in fact, it helps if the soil clumps are a little rough, ¼ to ¾ inch in diameter, so that the grass seeds will fall into the crevices in the surface.

## WHEN TO PLANT GRASS

The ideal time to plant a lawn is at the beginning of a period when grass growth is most aggressive and weed growth is slow. This period varies with the region and the climate.

Cool-climate grasses begin new growth in early spring, reach a peak of activity during the late spring and early summer, and then lapse into relative inactivity during midsummer. But by summer's end, when cool nights and autumn rains begin, they grow luxuriantly again until slowed by cold weather late in the fall. (During a mild winter a few years ago one of my New England neighbors mowed his lawn on New Year's Day when he ordinarily might have been shoveling snow.)

The growth patterns of most weeds in cool climates—particularly in Areas A, D and F—are different from those of grasses, much to the lawn builder's advantage. Perennial weeds such as mouse-ear chickweed, dandelion, ground ivy and others thrive in cool weather; they are in direct competition with desirable grasses throughout the year and the choice of planting time has no effect on competition from them. But annual weeds are easier to deal with. While many such as common chickweed, Mayweed and peppergrass compete with grasses in early spring, all slow or stop their growth in fall, and that most unruly nuisance, crab grass, is killed by the first cold snaps of early autumn.

With a fresh growing season just then commencing for perennial grasses, it is easy to see that the best possible time to sow grass seeds in cool climates is in late summer or early fall, up to two months before the ground freezes. From that point on, it is usually advisable to wait until early spring. However, seeds may be sown after the ground is frozen, so that they will begin to grow with the first warm weather of spring and get an early start in their competition with weeds. Some people have tried sowing grass seed on snow-covered ground on the theory that melting snow will provide moisture to aid germination, but many of the seeds are simply eaten up by birds before spring arrives.

In warm climates the habits of grasses dictate planting times, and variations in weed growth patterns cannot easily be taken advantage of. Warm-climate grasses, such as Bermuda grass, centipede grass, Zoysia grass, St. Augustine grass, carpet grass and Bahia grass, are at their best during the hot days of summer. The time to start a new lawn in warm regions is just before this period of rapid growth begins, in the spring or early summer, when daytime temperatures stay around 70°F. Grasses started then from sprigs or plugs and given proper care will become well established before they enter their dormant period and turn brown in fall.

For most homeowners starting a lawn from seed, the question of what seed to sow will be answered by choosing a mixture. Mixtures contain some grasses that thrive in sun and others that grow in shade, since most lawns have areas of both; each type of grass eventually predominates in the area best suited to it. But before you buy a mixture, you should know something about the nature of each of its ingredients; the species commonly used are described in the encyclopedia on pages 114-119. You should also check the package label for the amount of each grass type and its estimated rate of germination. Most grass seed is sold by weight, and the package specifies what percentage of the total weight is accounted for by each type of grass, as well as how large an area the seed should

**WHAT SEED TO USE**

cover. What the label does not mention is the number of seeds of each variety the mixture contains—a figure that varies immensely from one grass to another. Kentucky bluegrass, for instance, has about 2,250,000 seeds per pound; fescues average 600,000 seeds per pound; rye grasses contain only 275,000 seeds per pound. Thus a mixture labeled 52 per cent bluegrass, 80 per cent germination; 35 per cent creeping red fescue, 80 per cent germination; and 10 per cent Chewings fescue, 85 per cent germination, might seem to contain about half bluegrass, a sun-loving type, and half fescues, which are shade tolerant (the remaining 3 per cent is inert matter). In fact the mixture contains more than four times as many useful bluegrass as fescue seeds (928,000 bluegrass, 220,000 fescue); it is therefore suited to sunny lawns, not shady ones, because the proportion of shade-tolerant fescues is too small to be helpful. If you are looking for a "shade" mixture—which should be used on lawns where substantial areas receive less than three or four hours of sunshine a day—a better choice would be a mixture like this one: 25 per cent Kentucky bluegrass, 80 per cent germination; and 75 per cent red fescue, 90 per cent germination. A pound of this mixture should yield 450,000 live seeds of the bluegrass and 405,000 live seeds of shade-tolerant fescue—close to 50 per cent.

SOWING THE SEED   Once you have selected the right seed, there are two important things to remember when using it. Sow the seed as evenly as possible, and cover it with a very thin layer of soil. A trough-type spreader and a windless day are the best guarantees of even coverage. Follow the same instructions as those given for spreading fertilizer in the preceding chapter (*drawings, page 51*); first lay down a double swath of seeds at each end of the lawn as a turn-around area, then overlap all rows slightly to prevent bare strips. The setting for the spreader will depend on the size of the seed; the labels of grass-seed packages indicate the appropriate setting.

Lacking a spreader, you can still sow grass seed evenly by hand. The trick is to use a sweeping motion releasing the seed from a hollow fist, and to divide the total amount of seed for the area into two equal parts, sowing half in one direction and the other half at right angles to it.

Seeds of fine-textured grasses, which make the most attractive lawns, should be covered with soil to a depth no greater than $\frac{1}{8}$ to $\frac{1}{4}$ inch; more than that and the seeds may not germinate. There are two methods for covering seeds lightly; neither covers all the seeds, but do not worry—the first watering will carry most of the unburied seeds down into the soil crevices. In method one, especially useful for small areas, a leaf rake—either the steel or bamboo kind—is inverted and dragged with slight pressure across the seeded surface; the inverted tines bury some seeds and leave behind miniature furrows into which others fall, to be covered when the furrows disintegrate during the first sprinkling. Method two, for larger areas, employs a piece of chain-link fencing or a flexible wire-and-rubber door mat, to which a rope is attached. When it is pulled, it tumbles the soil, covering seeds as well as footprints and leaving behind a crumbly surface receptive to moisture.

After seeding a lawn many people roll it once lightly, but unless the soil is very loose and sandy, rolling is not necessary and it may compact the soil too much. I suggest that you simply water the lawn; sprinkling is necessary anyway, and it will settle the surface sufficiently in most cases. I also recommend mulching before you water. A mulch conserves the moisture the seeds need to germinate and reduces the number of waterings needed before the grass is established. Mulching also has another advantage: it protects the soil and seeds from driving rain, especially on slopes, holding them in place until the grass roots are well developed.

The cleanest, least objectionable-looking mulch for a lawn is probably straw. One bale of straw is enough to cover 1,000 square feet, since only a thin layer is needed, three or four straws deep. The soil should still be visible through the mulch. Straw has one shortcoming: it may contain seeds of undesirable plants. It is a good idea, therefore, to buy the straw several weeks in advance, and to open it and wet it down; this will allow any grain or weed seeds to germinate and die before you use the straw on the lawn. One caution: Be sure that you get straw, and not hay. Straw is the stems of cereal grains—wheat, buckwheat, oats—all of which are annual plants that die after one season; a stray seed or two that creeps into the lawn will cause no trouble. Hay is full of seeds of wild perennial meadow grasses and their presence can create problems for years to come. Salt hay is the exception. It is native to shore areas with marshy, slightly salty ground, and its seeds normally do not germinate in ordinary garden soil.

On steep embankments or in windy locations, a straw mulch should be anchored with string stretched between pegs and kept moist so that it will not blow away. You can also peg down lengths of light cheesecloth or the special nettings sold for erosion control. Natural mulches like straw can be left in place to rot into the soil, or can be raked up when the seedlings are 1 or 2 inches high; fabric mulches will also rot eventually, but in the meantime will disappear from sight as the grass grows up through them.

Even a mulched lawn needs regular watering, especially during hot or windy weather. The water should fall on the ground as a gentle mist without forming puddles and runnels that can wash the seed

## WATERING A NEW LAWN

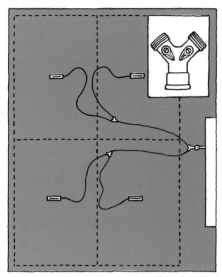

*To keep a newly seeded lawn watered without constantly trampling on it to rearrange hose lines, use several portable sprinklers placed to spray an interlocking pattern. In this diagram, a lawn is divided into quarters; at the center of each one is set an oscillating sprinkler capable of covering the rectangular area assigned to it. Each pair of sprinklers is connected to the water source by lengths of hose linked by Y joints; a special Y joint with shutoff valves (inset) is used at the hose faucet so that all the available water pressure can be channeled first to one pair of sprinklers, then to the other, in alternating watering periods. When the new grass is about 2 inches high, the hoses can be removed; the bare strips beneath them, where grass could not sprout, will soon be grown over.*

## WATERING AND MOWING

## HOW TO PLANT SPRIGS

1. *This method, used for grasses like centipede and Bermuda grass, employs pieces of lateral stems 4 to 6 inches long with roots and leaves attached. Sprigs are often shipped in airtight bags to keep them from drying out; if you buy unwrapped sprigs, keep them in moist burlap until planting.*

2. *After preparing the soil properly (page 93), and thoroughly soaking it a day in advance, dig furrows 3 to 4 inches deep and 12 inches apart—or 6 to 8 inches apart if you are willing to use more sprigs for faster coverage.*

3. *Place the sprigs at intervals of 6 to 12 inches, slanting each one upward from the bottom of the furrow and pressing it against the side to hold it. Make sure that some of the leafy part of each sprig projects above the surface.*

4. *Using your hands, cover all but the top leaves of the sprigs with soil, pressing it firmly in place and smoothing out the surface. Water thoroughly and keep the soil moist until plants grow together, in six to 12 months. Weed by hand or with a hoe; chemicals may damage the young plants.*

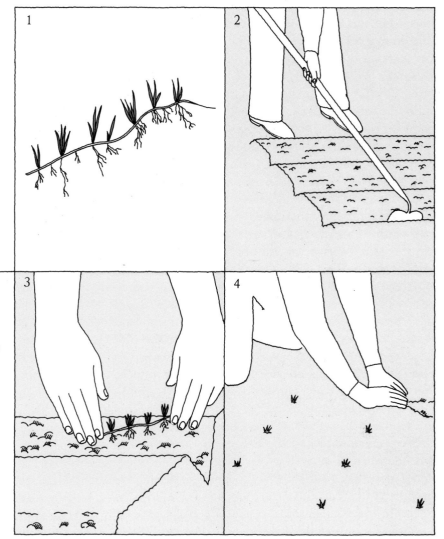

loose; such a fine spray can be produced by any of several types of sprinklers *(drawings, page 52)*. Set up the sprinklers and their connecting hose lines immediately after seeding, stepping on the lawn as little as possible, and leave this equipment in place until the grass is 1½ to 2 inches high. Do not worry about the grass seed beneath the hose lines; it will sprout as soon as the lines are removed.

The sensitive young plants of a new lawn need gentle treatment. Weed killers should not be applied for about a year after sowing seed. Nor should the lawn be mowed for some time. Wait until the grass is almost half again as high as its recommended mowing height—for example, 3 to 4 inches high if it contains grasses such as bluegrasses or fescues, which should normally be mowed to 2 to 3 inches. Then mow no lower than the recommended height. Cutting a new lawn too short could damage the young plants

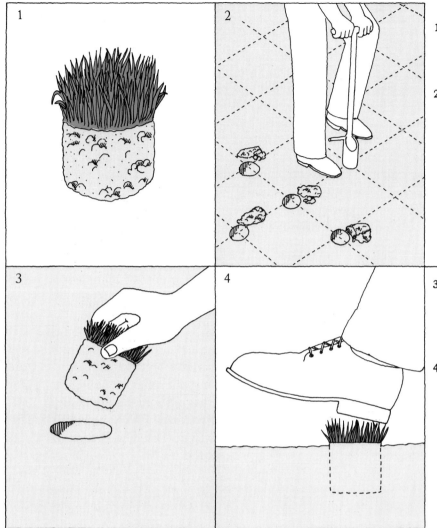

## HOW TO PLANT PLUGS

1. *Plugs, small pieces of sod 2 to 4 inches in diameter, are often used instead of sprigs (opposite page) for planting warm-climate grasses.*

2. *Digging holes is easiest with a plugging tool of the proper diameter. Press your foot down on the bar above the coring head, then lift out the core of soil. Space the holes 12 inches apart (6 or 8 inches if you are willing to buy more plugs for quicker coverage). One way to lay out such a grid is to hammer nails through a board at the desired intervals, then drag the board across the soil.*

3. *Insert each plug after you have filled the hole with water and allowed it to drain. Set the plug so that the base of the grass stems is slightly above ground level.*

4. *With your heel, press down on each plug to bring the roots firmly into contact with the soil. Smooth the surface between plugs with a rake and water thoroughly. Keep the soil moist until new growth has covered the bare areas between plugs; keep the soil free of weeds with a hoe rather than chemicals. Complete coverage can be expected in six to 12 months.*

permanently by preventing deep root growth. A sharp-bladed mower is essential and a reel mower preferable, since it cuts with a scissors action without pulling at the grass plants. If you use a rotary mower, be sure its blades are very sharp; otherwise it may jar the tender plants, tear their blades and dislodge their tiny roots. Never allow clippings to remain on the lawn to smother seedlings. And in removing clippings use a grass catcher rather than a rake, for a rake, even when wielded gently, can uproot young plants.

If you live in a warm climate (Areas B, C and E) you will probably start your new lawn not with seed but with pieces of growing grass. Soil preparation and post-planting care are essentially the same but the planting procedures are different. Live grass can be installed in three forms: sod, large rectangles of turf cut free of the

SPRIGS AND PLUGS

ground; plugs, which are small pieces of sod each about 2 to 4 inches across and 2 inches deep; and sprigs, which are bits of stems with several blades of grass and bits of root attached.

Sodding provides a lawn immediately, and for this reason it is used everywhere, on cool-climate as well as warm-climate lawns. It is an excellent way to patch stubborn bare spots and to establish lawns on steep slopes and the crests of embankments, where seeds tend to wash out with the first rain.

Sprigging and plugging are mainly used for lawns in the South and West. They employ grasses that may not breed true from seed, or sterile hybrids that do not set seeds at all. All sprigged and plugged grasses spread by moving along or under the ground on lateral stems called stolons or rhizomes—thus pieces of plant set in at intervals soon fill the bare spots between them.

Sprigs are cheaper than plugs; plugs are easier to handle. Sprigs are generally set 6 inches apart, plugs 12 inches apart, on a planting grid marked in the soil. Plugs are set into the ground upright, with the leaf bases level with the surface of the soil; sprigs are set into the ground at an angle with at least part of the leafy portion above the surface. After planting, firm the surrounding soil with your hands or feet to assure contact between the dirt and the roots, then water the lawn gently but thoroughly. Mulching is not necessary because the plants spread rapidly and soon come together. Until they do, weeds can be kept down by hoeing; using weed-killing chemicals on a newly sprigged or plugged lawn is as dangerous as it is on a newly seeded one.

INSTANT LAWNS Sodding, laying a growing turf in place piece by piece, like tiles on a floor, is the fastest way to create a lawn. Sod can be bought at sod farms and nurseries in strips a foot or 18 inches wide and up to 6 or more feet long. Ideally, the strips should be cut from their original growing bed so that the root zone in the strips is no deeper than an inch. This requirement may seem contrary to good garden practice, which ordinarily demands the deepest roots possible for transplanting. But in fact, thick sod will take a long time to push roots down into the soil beneath and take hold, while a 1-inch sod, given plenty of moisture, will begin to send out new feeder roots that will knit to the soil beneath it in a few days.

While sod makes a lawn with miraculous speed, it is not foolproof. If the soil has not been properly prepared with sufficient food and organic matter, sodded grass soon thins out and loses vigor. And if the soil is bumpy or uneven, the sod will conform, producing a lawn that is bumpy and uneven too. In laying sod the time that elapses between cutting and laying is critical. Do not order sod for delivery until the site is completely ready, and plan to

## USING SOD TO BUILD OR REBUILD A LAWN

1. *To replant small areas of lawn with sod use 12-by-12-inch squares (top); for large sections buy rolls 12 inches wide and 6 feet long. Neither should be more than 1 inch thick, otherwise it will not root easily. Prepare the soil as for seeding (page 93).*

2. *Avoid gaps between strips by working inward from a guideline strung to stakes. Lay the sod in a bricklike pattern so that end joints overlap. To prevent making depressions in the sod support your weight on a piece of board.*

3. *Fill in joints with a mixture of equal amounts of peat moss and soil; press it down firmly with your fingers so that the seams are completely filled (inset). Grass will grow into the filled seams from the sod in about 10 days.*

4. *After all the sod has been laid, tamp it to press the roots into the soil, using a tamping tool as shown, the back of a spade, or a board tapped with a mallet. Water thoroughly, and water once or twice a week for a month or two. Do not mow until the grass has grown 2 to 3 inches high.*

lay the sod immediately. If for some reason there is a delay, unroll the pieces of sod and store them flat, grass side up, on pieces of plastic so the roots will not grow into the soil beneath it. Keep the strips moist, but not wet.

The proper way to lay sod is shown in the drawings above. If you are going to do it yourself, be prepared for exercise from lugging the heavy strips around and squatting on boards to set them in place. Once the work is finished, however, you will have the immediate satisfaction of seeing a nice green lawn marred only by a faint, and temporary, checkerboard pattern. With no need to mulch or to worry about washouts, and with only an occasional watering to keep the new sod damp, you can sit back and relax with a head start against weeds—until you have to get out the lawn mower perhaps sooner than you thought.

# Choosing and growing ground covers 4

Once upon a time—only a few years ago, actually—there was a home-loving, middle-aged couple who had the most beautiful lawn on their street in a San Francisco suburb. Then, after three years during which they nurtured it fondly, the lawn began to sicken. In the belief that it might not have been getting enough water, the husband installed an elaborate underground watering system. The lawn grew worse. When a gardener suggested that it might be getting too much water, the husband dug up the watering system, replaced the turf and went back to cautious hosing. The lawn got even sicker. The husband tried fertilizers, insecticides, humus, in vain. He called in an expert who recommended digging the whole lawn up and starting over. He called in another expert who diagnosed the trouble as a fungus in the grass, but did not specify what kind. He sent off a sample of grass and soil to the U.S. Department of Agriculture, in the hope that it could identify the culprit. He got back a bulletin on lawn fungi and diseases. Husband and wife studied the bulletin; it quickly became clear that their lawn suffered from an incurable disease and grass would not grow in the soil on their lot. So they gave up on grass and bought 1,100 plants of Hahn's ivy. With the help of a gardener, they dug up the lawn and set out the ivy plants. The result was beautiful and delighted them and their immediate neighbors.

The story should have a happy ending right here, of course. Unfortunately for the couple, however, the civic association that controlled the suburb thought ivy was pretty radical. Anonymous phone calls accused the couple of being too lazy to maintain a lawn, and even of being Communists. The civic association took them to court on charges of violating a covenant that prescribed grass lawns for the neighborhood. The happy ending finally came when the court termed the case silly and the association withdrew its complaint. The ivy is still there.

Whatever its legality, the couple's decision was correct horticulturally. Ground covers such as ivy, and scores of other more col-

*Clippers, scythe, watering can, rake, hoe, pruning knife—tools to tend the fashionable lawn and ground-cover parterres in the background—are carried by a late 17th Century French "gardener" in fancy dress.*

*Since Colonial times the bayberry (Myrica pensylvanica), a tall ground-cover shrub native to the Northeast Coast, has provided a way of making holiday candles. The shrub's gray, waxy berries, which are aromatic when crushed, are gathered in the autumn and rendered in a pot of boiling water until the wax floats on the surface. The water is allowed to cool and the hardened wax is removed and set aside to allow the moisture to evaporate. The wax is then remelted and poured into containers around upright wicks (milk cartons, cut to the desired height, can be used and cut away after the wax has hardened). When the candles are burned they give off the fragrance of the fresh berries.*

orful plants, are as useful and decorative as grass, and sometimes more so, in many areas around the home. (In fact, the ground cover called periwinkle was recommended by an early English writer and herbalist named Culpeper, who claimed a further virtue for it: if a husband and wife both ate its leaves, he said, it would "cause love between them.") In the broadest sense, the term "ground cover" applies to any vegetation that blankets the soil, from moss to pine forest. In horticulture, however, it means low-growing plants in close proximity, used to adorn areas that otherwise would have only grass, or would remain bare. The description "low-growing" is relative and does not mean that the plants rise no taller than mown grass: often it is a matter of scale rather than of measurement. For an average-size home a low-growing cover might be anything up to 12 inches high; for a small one it would probably not exceed 3 inches. On the other hand, Santa Cruz fire thorn, which attains 3 feet in height, or tamarisk juniper, which may grow 2 feet tall, might well qualify as a low-growing ground cover on a large estate. In any event, there are no rigid rules, and overall appearance as well as actual size might make a particular ground cover seem perfectly suitable on an open, rolling terrain and wholly out of place in a confined area.

Apart from height, ground covers vary in other ways. Some are shrubs like rosemary, which was praised by Shakespeare and Sir Thomas More. Some are vines like ivy, which legend says adorned the mast of the ship that first carried Dionysus, the god of wine, to Greece. There are evergreen ground covers such as bearberry, deciduous ground covers such as dwarf forsythia and ground covers that are herbaceous perennials—nonwoody plants such as lily of the valley that die back to the ground in late fall and reappear the following spring. Their foliage may range in color from the dark green of sweet fern through the blue green of dwarf holly grape to the gray green of Silver Mound artemisia, and in shape from smooth edged to serrated. Among them all, there is no one perfect ground cover. Each of them does an outstanding job under the conditions for which it is best suited and each of them also deserves to be appreciated for its beauty as well as its utility.

Ground covers frequently make a greater contribution to the overall design of the landscape than grass can; if they are chosen with this in mind, the opportunities for enriching your home grounds with beauty and interest are endless. Consider, for example, how a slope might look if planted in steel-blue juniper or in dark green Aaronsbeard St.-John's-wort studded with yellow blossoms. Imagine a shaded area as a ferny glen or visualize it sheathed in the gleaming leaves of galax. Picture a hot, dry area above a retaining wall, difficult and dangerous to mow, carpeted in any one of a number of delightful plants that are capable of turning this garden liability into an asset. Whatever effect you want to achieve, there are ground covers to help you achieve it, and the detailed descriptions of 88 of them in the encyclopedia section of this book should serve as both stimulus and guide. In choosing a ground cover, consider first the effect it will produce; then, among the plants that will achieve the effect, select the one whose horticultural requirements are best suited to the conditions on the site.

Ground covers have another advantage over grass: they are useful plants for trying situations. There are ground covers that will grow in wetter places or drier places than grass will tolerate. Many of them—those that are native to the forest floor—actually prefer dense shade to sunlight, and over the years have acquired the ability to compete successfully with the roots of trees for the available supply of nutrients and moisture. Wherever soil erosion is a problem, ground covers are a natural ally. Not only do their roots stabilize the soil, but their thick foliage breaks the force of lashing rains and channels it into gentle dripping onto the ground beneath. Ground covers also provide a living mulch for rhododendrons, azaleas and clematis—in fact, for any plant that does best under cool soil conditions. In a bed of spring-flowering bulbs an evergreen ground cover not only sets off the blossoms, it also hides the fading leaves after the bloom is past.

Ground covers can lighten the burden of lawn maintenance on steep slopes and rocky terrain, where mowing is arduous and sometimes dangerous—and where a lot of hand clipping is generally required. But those gardeners who choose ground covers over grass in the expectation of avoiding maintenance are in for a surprise. Ground covers need to be groomed too. It is true that they need to be groomed less frequently than grass needs to be mowed; the standards for ground covers are different. The sight of a billowing surface of Sprenger asparagus is pleasing, while a billowing stand of uncut bluegrass is not. Nevertheless, ground covers need care, and most of the work must be done by hand. Unlike grass, which heals quickly when stepped on, most ground covers do not. (For information on the few that do, see the encyclopedia section.)

## PREPARING THE SITE

With a few exceptions the procedures for planting ground covers are essentially the same as those for grass. Both are permanent plantings meant to last for a number of years, and therefore such matters as irrigation, drainage and soil preparation must be handled with special care. There will be few opportunities to alter them after the ground cover is in place.

In a previous chapter, I spoke of underground sprinkler systems in conjunction with lawns in dry parts of the country, notably

## THE ANCIENT SHAMROCK

*Few ground-cover plants are more firmly rooted in the heart and history of a nation than the shamrock is in Ireland. The association goes back to the Fifth Century, when St. Patrick is supposed to have held up the three-leaved plant as an emblem of the Holy Trinity. Exactly which species the "true" shamrock is remains in dispute; the leading contenders are yellow-flowered clover (Trifolium minus) and white-flowered clover (Trifolium repens); one variety of the latter, purpureum, is noted for producing the most four-leaf clovers (page 148). On St. Patrick's Day great numbers of both species—including more than a quarter of a million plants flown to the U.S. for the festivities—are worn with fine impartiality by loyal sons of Erin.*

in the West and Southwest. The same frequent and regular supplemental moisture is needed by ground covers, especially in such dry areas. And the time to install the equipment is after the final grade is established, so that the spray heads can be set to the proper height and in the proper location for the particular ground cover you intend to use. The height should be 3 to 4 inches above the height of the ground cover at maturity (not its height when planted) and there should be enough spray heads to cover the whole bed evenly; the spray should be such that the water will fall like a gentle spring rain.

But just as the ground covers need regular moisture, they also need good drainage. Although there are a few ground covers that will grow in wet or soggy soil, by far the majority of them prefer, and in fact demand, well-drained soil. And, as with the sprinklers, the drainage should be considered when the grading is done, not afterward—particularly if water does not drain off from the site naturally, and it appears likely that an underground drainage system will have to be installed to cope with the problem.

**PREPARING THE SOIL**  Once the grading is finished, the ground can be made ready for its cover. The first step, of course, is to add some organic material to improve the soil's texture, plus a fertilizer and whatever soil sup-

HOW TO PLANT GROUND COVERS

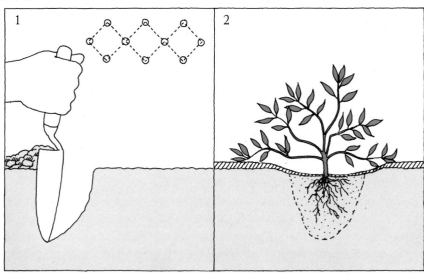

*Dig holes in well-prepared soil at intervals specified for the plant (Chapter 5), plunging a trowel into the ground and pulling it toward you. On a slope, staggered rows (inset) will keep rain from forming gullies.*

*Set each plant in a slight depression that catches rain water—the plant should be set lower than ground level, while its stem projects from the soil as much as before transplanting. Spread mulch, and water thoroughly.*

plements may be needed to bring the soil into the proper pH range.

Any number of organic materials are suitable for ground covers—well-rotted manure, spent mushroom soil, compost, leaf mold. One of the most popular and most widely available types is peat moss. It is beneficial even to ground covers that have no special soil requirements. A 2- to 3-inch layer of peat moss spread evenly on the surface and thoroughly incorporated to a depth of 6 to 8 inches will be adequate for most soils. Be sure the peat moss is damp, so it can be handled easily and will not blow away.

Ground covers do not have the same fertilizer requirements as grass. Still, it is advisable to add some nutrients to the soil to get the young plants off to a good start. Ground-cover fertilizers, unlike grass fertilizers, which are high in nitrogen to encourage lush green foliage, have less nitrogen and larger amounts of phosphorus and potassium, which produce strong roots and healthy top growth. Almost any all-purpose fertilizer will contain these elements in the right proportion; two good ones, among others, are 5-10-5 and 5-10-10 (grass fertilizers are usually 10-6-4 or 20-8-5). The fertilizer sold as "all-purpose" in your area usually is formulated to compensate for whatever the local soil lacks, and it should give good results. Spread the fertilizer evenly over the soil at the rate of 20 to 40 pounds per 1,000 square feet, working it in thoroughly along with the peat moss.

Whatever soil amendment may be needed to alter the pH factor should also go into the soil at this time. As you will see when you read the encyclopedia section, some of the plants used for ground covers require soils that are acid whereas others prefer alkaline conditions. The testing procedures for soil acidity and the materials and methods used in altering them are discussed in detail in Chapter 2. They are equally relevant here. And while the pH factor may be manipulated, you can reduce future maintenance if in selecting a ground cover you make sure to choose a plant whose pH preferences are close to the natural pH of the soil in which you intend to put it.

The peat moss, fertilizer and/or other materials can be worked into the soil quite satisfactorily with a four-tined spading fork if the area is relatively small; when the area to be worked is of any appreciable size, it is easier to use a rotary tiller.

Once the soil is prepared, the planting itself poses few problems. On slopes, a diamond pattern (*diagram, page 106*) will help prevent gullies from forming during a rainfall. There are two steps that should be taken to protect the soil around the roots of new plants. The first consists of setting the plants into scooped-out pockets, which serve as catch basins for rainfall and act as moisture res-

**HOW TO PLANT**

ervoirs for the young plants. Then the entire area should be mulched. The kind of mulch depends on the size and scale of the plant. Around vigorous woody plants like juniper and bearberry, a coarse mulch like wood chips is suitable. For small creeping plants like Corsican mint or thyme, a fine-textured mulch like buckwheat hulls or finely ground bark is more appropriate. Whatever the material used, it should be as natural looking as possible—bark, for instance, is an attractive dark brown earth color.

## HOW TO PROPAGATE PLANTS

One deterrent to using ground covers is, I think, exaggerated. That is their cost. Although some varieties can be started from seed, for quicker results most are purchased as young plants, and plants in large numbers can be expensive. But gardeners who want to economize can purchase only enough stock for one small area, and then propagate their own new plants from that parent stock. Many ground covers root and transplant rather easily, and even an inexperienced gardener can learn to propagate them by one of several standard methods.

The most familiar form of propagation is to take cuttings from the ends of the stems. A cutting should be 3 to 6 inches long. Strip the cutting of its lower leaves and dip the end of the cutting in a rooting hormone powder (available in any nursery or hardware

## USING GROUND COVERS ON SLOPES

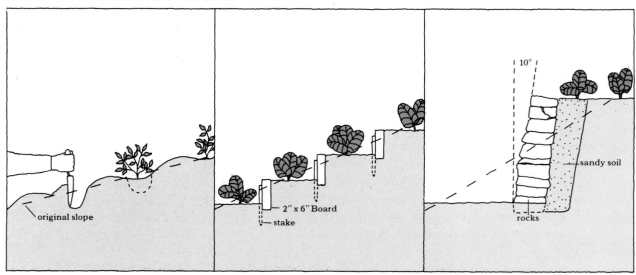

*On gentle slopes (up to about 20°), ground-cover plants can be set in shallow trenches dug across the slope and banked to catch water. Larger plants should be placed in individual holes (page 106).*

*On steeper banks, hold the soil by cutting and filling to create shallow terraces before planting; creosoted logs, railroad ties or boards staked in place will keep the filled edges of the terraces from eroding.*

*On extremely steep slopes, a mortarless retaining wall can be used. To offset the pressure of soil and water, slant the wall back 10° or more and pack sandy soil behind it and between rocks for drainage.*

store). Then plant the cutting in a 3-inch pot filled with coarse sand, peat moss, vermiculite, perlite or a mixture of equal parts of coarse sand and peat moss. Water the cutting well and then slip it, pot and all, inside a clear plastic bag that will serve for the rooting period as an individual "greenhouse." Tuck the end of the bag under the pot, and place the encased cutting in a warm, partly shaded place until new growth begins, indicating that roots have formed. If a number of cuttings are being grown, they can be set in a flat, a shallow box in which seedlings are started, filled to within 1 inch of the top with damp rooting medium. A single sheet of clear plastic or a pane of glass across the top will serve as a covering. Once the roots have formed, remove the cutting from the plastic bag or the glass-topped rooting medium, knock it out of the pot, soil mixture and all, and plant it where you want it in the garden. Do not transplant any rooted cuttings outdoors later than two months before frost is expected. If in doubt, it is a good idea to keep the plants through the winter in a cold frame and set them out in the spring.

There are some ground covers from which you should not take cuttings until just before frost, when the growth is mature. In the case of these cuttings, follow the same procedure as above but keep them through the winter. The best rooting bed for these cuttings is a flat, 3 to 4 inches deep, containing a mixture of equal parts of peat moss and coarse sand. If kept in a cool place (40° to 50° F.), they should have rooted by spring. At this point it is a good idea to plant them outdoors in a protected spot until they have become well established; the following year they will be sturdy enough to flourish wherever you want them. To find out when to take a cutting from your ground cover, see the encyclopedia.

Another method of propagating ground covers, especially herbaceous plants, is by division—these plants develop thick crowns of roots and stems, which can be broken apart (drawings, page 111). Some plants should be dug up for division while they are still dormant; for others it is best to wait until they show new growth or have flowered. Plant the separated sections quickly, before the roots dry, water them thoroughly, and they should flourish as additional plants in your ground-cover bed.

A third method, propagation by layering, is also relatively simple; in fact many herbaceous plants used for ground covers do it naturally, rooting and producing new plants wherever they touch moist soil. Layering is best begun in early spring. To layer a woody plant, notch the underside of a stem and dust it with rooting hormone powder, then pin it against the ground with a forked stick or a loop of wire and cover it with a mound of soil. The soil should be kept constantly damp; a mulch will help. Roots will eventually sprout from the notched section of the stem, which can then be removed from the ground, severed from the parent plant and set out as a new plant. Again, the encyclopedia will tell you which of the propagation methods to use on your particular ground cover, and when.

CARE OF GROUND COVERS Most new beds of ground cover benefit from a mulch to help hold down weeds and keep the soil moist. Not only does the mulch shade the ground to prevent weed seeds from sprouting, its soft texture also makes stray weeds easier to pull out. Weeds can be very troublesome in ground cover because they are so inaccessible, and perennial weeds can be a particular problem because they will continue to sprout from any stray pieces of root left in the ground. In pulling a perennial weed, always try to pull every bit of it, however tedious and time consuming the job may seem.

Mulching not only keeps weeds away from ground covers but also insulates the soil, keeping it cool and moist. And even after the ground cover has overgrown it, the mulch will continue to serve as a water-absorbing medium beneath the plants. For the first year or so, a bed of ground cover will probably need an occasional watering even in areas where the annual rainfall is normally sufficient. This is especially important during dry spells. Be sure to water deeply, penetrating the soil 6 to 8 inches.

In cold climates a new bed of ground cover may need winter protection for a year or so. The purpose of winter protection is not to keep the ground warm, but to prevent it from thawing and freezing, with the resultant heaving that forces plant roots out of the soil; the breaking and drying of the roots will kill the plant. The best protection any ground cover can have is a blanket of snow. Barring that, it can be kept evenly cool during alternating warm and cold spells with a light covering of evergreen boughs or salt hay (not ordinary hay, which is loaded with weed seeds). Do not put the protective covering on before the ground is frozen, and do not remove it until the ground has thawed in the spring.

From time to time most ground covers develop a wayward stem or two that must be clipped off, and occasionally a stray branch will fail to come through the winter. Pruning unwanted stems and branches is a regular routine of ground-cover care and should be performed early in the spring. An occasional shearing encourages bushier growth in plants that tend to become stringy, and sometimes it is even a good idea to cut such plants back nearly to the ground. Treated this way, species like Aaronsbeard St.-John's-wort and Algerian and English ivy take a new lease on life and produce a dense mat of low-growing fresh foliage. Pruning is also vital for such fast-growing, invasive vines as Hall's Japanese honeysuckle, a useful semievergreen ground cover that has a tendency to grow so rapidly that it can very easily get quite out of hand.

The tools for grooming ground covers vary with the plant and the size of the grooming problem. For a dead branch or two, a small pruning tool will do, but if you are clipping the surface of an entire bed, the most efficient tool is hedge shears. Low-growing ground covers like dichondra, which do not bruise easily and are common grass substitutes in the Southwest and southern California, can be cut with a rotary lawn mower.

Ground covers, like all plants, benefit from an annual application of fertilizer in the spring just as their season of new growth begins. A typical fertilizer application would be 20 pounds per 1,000 square feet of the same all-purpose mixture (5-10-5 or 5-10-10) used in setting out the plants. Fertilizer should be sprinkled over the surface of the ground on a day when the foliage is completely dry, and watered in thoroughly so that none remains on the foliage to burn it.

After that, maintenance is of minor concern for the balance of the season. About the only chore left is the removal of leaves that fall among ground-cover plants, and they can be dispatched easily with a stream of water from a garden hose.

All you need do now is enjoy your efforts. Ground covers may not fulfill Mr. Culpeper's promise to "cause love" between man and wife, but they can be counted on to enhance man's estate.

## MULTIPLYING GROUND COVERS BY DIVISION

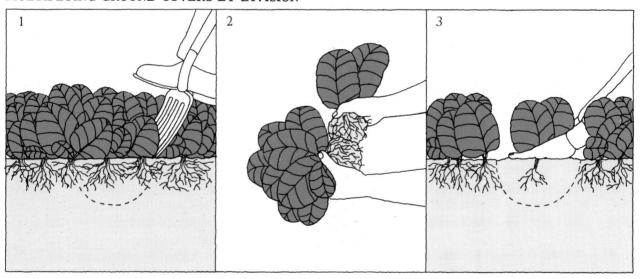

*To extend an established patch of ground cover or start a new one, fork up clumps of plants from a densely growing area, preferably in spring. Many ground-cover plants can be multiplied this way (Chapter 5).*

*Gently shake dirt off the clump and pull it apart to separate it into smaller ones. You may get a dozen or more plants from a large clump. Do not leave the dug-up plants lying around lest their roots dry out.*

*Replace a plant or two in the center of each old hole, using your hands to fill in and firm the soil, and set out most of the newly divided plants in prepared soil (drawings, page 106). Water with a hose after planting.*

# 5 An illustrated encyclopedia of grasses and ground covers

When it comes to choosing a grass for your lawn, the most important consideration is the kind of climate in which you live. In picking ground covers you open a door somewhat wider: here the choice is governed not only by climate but by personal taste and the purpose that the ground cover is to serve; in addition, there are a great many more ground covers to choose from than there are grasses. To help you make the best selections in both categories, the following chapter is devoted to the characteristics and culture of the 13 grasses that are most widely used in the United States and Canada (the encyclopedic entries for them begin on page 114), and 88 outstanding ground covers that have been chosen from among the hundreds that are available to home gardeners today (their entries begin on page 120).

Each entry in the encyclopedia specifies the regions in which the plant discussed grows most satisfactorily. In the case of the grasses, the recommended growing areas are keyed by letter to a special climate map that appears on page 150; the ground covers are keyed by number to a zone map of winter hardiness that will be found on page 151.

Within each group the plants are listed alphabetically by their Latin botanical names, which serve to identify them immediately to growers and botanists everywhere in the world, whatever the plants may be called locally. For example, in the case of the first grass discussed, *Agropyron cristatum* (crested wheat grass), the genus name, *Agropyron,* is followed by the species name, *cristatum.* Occasionally a third name is added to indicate that the plant is a particular variety of a species. Common genus names are cross-referenced to the Latin botanical names; thus, if you wish to find "crested wheat grass," and you do not know its Latin name, look under "wheat grass"; you will then be referred to the listing for *Agropyron.* For quick and easy reference, a chart of the characteristics and uses of all the ground covers described in detail in the encyclopedia appears on pages 152-153.

*An opulent bouquet of grasses and ground covers with their blossoms, painted by Allianora Rosse, indicates the scope of color and texture available to gardeners who want to add variety to their lawns.*

COLONIAL BENT GRASS
*Agrostis tenuis*

REDTOP
*Agrostis alba*

# Grasses
## A
### AGROPYRON
*A. cristatum* (crested wheat grass),
*A. smithii* (western wheat grass)

Crested wheat grass and western wheat grass are exceptionally tolerant of drought and are sometimes combined for use in nonirrigated sections of Areas D and E. Crested wheat grows in dense bunches and has somewhat hairy leaves; the western species spreads by underground stems and has erect wheatlike leaves. Both are bluish green except in midsummer when they become dormant and turn straw colored. They are exceptionally immune to pests and diseases unless irrigated or fertilized too generously.

HOW TO GROW. Wheat grasses do best in soils with a pH between 6.0 and 8.5; they require a minimum of four to six hours of full sun a day. Seeds should be sown in fall or early spring at a rate of 1 to 2 pounds per 1,000 square feet. Fertilize in early spring and early fall. Mow to a height of 2 to 2½ inches.

### AGROSTIS
*A. alba* (redtop), *A. canina* (velvet bent), *A. palustris* (creeping bent), *A. tenuis* (Colonial bent)

Bent grasses produce some of the most attractive lawns in the world, since most species produce fine-textured, thick, shiny green turf. They thrive in the cool, humid climates of Areas A and F, but may be grown with irrigation in the drier Northwest, Area D, and in high altitudes or near the sea in the Southwest, Area E. However, they require so much care they are mainly used on golf courses and are not recommended for a home lawn unless you are willing to devote time and effort to feeding, watering, mowing and spraying. Redtop, although a bent, differs in major respects from the other species listed above. It is a perennial that germinates and spreads rapidly by underground stems but soon dies out. While land developers sometimes include its seeds in mixtures to make a quick temporary lawn, it does not make a good turf because it has a coarse texture and competes too vigorously with permanent grasses. The other bents—velvet, creeping and Colonial—are also perennials. Velvet spreads out along the surface of the ground but is usually propagated from seeds; the variety is seldom named on the box although improved types such as Kingston have been developed. Creeping bents, as their name suggests, also spread on the surface and can be grown either from sprigs or from seeds; the recommended varieties of the species include Arlington, Congressional, Penncross, Pennlu, Seaside and Toronto. Colonial bents grow in clumps and are started from seeds; Astoria, Exeter, Holfior, Highland, Oregon Colonial and New Zealand Colonial are recommended types.

HOW TO GROW. Bent grasses grow best in a rich, moist, highly organic soil with a pH between 5.3 and 7.5; they require constant moisture and do best with four to six hours of sun per day but can tolerate light shade. Sow seeds at a rate of 1 to 2 pounds per 1,000 square feet. If sprigs are to be used, they should be planted by a technique different from the one ordinarily recommended. Spread the sprigs in a thin layer over prepared soil, barely cover them with a fine mixture of half soil and half peat moss, then roll lightly to press the sprigs into the ground. Keep the ground moist until the grass grows and makes a solid turf. Fertilize every other month. Daily watering may be necessary in dry weather. Spray every 10 days to prevent disease. Mow no higher than ¾ inch with a reel mower; dethatch in early spring or fall.

## AXONOPUS
### A. affinis (carpet grass)

Although carpet grass does not make a premium turf, it requires little care and can take hard wear. Grown only in the Deep South, Area C, carpet grass has creeping, above-ground stems that root as they grow and light green, coarse leaves that turn brown when the temperature goes below freezing. Nematodes, sod webworms, army worms and fungus diseases attack this species occasionally.

HOW TO GROW. Carpet grass will grow in acid, sandy or poorly drained soils with a pH between 4.7 and 7.0. It thrives in full sun or light shade and will grow in wetter places than most grasses. It can be grown from sprigs or plugs set 6 to 12 inches apart in early spring, but is commonly propagated from seeds sown in spring or early summer, 4 to 5 pounds per 1,000 square feet. Fertilize in spring and summer. Mow to a height of 1 to 2 inches.

## B

BAHIA GRASS See *Paspalum*
BENT GRASS, COLONIAL See *Agrostis*
BENT GRASS, CREEPING See *Agrostis*
BENT GRASS, VELVET See *Agrostis*
BERMUDA GRASS See *Cynodon*
BLUEGRASS, CANADA See *Poa*
BLUEGRASS, KENTUCKY See *Poa*
BLUEGRASS, ROUGHSTALK See *Poa*

## BOUTELOUA
### B. gracilis (blue grama grass)

Low-growing blue grama is so drought resistant that it can be used in nonirrigated sections of the West, Areas D and E, where more common lawn grasses fail. It spreads by short underground stems and has small, grayish green, slightly hairy leaves that grow in low tufts; the tufts run together as they enlarge. In hot, dry weather blue grama becomes dormant and the leaves turn brown. Unless very generously irrigated and overfed, this species is not usually bothered by insects and diseases.

HOW TO GROW. Blue grama grows in soils with a pH between 6.0 and 8.5; it requires four to six hours of sun a day. Sow seeds in early spring at a rate of 1 to 2 pounds per 1,000 square feet. Fertilize in early spring and early fall. Mow to a height of 2 to 2½ inches.

## BUCHLOË
### B. dactyloides (buffalo grass)

Buffalo grass is a tough native of arid sections of the West, Areas D and E, that grows so slowly it usually requires no more than two or three mowings a year. It creeps along the surface, rooting as it goes; the low-growing foliage, fine bladed and hairy, is gray green but turns straw colored in midsummer, when the grass becomes dormant. This species has separate male and female plants; females, whose seed stems are shorter than those of the males, make smoother-textured lawns. Buffalo grass is rarely troubled by insects or disease if it is not irrigated or overfed.

HOW TO GROW. Buffalo grass does best in a rich, well-drained clay soil with a pH between 6.0 and 8.5; it will not survive where rainfall averages over 25 inches a year, and it cannot tolerate shade. Plant plugs 6 to 12 inches apart in spring or sow seeds at the rate of 1 to 1½ pounds per 1,000 square feet. Plant seeds in spring if they have been soaked and chilled so that they can germinate in the hot summer; otherwise sow in fall. Fertilize in early spring and early summer. Cut to a height of 2 to 2½ inches.

BUFFALO GRASS See *Buchloë*

*For growing areas, see map on page 150.*

**CARPET GRASS**
*Axonopus affinis*

**BUFFALO GRASS**
*Buchloë dactyloides*

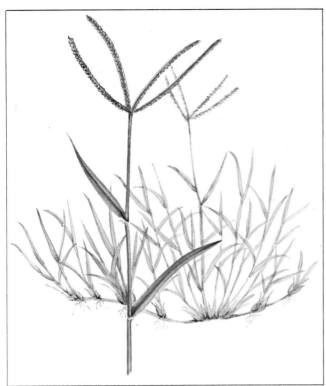

**BERMUDA GRASS**
*Cynodon dactylon*

**CENTIPEDE GRASS**
*Eremochloa ophiuroides*

# C

CARPET GRASS  See *Axonopus*
CENTIPEDE GRASS  See *Eremochloa*

## CYNODON
*C. dactylon* (Bermuda grass)

Common Bermuda grass is a long-jointed, creeping species that spreads rapidly and vigorously. It is the most widely used lawn grass in the warm climates of Areas B, C and E, and the hybrid forms produce some of the most beautiful of all lawns, noteworthy for their texture and density. The following Bermuda hybrids are recommended for home lawns: Ormond (also known as Everglades 3), vigorous and fast growing with upright, blue-green blades; Santa Ana, a dark green, medium-textured variety especially well suited for use in southern California because of its resistance to smog; Sunturf, cold resistant with fine, wear-resistant foliage; Tifdwarf, a variety with miniature leaves that requires less frequent mowing; Tifgreen, a fine-textured, dark green variety that tolerates partial shade; Tiflawn, a very tough grass; Tifway, a dark green variety that keeps its color late into fall and has better than average resistance to insects and diseases; U-3, an older, vigorous variety that does well even in the cooler northern edges of Areas B and E. All Bermuda grasses, like other warm-climate species, turn brown in cool weather. They can suffer damage by chinch bugs, mites, nematodes, sod webworms, army worms, mole crickets and fungus diseases.

HOW TO GROW. Bermuda grass does best in rich, moist soil with a pH between 5.2 and 7.0. Most varieties require full sun, but some hybrids tolerate light shade; all have a good resistance to salt injury. Common Bermuda grass may be grown from sprigs or plugs set 6 to 12 inches apart or from seeds sown at the rate of 2 to 3 pounds per 1,000 square feet in late spring or early summer; all the hybrids must be grown from sprigs or plugs set 6 to 12 inches apart. Bermuda grasses require three or four feedings a year; in the Deep South they should be fed every two months. Mow with a sharp reel mower, cutting the common variety to a height of 1 to 1½ inches, the hybrids to a height of ½ to ¾ inch. You can reduce thatching by always using a grass catcher or rake after mowing, but you will also have to dethatch in early spring.

# E

## EREMOCHLOA
*E. ophiuroides* (centipede grass)

Centipede grass, which seldom needs mowing because it grows slowly and never gets taller than 4 or 5 inches, is considered the easiest grass to maintain by many gardeners in Area C and in the southern sections of Areas B and E. It acquired its name because its thick spreading stems send out many roots, giving the plant a centipedelike appearance. The light yellowish green leaves are somewhat coarse and, like all warm-climate grasses, turn brown in the cooler fall weather. Centipede grass is sometimes attacked by nematodes, chinch bugs, leaf hoppers, mole crickets and sod webworms, but is moderately drought resistant.

HOW TO GROW. This species will grow well in soils that are on the acid side (pH 6.0 and less), including those with a pH as low as 4.0, much more acid than can be tolerated by most other grasses. It survives in light shade, but does not do particularly well close to the sea. Regular irrigation is needed if it is to flourish. Although centipede can be grown from seeds sown in spring at the rate of 2 to 4 ounces per 1,000 square feet, most lawns are propagated from sprigs or plugs set 6 to 12 inches apart in spring. Fertilize in spring and early fall. Mow to a height of 2 inches.

# F

FESCUE, RED See *Festuca*
FESCUE, TALL See *Festuca*

## FESTUCA
*F. arundinacea* (tall fescue), *F. rubra* (red fescue)

Tall fescue is a tough, coarse grass mainly used on athletic fields and to prevent erosion on banks; red fescue forms a fine-textured, sturdy lawn when mixed with bluegrass. Both fescues grow well in cool-climate regions: Areas A and F, the northern sections of Areas B and E, and, with irrigation, Area D. Tall fescue grows in clumps and has relatively large medium green leaves; recommended varieties are Alta, Goar and Kentucky-31. Some kinds of red fescue form clumps but others spread by creeping; all have dark green needlelike leaves that are hard to cut smooth with a rotary mower. Noteworthy types are Chewings and creeping red, with its varieties Illahee, Pennlawn and Rainier. Disease seldom strikes tall fescue but red fescue is subject to fungus. Both are moderately drought resistant.

HOW TO GROW. Fescues prosper in moist as well as dry soil, even if it is infertile, so long as the pH is between 5.3 and 7.5; they grow in shade as well as sun. Sow tall fescue seeds in early fall, seeding heavily—at the rate of 4 to 8 pounds per 1,000 square feet—so that the plants will be crowded and the clumps less conspicuous; sow red fescue seeds at the rate of 3 to 5 pounds per 1,000 square feet in early fall or early spring. Fescues, if grown alone, require fertilization only in late summer and early spring, but if you mix red fescue and bluegrass, give them the three feedings recommended for bluegrass—early spring, early summer and early fall. Mow fescues to a height of 2 to 2½ inches—in hot weather raise the height to 3 inches.

# G

GRAMA GRASS, BLUE See *Bouteloua*

# J

JAPANESE LAWN GRASS See *Zoysia*

# K

KOREAN LAWN GRASS See *Zoysia*

# L

## LOLIUM
*L. multiflorum* (Italian rye grass, annual rye grass),
*L. perenne* (perennial rye grass)

A fast-growing annual grass, Italian rye is widely used in the South, Areas B, C and E, to "overseed" a lawn and keep it green during the winter, when permanent grasses are brown; if Italian rye is sown over the permanent lawn in fall, it flourishes during the cool winter months and then is crowded out when the permanent grasses begin to grow again in the spring. It, as well as perennial rye, which usually lives only four to five years, can be used to create a tough temporary turf in cool climates. Neither lasts long enough for a permanent lawn, but seed mixtures sometimes contain one or both mixed with other grasses on the theory that the quick-growing ryes shelter slower-growing permanent grasses while the lawn is establishing itself. It often turns out, however, that ryes simply compete with the permanent grasses for moisture and nutrients and undermine their strength. Ryes grow in clumps and have rather coarse, shiny, bright green leaves on upright stems.

HOW TO GROW. Rye grasses grow in any soil with a pH between 5.5 and 8.0; they tolerate partial shade and salt air. To overseed a lawn for winter, sow Italian rye at the rate of 5 pounds per 1,000 square feet a few weeks before the

TALL FESCUE
*Festuca arundinacea*

RED FESCUE
*Festuca rubra*

PERENNIAL RYE GRASS
*Lolium perenne*

*For growing areas, see map on page 150.*

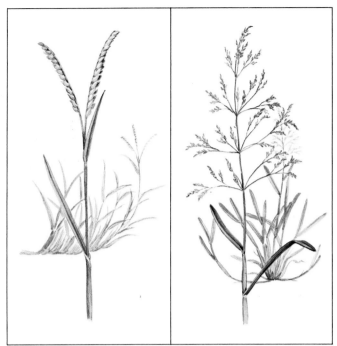

**BAHIA GRASS**
*Paspalum notatum*

**KENTUCKY BLUEGRASS**
*Poa pratensis*

**ROUGHSTALK BLUEGRASS**
*Poa trivialis*

lawns in your area generally begin to brown. If the grass comes up yellowish green, a sign of nitrogen deficiency, apply fertilizer. Mow to a height of 2 inches.

# M

MANILA GRASS See *Zoysia*
MASCARENE GRASS See *Zoysia*

# P

## PASPALUM
*P. notatum* (Bahia grass)

Common Bahia grass, too coarse for planting around a home, is widely used for pasture and forage, but varieties such as Pensacola, Argentine and Paraguay are popular in the southern coastal region of Area C. Bahia stays green most of the year in this area, turning brown only after the temperature falls below 30°. It creeps along the surface with short, heavy runners that root as they go; its light green blades are tough and slightly hairy. Bahia is not usually bothered by nematodes but sod webworms, leaf hoppers, army worms, dollar spot and brown patch do on occasion prove troublesome.

HOW TO GROW. Bahia thrives in sandy soil with a pH between 5.0 and 6.5. It requires ample moisture but can survive some drought because it sends down deep roots. It withstands salt injury fairly well and tolerates partial shade. Sow seeds at the rate of 4 to 6 pounds per 1,000 square feet in spring. Fertilize in early spring, early summer and late fall. Mow to a height of 2½ to 3 inches.

## POA
*P. compressa* (Canada bluegrass), *P. pratensis* (Kentucky bluegrass), *P. trivialis* (roughstalk bluegrass)

Kentucky bluegrass and its varieties are premium lawn grasses, prized for their rich green color, fine texture and dense growth. They are used across the northern half of the U.S.—Areas A and F—and also in irrigated sections of Area D. Common Kentucky bluegrass spreads by underground stems and has medium-textured, upright, bright green foliage distinguished by boat-shaped tips. Among available varieties are Merion, Arboretum, Fylking, Newport, Nugget, Pennstar and Windsor. Canada bluegrass and roughstalk are special-purpose grasses, adaptable to shady plots and cold climates. Both grow well in such rigorous climates as that of Maine or South Dakota. The Canada species makes a very tough sod; it spreads underground and has a fine-textured, blue-green foliage. Roughstalk, which will not stand heavy wear, creeps along the ground; its leaves are bright green, often tinted with purple. All bluegrasses are subject to injury by root-eating grubs and are susceptible to fungus diseases.

HOW TO GROW. Kentucky bluegrasses grow best in rich, loamy, well-drained soil with a pH between 6.0 and 7.5. These grasses are drought resistant, becoming semidormant in dry weather if the soil temperature goes above 80°. Full sun is needed in the more northern areas; more shade can be tolerated farther south. Sow Kentucky bluegrass seeds at the rate of 2 to 4 pounds per 1,000 square feet in fall or early spring. Fertilize in early spring, early summer and early fall. Mow to a height of 2 to 2½ inches or 3 inches in very hot weather; low-growing varieties such as Merion may be mowed as low as 1 inch but will then require extra protection against weeds. Canada bluegrass grows in soils with a pH between 5.5 and 7.5; it will do reasonably well in shady places and in dry soil with little fertilizing. Mow to a height of 2 to 2½ inches. Roughstalk grows in very damp soil with a pH between 5.8 and 7.5; it will not stand drought and must be fertilized as frequently as Kentucky bluegrass. Mow to a height of 2 to 2½ inches. Both Canada bluegrass and roughstalk are usually sold in seed mixtures that are sown in spring or fall at the rate of 2 to 4 pounds per 1,000 square feet.

# R

REDTOP See *Agrostis*
RYE GRASS, ANNUAL See *Lolium*
RYE GRASS, ITALIAN See *Lolium*
RYE GRASS, PERENNIAL See *Lolium*

# S

ST. AUGUSTINE GRASS See *Stenotaphrum*

## STENOTAPHRUM
*S. secundatum* (St. Augustine grass)

St. Augustine grass provides many attractive lawns in Florida and along the Gulf Coast, Area C, as well as in the southern parts of Areas B and E; in all but the coldest sections it remains green through the winter. St. Augustine spreads along the ground, rooting as it goes, usually producing a solid, almost weedproof turf in its first season; its leaves are blue green, low growing and coarse. An excellent variety is Bitter Blue. These grasses are susceptible to fungus diseases, chinch bugs, army worms, sod webworms, mole crickets and nematodes—as well as to an apparently incurable disease called simply St. Augustine decline.

HOW TO GROW. St. Augustine must have very moist soil with a pH between 6.0 and 7.0; it will grow in full sun, partial shade, and even in heavy shade if given extra fertilizer and water. It is also very tolerant of salt spray. Plant sprigs or plugs 6 to 12 inches apart in early spring. Fertilize in early spring, early summer and late fall. Mow to a height of 1 to 2 inches. Dethatch once a year in spring or fall.

# W

WHEAT GRASS, CRESTED See *Agropyron*
WHEAT GRASS, WESTERN See *Agropyron*

# Z

## ZOYSIA
*Z. japonica* (Japanese or Korean lawn grass), *Z. matrella* (Manila grass), *Z. tenuifolia* (Mascarene grass)

Zoysias grow well in Areas B, C, and E and are often used in the coastal sections of Areas A and F because they are salt tolerant. Like other grasses adapted to warm climates, however, their leaves turn brown at the first frost and do not turn green again until night temperatures stay above 50°. All three Zoysias spread by means of lateral stems above and below ground. Japanese lawn grass has coarse, upright, gray-green leaves but its improved forms, such as Meyer and Emerald, have fine, dark green foliage not unlike that of Kentucky bluegrass. Manila is similar to the finer Japanese varieties. Mascarene has mosslike bright green leaves. Zoysias are attacked by nematodes, mole crickets, sod webworms, army worms, chinch bugs and fungus diseases.

HOW TO GROW. Zoysias thrive in soil with a pH of 5.5 to 7.0, but if given adequate moisture and fertilizer, they can grow in soil as acid as pH 4.5 or as alkaline as pH 7.5. They prosper in fairly dense shade and in full sun; however, if a Zoysia is grown with Bermuda grass—a popular mixture for partly shaded lawns—the Bermuda will crowd out the Zoysia in the sunny areas. For a solid turf in one season plant sprigs or plugs 6 inches apart in late April or May. Fertilize in early spring, midsummer and early fall. Mow Japanese grass to a height of 1½ inches, Manila and Mascarene to ½ to 1 inch.

ST. AUGUSTINE GRASS
*Stenotaphrum secundatum*

ZOYSIA (MANILA GRASS)
*Zoysia matrella*

*For growing areas, see map on page 150.*

# Ground covers
## A

AARONSBEARD ST.-JOHN'S-WORT  See *Hypericum*

### ACHILLEA
*A. tomentosa* (woolly yarrow)

Woolly yarrow is an evergreen with fernlike, gray-green leaves 1½ to 5 inches long that grow in clumps, forming a thick matlike covering 2 to 4 inches high; above the leaves rise 6- to 12-inch flower stems crowned by clusters of tiny yellow blossoms from spring until fall. Plants spread rapidly by runners that root in all directions.

USES. Woolly yarrow is suitable for edgings and between stones in a terrace or path that does not bear heavy traffic. If no flowers are desired it can be mowed to a height of 1 or 2 inches. It is exceptionally hardy, thriving in Zones 2-10; it withstands drought and salt air and, given full sun, grows in almost any well-drained soil, even poor, dry ones.

HOW TO GROW. Plant in spring, setting plants 6 to 12 inches apart. New plants may be propagated by seeds, by cuttings, or by dividing plants in early spring while dormant or in early fall when the season's growth has matured.

### AEGOPODIUM
*A. podagraria variegatum* (silveredge goutweed, silveredge bishop's weed)

This ground cover provides a thick mass of coarse green and white leaves with saw-tooth edges; the foliage becomes 8 to 10 inches tall, but dies down to the ground in the winter. Clusters of small white flowers come into bloom in midsummer. Plants spread rapidly by underground roots.

USES. Silveredge goutweed is suitable for areas where barriers can contain its vigorous growth, such as a strip between a house and a paved path. It will grow in almost any soil in sun or shade in Zones 3-10 and will thrive under most trees.

HOW TO GROW. Plant in spring, setting plants 6 to 12 inches apart. New plants are propagated by dividing old ones in early spring while dormant, or in early fall when the season's growth has matured. Unkempt foliage can be mowed close to the ground and will quickly grow back.

AFRICAN DAISY, TRAILING  See *Osteospermum*

### AJUGA
*A. reptans* (bugleweed, carpet bugle)

Bugleweed, one of the finest of all the ground covers, has slender shiny leaves 2 to 4 inches long that form rosettes lying flat on the ground or mounding as high as 6 inches. The foliage is a deep green in the original species, but there are also varieties whose leaves are purple (*A. reptans rubra*), bronze (*A. reptans atropurpurea*) or splashed with creamy white or pink markings (*A. reptans variegata*); all varieties turn reddish bronze in fall and, in cooler zones, drop their leaves. In spring clusters of small blue, purple, red or white blossoms are borne in compact flower heads held 4 to 6 inches above the leaves. Plants spread rapidly by means of runners.

USES. Bugleweed grows in Zones 4-10 and is particularly useful in deeply shaded areas, although it will also thrive in full or partial sun. Its handsome foliage is low enough to border a path and the colorful varieties can provide unusual landscaping effects. It grows best in rich, moist soil.

HOW TO GROW. Plant in spring, setting plants 6 to 12 inches apart. Propagate by dividing the young plants that develop from the parent plant at the ends of runners, after first spring growth.

WOOLLY YARROW
*Achillea tomentosa*

SILVEREDGE GOUTWEED
*Aegopodium podagraria variegatum*

BUGLEWEED
*Ajuga reptans*

## AKEBIA

### A. quinata (five-leaf akebia)

This twining vine is named for its large leaves, each of which is divided into five smooth, rounded shiny leaflets 3 to 5 inches long. The foliage remains green and stays on the vines the year round in warm climates from Zone 7 southward. The trailing shoots of akebias spread rapidly and their underground runners send up shoots to produce a billowy carpet that is several inches to about a foot high. In early spring the plants bear clusters of fragrant purple flowers that are about ½ inch across but are almost entirely hidden beneath the leaves.

USES. Five-leaf akebia can be used to ramble over open areas or slopes. It must be planted well away from shrubs and trees, however, for it can quickly climb and smother them. Akebias are deep rooted and drought resistant and will grow in Zones 4-10 in nearly any well-drained soil in full sun or light shade.

HOW TO GROW. Plant in spring, setting plants about 2 feet apart. New plants can be propagated by cuttings taken in early summer or by division, layering or seeds.

FIVE-LEAF AKEBIA
*Akebia quinata*

## ANGEL'S TEARS See *Helxine*

## ANTHEMIS

### A. nobilis (Roman chamomile, English chamomile)

Though not a grass, chamomile has long been used for lawns in Europe and to a lesser extent in this country. Its fernlike semievergreen leaves form a mat 3 to 10 inches high; its slender stalks are topped with tiny daisylike white flowers through much of the summer. It can be allowed to grow naturally, or can be mowed and walked on; one of the delights of a chamomile lawn is the pungent fragrance released by its bruised leaves. Plants spread fairly rapidly by means of creeping stems that root as they go.

USES. Chamomile grows in Zones 3-10 and does well in a variety of soils, including sandy ones; it grows and flowers best in full sun but will tolerate partial shade. Deep rooted and drought resistant, it is often used for lawns in areas where dry weather turns grasses brown.

HOW TO GROW. Plant in spring, setting plants 4 to 12 inches apart. New plants can be grown from seeds but are most easily started from divisions while plants are dormant in early spring, or in early fall when the season's growth has matured. To make a lawnlike surface, mow off the flower heads; occasional rolling may be needed to press down clumps and keep the surface smooth.

CHAMOMILE
*Anthemis nobilis*

## ARABIS

### A. albida, also called A. caucasica (wall rockcress)

Rock-garden fanciers have cherished wall rockcress for generations, not only for the clouds of small white, pink or lavender flowers that cover the plants in early spring, but for its soft gray-green leaves. The foliage grows in mounds 6 inches high and may spread moderately rapidly from a single plant to cover an area 18 inches across. The leaves remain green the year round in warm climates but die down to the ground in colder areas.

USES. Wall rockcress is most effective in relatively small areas where its flowers can be appreciated at close range. It can be grown throughout Zones 3-10 but needs a very well drained location and full sun or, in hot, dry areas, light shade. It does best in rather sandy or gritty soil.

HOW TO GROW. Plant in very early spring or in early fall, setting plants 10 to 12 inches apart. New plants are most easily started from divisions or cuttings made immediately after the first flowering, but can also be grown from seeds. After the flowers fade, the flower stalks and

WALL ROCKCRESS
*Arabis albida*

*For growing zones, see map on page 151.*

**BEARBERRY**
*Arctostaphylos uva-ursi*

**COMMON THRIFT**
*Armeria maritima*

**SILVER MOUND ARTEMISIA**
*Artemisia schmidtiana* 'Silver Mound'

about half the length of the stems should be sheared back; this trimming will force new crowns of foliage to develop; cuttings can be rooted to make new plants.

## ARCTOSTAPHYLOS
*A. uva-ursi* (bearberry, kinnikinnick)

Bearberry is an evergreen shrub that grows 6 to 12 inches tall and spreads widely by sending out shoots that root as they trail over the ground; a single plant may eventually cover an area 15 feet across, although growth is slow. The inch-long shiny dark green leaves take on a handsome bronze cast in fall. Tiny (¼ inch) bell-shaped pink flowers in spring are followed by bright red berries, which remain on the shrubs during late summer and attract birds.

USES. Bearberries are hardy in Zones 2-10 and do well in dry, windy, exposed sites in full sun or light shade. In the wild they often grow on sandy dunes by the seaside or high on mountains and they make excellent plants for holding slopes against erosion. Bearberries need a sandy, acid soil (pH 4.5 to 5.5).

HOW TO GROW. Plant in early spring or late fall, setting plants 12 to 24 inches apart. Propagation is very difficult; most gardeners buy new plants.

## ARMERIA
*A. maritima* (common thrift, sea pink)

When common thrift is not in bloom, its clumps of narrow 6-inch-high evergreen leaves could easily be mistaken for grass. In the spring, however, and through most of the summer in cool locations, the plants send up stems 10 to 12 inches tall bearing ½- to ¾-inch globelike clusters made up of numerous tiny pink, rose, lilac or white flowers; in warm zones flowers bloom intermittently through the year. Growth is fairly rapid.

USES. Common thrift's billowing mounds of foliage make a delightful irregular ground cover in beds, edgings and rock gardens. It thrives in Zones 2-10 in full sun and well-drained sandy soil, particularly near the seashore.

HOW TO GROW. Plant in early spring or early fall, setting new plants 12 inches apart. New plants may be started from seeds but are most easily grown from divisions made after the first flowering. Since the centers of old plants eventually die, it is a good idea to dig up plants, divide them and reset the divisions 12 inches apart every three years. They thrive in rather poor, dry soil; flower production will be reduced if the plants receive too much fertilizer and moisture. Mulch to keep out weeds.

## ARNOLD DWARF  See *Forsythia*

## ARTEMISIA
*A. schmidtiana* (satiny wormwood)

Artemisias make tufted carpets of fragrant, silvery gray foliage that dies down to the ground in the winter. The variety *A. schmidtiana* 'Silver Mound' is a dome-shaped plant a foot or more high, while *A. schmidtiana nana* (angel's hair) grows only 2 to 6 inches tall. Clusters of tiny yellowish flowers appear in late summer or early fall but are inconspicuous. Plants grow together rapidly.

USES. Artemisias provide unusual areas of accent in a garden because of their color. They grow in Zones 3-10 in full sun and almost any well-drained soil; they are drought resistant and require little care.

HOW TO GROW. The best time to plant is in spring. Angel's hair should be set 6 inches apart, Silver Mound 12 to 15 inches apart. New plants may be started from cuttings, or by dividing old plants in early spring while dormant or in early fall when the season's growth has matured.

## ASARUM

*A. caudatum* (British Columbia wild ginger, wild ginger)

Wild ginger has shiny heart-shaped evergreen leaves 2 to 6 inches across, often tinged bronze, that form a thick, undulating carpet 6 to 10 inches high and smell of ginger when bruised. In late spring the plants bear small, cuplike brownish or reddish purple flowers with curious 2-inch "tails," usually hidden under the leaves. Plants spread at a moderate rate by means of creeping underground stems that send up shoots.

USES. Wild ginger thrives in partial to deep shade in Zones 4-10 and is especially suited for growing under such plants as rhododendrons and mountain laurels; it requires a moist, shady location and does best in a highly organic, slightly acid soil (pH 5.5 to 6.5).

HOW TO GROW. Plant in spring, setting plants about 12 inches apart. New plants are grown from divisions made in early spring when the old plants are dormant.

## ASPARAGUS

*A. sprengerii* (Sprenger asparagus)

Sprenger asparagus is valued for its arching sprays of light green needlelike leaves, which grow on stems 3 to 6 feet long to form soft, loose billows of foliage about 18 inches high. In spring clusters of misty pinkish white flowers appear, followed by tiny bright red berries less than ¼ inch across. Plants grow moderately rapidly.

USES. Sprenger asparagus cannot withstand cold but in the warm climate of Zones 9 and 10 it does well outdoors. (In colder climates it is often used as a house plant.) It grows best in full sun or partial shade in soil that is rich in organic matter. Sprenger asparagus is armed with small prickles and has a tendency to climb among small shrubs, so it should be planted in open ground.

HOW TO GROW. Plant in spring, setting plants 15 to 18 inches apart. New plants may be started from seeds or from divisions made at any time; cut old stems to soil level and divide the roots with a heavy knife. Plants should be fed twice a year, in spring and early fall, and sheared once a year in early spring to a height of 6 to 8 inches; within a short time new sprays of foliage will cover the ground again. Although the tuberous roots can go without moisture for some time, Sprenger asparagus grows much more luxuriantly when watered freely.

## ASPERULA

*A. odorata* (woodruff, sweet woodruff)

Woodruff, a dense ground cover that dies to the ground each fall and reappears in spring, is distinguished by 1- to 2-inch leaves set in starlike whorls around stems that are square in cross section and grow 6 to 8 inches high. In spring and early summer the top of each stem is crowned with a cluster of tiny four-petaled white flowers. The creeping stems of woodruff plants will spread rapidly to provide a thick carpeting.

USES. This species, which grows in partial to deep shade in Zones 4-10, is especially useful in moist, shady places such as the ground beneath rhododendrons; it will even grow in such notoriously hard to cultivate areas as the space around maple trees. Its dried leaves and stems have the fragrance of new-mown hay and are used in making May wine. Woodruff does best in moist, highly organic, acid soil (pH 4.5 to 5.5).

HOW TO GROW. Plant in early fall or spring, setting new plants 10 to 12 inches apart. New plants are most easily propagated from divisions in early spring, while the old plants are dormant, or in early fall when the season's growth has matured.

**BRITISH COLUMBIA WILD GINGER**
*Asarum caudatum*

**SPRENGER ASPARAGUS**
*Asparagus sprengerii*

**WOODRUFF**
*Asperula odorata*

*For growing zones, see map on page 151.*

**COYOTE BUSH**
*Baccharis pilularis*

**LEATHER BERGENIA**
*Bergenia crassifolia*

**CRIMSON JEWEL BOUGAINVILLEA**
*Bougainvillea* 'Crimson Jewel'

# B

BABY'S TEARS  See *Helxine*

## BACCHARIS
*B. pilularis* (coyote bush, chaparral broom)

This evergreen shrub, a native of the West Coast, has ½-inch gray-green hollylike leaves, and though it grows only about 1 to 2 feet tall it spreads rapidly to make a dense mat, a single plant eventually reaching 6 to 10 feet across. Inconspicuous white flowers appear in the summer.

USES. Coyote bush makes a fine ground cover and provides excellent erosion control in Zones 8-10 on the West Coast. It grows in full sun in almost any soil and can stand salt spray, wet conditions, drought and heat.

HOW TO GROW. Buy nursery-grown male plants; females bear cottony seeds that are unsightly and a nuisance. Plant in spring, setting plants 4 to 5 feet apart in soil mulched to inhibit weed growth; water occasionally the first season to get the plants established. In early spring prune any dead wood or high-growing canes. Start new plants from cuttings in early summer.

BEARBERRY  See *Arctostaphylos*
BELLFLOWER, POSCHARSKY  See *Campanula*
BELLFLOWER, SERBIAN  See *Campanula*

## BERGENIA
*B. crassifolia* (leather bergenia)

Bergenias have thick shiny cabbage-shaped leaves, 8 inches or more across, that grow in rosettes from heavy rootstalks and form a dense cover. Very early in the spring plants send up leafless flower stalks to a height of 10 to 12 inches topped by clusters of ¾-inch bright pink flowers. The foliage, evergreen in Zones 7-10, turns shades of bronzy green in the fall in the colder areas of Zones 4-6.

USES. Bergenias are grown in Zones 4-10 except in Florida and along the Gulf Coast, both for the effect of their bold foliage and their masses of pink flowers. They thrive in moist, organically rich, slightly acid soil (pH 5.5 to 6.5) in partial shade.

HOW TO GROW. Plant in spring, setting plants about 12 to 15 inches apart. Propagation is by division, which should be done immediately after flowering in early spring.

BIRD'S-FOOT TREFOIL  See *Lotus*
BISHOP'S WEED  See *Aegopodium*
BLUE FESCUE  See *Festuca*

## BOUGAINVILLEA
*B.* 'Crimson Jewel' (Crimson Jewel bougainvillea)

Most bougainvilleas are enormous evergreen vines that can climb to the tops of tall trees, but the Crimson Jewel variety is a bushy type that forms a striking, luxuriant and thorny ground cover 18 to 24 inches high. Through much of the year it is laden with masses of brilliant red bracts, leaflike growths 1 to 1½ inches across that surround the tiny true flowers. Plants spread rapidly, eventually becoming 4 to 5 feet in diameter.

USES. The bushy growth of this colorful species makes a fine covering for large areas; the thorn-bearing stems will also discourage traffic. Bougainvilleas are tender tropical plants, however, and can be grown only in Zone 10; even there they are sometimes nipped by frost. They do best in hot, sunny locations, though they will tolerate very light shade and will grow in a variety of soils.

HOW TO GROW. Crimson Jewel bougainvillea is a patented plant and must be purchased in containers. Plant in late spring, setting plants about 6 feet apart; take great care not to disturb the soil ball in transplanting. Nip back tips during summer to encourage branching, but do not prune from October to March.

BRITISH COLUMBIA WILD GINGER See *Asarum*
BUGLEWEED See *Ajuga*

# C

## CALLUNA
*C. vulgaris* (Scotch heather)

The many varieties of Scotch heather are bushy miniature shrubs, 4 to 24 inches high with tiny needlelike evergreen leaves. They bear a profusion of tiny white, pink, lavender or reddish purple bell-like flowers from midsummer until fall. Roots spread slowly and a thick covering should not be expected until the second year.

USES. Scotch heather is an excellent flowering ground cover for large or small areas, especially in coastal locations; it withstands wind and salt air, roots deeply and is useful on steep, open slopes to prevent soil erosion. It will grow in almost any well-drained soil in Zones 4-10, but flourishes in moist, highly organic acid soil (pH 4.5 to 5.5) in full sun or light shade.

HOW TO GROW. Plant in early spring in Zones 4-6, spring or fall in Zones 7-10, setting plants about 12 inches apart and mulching to discourage weeds. New plants are easily started from divisions in spring or from cuttings taken in fall and kept in a cold frame over the winter. In early spring, feed with a fertilizer made for acid-loving plants, and gently shear back old plants to about half their height to encourage a thick, uniform growth.

## CAMPANULA
*C. poscharskyana* (Poscharsky or Serbian bellflower)

Serbian bellflower, which grows about a foot high, forms a loose, casually tumbling cover of 1½-inch heart-shaped leaves that are adorned by 1-inch star-shaped lavender blossoms from spring to early summer. It spreads rapidly by creeping runners, dying down to the ground in winter.

USES. This highly decorative species is especially pleasing at close range, where its attractive flowers can be appreciated. It thrives for years without care in dry or moist soils and seashore locations, in sun or light shade in Zones 3-7 and light shade in Zones 8-10.

HOW TO GROW. Plant in spring or fall, setting plants 10 to 12 inches apart. Propagate by dividing plants in spring or fall or by taking cuttings in summer and planting them by early fall.

## CARISSA
*C. macrocarpa* 'Green Carpet', also called *C. grandiflora* (Green Carpet Natal plum)

Most Natal plums are large evergreen shrubs, but the variety known as Green Carpet grows only 12 to 18 inches high, spreading to a diameter of 4 feet. It has shiny oval evergreen leaves about an inch long. Not as free-flowering as the tall-growing species, Green Carpet bears fragrant 1-inch white flowers sporadically through the year followed by edible red fruit, which look like plums and taste somewhat like cranberries.

USES. Green Carpet provides a handsome year-round ground cover in Zone 10 and requires little attention. A tender tropical plant, it grows best in hot, sunny locations, although it will do quite well in partial shade; it thrives in a variety of soils and will stand salt spray and wind.

HOW TO GROW. Plant container-grown plants any time of the year, setting plants about 2 feet apart. Propagate from cuttings taken any time of the year.

SCOTCH HEATHER
*Calluna vulgaris*

POSCHARSKY BELLFLOWER
*Campanula poscharskyana*

GREEN CARPET NATAL PLUM
*Carissa macrocarpa* 'Green Carpet'

*For growing zones, see map on page 151.*

**HOTTENTOT FIG**
*Carpobrotus edulis*

**CARMEL CREEPER**
*Ceanothus griseus horizontalis*

**SNOW-IN-SUMMER**
*Cerastium tomentosum*

**CARMEL CREEPER** See *Ceanothus*
**CARPET BUGLE** See *Ajuga*

## CARPOBROTUS
*C. edulis* (Hottentot fig, sea fig)

Hottentot figs, natives of South Africa, are among the most common roadside plants in southern California, where they are used on gentle slopes to control erosion and to beautify the landscape. Their succulent, spiky, 3- to 5-inch leaves, grayish green throughout the year, grow thickly along trailing vines that quickly form a dense carpeting 4 to 6 inches high. Large daisylike flowers, about 4 inches across and pale yellow to rose in color, appear in spring and are followed in midsummer by edible but not very tasty fig-shaped fruit.

USES. Hottentot figs thrive only in Zone 10 on the West Coast but grow in a variety of soils, including seaside sand, demanding only sunshine and good drainage; they can be used to hold soil on gentle slopes (25° or less) and provide colorful decoration in gardens.

HOW TO GROW. Plant any time, setting plants 18 to 24 inches apart for quick coverage. Propagation is by cuttings, which do not have to be rooted beforehand.

**CATMINT, MAUVE** See *Nepeta*

## CEANOTHUS
*C. griseus horizontalis* (Carmel creeper)

Visitors who drive along the coastal highway between Los Angeles and San Francisco from March to May are captivated by handsome lilaclike shrubs whose blue blossoms blanket the hillsides like a smoky haze. Sometimes called "wild lilac," although it is not of the lilac genus *(Syringa)*, Carmel creeper grows only 18 to 30 inches tall but may spread to 10 to 15 feet, creating a dense, bushy evergreen covering. Flower clusters about 2 inches long appear above small dark green leaves.

USES. Resistance to wind and salt spray makes this shrub outstanding for seaside gardens in West Coast areas of Zones 7-10. It requires full sun and light, sandy soil; good drainage is essential.

HOW TO GROW. Plant in fall, setting plants 3 to 4 feet apart. Give them little or no fertilizer, but mulch with leaf mold to discourage weeds. Limit pruning to a minimum, pinching back stems during the growing season rather than cutting away large branches. Plants are short-lived if overwatered. Propagation is from cuttings but is difficult; most gardeners buy plants from nurserymen.

## CERASTIUM
*C. tomentosum* (snow-in-summer)

The tiny, fuzzy, silvery-gray leaves of this species make a solid evergreen mat 3 to 6 inches high, covered in spring and early summer with masses of ½-inch white flowers. The creeping stems spread rapidly, single plants growing 2 to 4 feet across.

USES. Although snow-in-summer has long been planted in rock gardens, its aggressive growth makes it better suited for use as a decorative ground cover where it can be given room to spread. It will do well in almost any soil in Zones 2-10, in seacoast, desert or mountain sites, but requires full sun and very good drainage to achieve long life.

HOW TO GROW. Plant in spring, setting plants 1 to 2 feet apart. New plants can be started easily from seeds, from cuttings, or from divisions made in early spring while plants are dormant or in early fall when the season's growth has matured. Snow-in-summer may be sheared after flowering to remove dead flower heads.

## CERATOSTIGMA
*C. plumbaginoides,* also called *Plumbago larpentae* (leadwort)

Leadwort is an attractive evergreen species that grows 9 to 12 inches high and bears clusters of deep purplish blue ¾-inch flowers in late summer and early fall. In cooler climates the top leaves take on a bronze hue in fall. Plants spread rapidly by underground stems.

USES. Leadwort is particularly appealing in small areas where its blossoms can be appreciated. It grows almost anywhere in Zones 6-10 in sun or light shade, provided it has soil rich in organic matter. Good drainage is essential.

HOW TO GROW. Plant in spring, setting plants 18 to 24 inches apart and mulching to discourage weeds. Leadwort is best sheared to the ground early each spring so that new growth, which is late in appearing, will be stimulated to make fresh foliage for each season (flowers are borne at the ends of new growth). After shearing, new plants may be started by dividing the roots.

## CHAMAEDRYS GERMANDER  See *Teucrium*
## CHAMOMILE  See *Anthemis*
## CHAPARRAL BROOM  See *Baccharis*
## COMMON PERIWINKLE  See *Vinca*
## COMMON THRIFT  See *Armeria*

## COMPTONIA
*C. peregrina,* also called *C. asplenifolia* (sweet fern)

If you have ever hiked through open woodlands or abandoned farms in eastern North America you have probably seen graceful stands of sweet fern, a deciduous woody shrub with fragrant, dark green, finely divided leaves. It forms a lush thicket of foliage that generally grows 18 to 24 inches high but may reach a height of 4 feet. Tiny greenish catkinlike flowers are borne in early spring at the same time the new leaves unfold.

USES. Sweet fern makes a stunning ground cover on sunny, sandy embankments; its tightly knit roots form a thick erosion-controlling mat. It thrives in well-drained slightly acid soils (pH 5.5 to 6.5) almost anywhere in Zones 2-7 but will not tolerate shade.

HOW TO GROW. Plant in early spring, setting plants 18 to 24 inches apart. Cut stems to the ground to increase chances of survival.

## CONFEDERATE JASMINE  See *Trachelospermum*

## CONVALLARIA
*C. majalis* (lily of the valley)

The bell-like, white or pale pink ¼-inch flowers of the lily of the valley, traditional favorites in wedding bouquets, rise above a carpet of graceful 8-inch leaves in early spring, providing one of the most delicate and fragrant displays of any plant used as a ground cover. Each plant sends up two leaves each year; these die down in the fall and emerge again each spring, thriving for generations with little or no care. Plants multiply from underground stems that spread slowly to make a dense carpet.

USES. Lilies of the valley flourish in Zones 3-7 in partial to quite dense shade, but are at their best in light shade and rich, moist soil. They are often used in beds around the base of trees and are effective in small, shaded areas where few other plants will survive.

HOW TO GROW. Plant "pips" (the little "eyes" or shoots that appear along the roots) in very early spring or in fall, setting them about 4 inches apart, or plant 6- to 8-inch sods with their centers about 1 foot apart at any time the ground can be worked. Mulch to conserve moisture and pre-

**LEADWORT**
*Ceratostigma plumbaginoides*

**SWEET FERN**
*Comptonia peregrina*

**LILY OF THE VALLEY**
*Convallaria majalis*

*For growing zones, see map on page 151.*

GROUND MORNING GLORY
*Convolvulus mauritanicus*

CROWN VETCH
*Coronilla varia*

BEARBERRY COTONEASTER
*Cotoneaster dammeri*

vent weed growth. Propagate by digging up and dividing pips when plants are dormant in early spring or fall.

## CONVOLVULUS
### *C. mauritanicus* (ground morning glory)

This species is notable for its profusion of trumpet-shaped lavender-blue flowers as large as 2 inches across, which bloom from late spring to late fall and, unlike the blossoms of true morning glories, stay open all day. The leaves remain on the plants through the year, providing a loose mass of foliage 1 to 2 feet tall that spreads along the ground on trailing stems.

USES. Ground morning glories are often used in small decorative beds and make an excellent covering for hot, dry, sunny slopes. They do best on the West Coast and in the Southwest in Zones 8-10 and will grow in a variety of soils but require sun or light shade and good drainage.

HOW TO GROW. Plant in spring, setting plants about 2 to 3 feet apart. Avoid overwatering, especially in shady locations. Ground morning glories eventually develop woody stems and become straggly; they should be pruned in early spring before new growth begins. Propagate from seeds, or from cuttings taken in spring.

## CORAL GEM See *Lotus*

## CORONILLA
### *C. varia* (crown vetch)

Crown vetch trails along the ground to form a dense, straggling cover 1 to 2 feet high made up of glossy, fern-like leaves 6 to 10 inches long; clusters of pink and white flowers resembling tiny sweet peas bloom from spring through fall, followed by finger-length brown seed pods. The plants grow rampantly, their tough, far-ranging underground stems spreading to form a thick covering.

USES. Crown vetch is an excellent cover for areas where its growth does not have to be contained. It is particularly useful on banks, for its roots penetrate deeply to create an erosion-resisting sod. It thrives in Zones 3-10 in full sun in almost any soil and survives drought well.

HOW TO GROW. Plant in spring or fall, setting plants 4 to 6 feet apart on level ground, 3 to 4 feet apart on slopes; or sow hulled seeds at the rate of 1 pound per 1,000 square feet early in the spring. Shear to the ground in fall or early spring to encourage bushy new growth. New plants may be started by dividing old ones in early spring when the plants are dormant, or in early fall when growth has matured.

## CORSICAN MINT See *Mentha*
## CORSICAN PEARLWORT See *Sagina*

## COTONEASTER
### *C. dammeri* (bearberry cotoneaster)

This ground-hugging evergreen flows across the surface of the soil like a shining carpet 6 to 12 inches high, studded in spring with thousands of tiny white flowers that are followed by masses of bright red berries. Plants spread fairly slowly by trailing shoots that root as they go.

USES. A good cover for rocky areas and seashore sites, bearberry cotoneasters fall gracefully over large boulders and root well on steep banks. They thrive in almost any soil in Zones 5-10, in full sun or very light shade, but require good drainage.

HOW TO GROW. Plant in spring, setting plants 3 to 4 feet apart in areas where they have room to grow without heavy pruning, which can destroy their natural symmetry. Propagate in summer from cuttings taken after the season's growth matures, but before it hardens.

## COTULA
### *C. squalida* (New Zealand brass buttons)

A summer sod of *Cotula squalida* is an odd but delightful sight, for among its soft, hairy, fernlike leaves, which rise only 2 to 3 inches high, are numerous tiny yellow "buttons" resembling petalless daisies. Foliage stays green in Zones 8-10; it may die back in winter in the cooler areas of Zones 6-7 but forms another thick carpet in spring. Plants spread fairly rapidly by creeping and rooting.

USES. This ground cover makes an attractive alternative to grass in smaller areas; it is also a fine plant to grow between stones on a path or terrace. It will thrive in Zones 6-10 in rich, moist soil and full sun or light shade.

HOW TO GROW. Plant in early spring, setting plants 4 to 6 inches apart. Propagation is by division in spring.

COYOTE BUSH  See *Baccharis*
CREEPING JENNY  See *Lysimachia*
CREEPING LILY-TURF  See *Liriope*
CREEPING ROSEMARY  See *Rosmarinus*
CREEPING SPEEDWELL  See *Veronica*
CROWN VETCH  See *Coronilla*
CYPRESS SPURGE  See *Euphorbia*

## CYTISUS
### *C. kewensis* (Kew broom)

Kew broom, a low-growing deciduous shrub of the pea family, sprouts trailing branches that seldom grow more than 6 inches high but may spread rapidly to cover an area 6 feet in diameter. The leaves are tiny, and the stems resemble long green reeds, giving the plant the appearance of being evergreen even after its leaves have fallen. In spring it is covered with masses of ½-inch pale yellow or creamy white flowers shaped like peas.

USES. Kew broom is especially attractive when planted at the top of a wall, where its trailing stems can be allowed to cascade. It grows in Zones 6-8 and the cooler coastal sections of Zone 9. It does best in full sun or very light shade, in rather light soil with excellent drainage. It is drought resistant and tolerates salt air.

HOW TO GROW. Mature Kew broom is very difficult to move successfully, but container-grown plants can be transplanted with little risk of loss. Set plants out in the spring at intervals of 3 to 4 feet. Kew broom can be multiplied by cuttings or layering in spring.

# D

DAY LILY, TAWNY  See *Hemerocallis*

## DIANTHUS
### *D. deltoides* (maiden pink)

Maiden pink has evergreen foliage 2 to 6 inches high. Great numbers of slender flower stalks rise to a height of about 8 inches in late spring and are topped by small fragrant five-petaled pink, red or white flowers. Plants spread at a moderate rate.

USES. Maiden pink is easy to grow; it does well in full sun and almost any well-drained soil in Zones 2-10. When not in flower, it closely resembles grass. Slow and neat in growth habit, it is suitable for planting between flagstones.

HOW TO GROW. Plant in spring, setting new plants 6 to 8 inches apart. New plants are easily started from cuttings, or from divisions made in early spring while the plants are dormant or in early fall when the season's growth has matured. Replanting may be necessary from time to time if grass grows among the plants—the grass is hard to pick out because it looks much like maiden pink. For a neater appearance, shear plants back slightly after flowering.

NEW ZEALAND BRASS BUTTONS
*Cotula squalida*

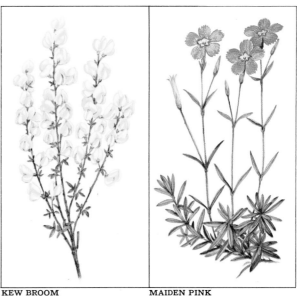

KEW BROOM
*Cytisus kewensis*

MAIDEN PINK
*Dianthus deltoides*

*For growing zones, see map on page 151.*

**DICHONDRA**
*Dichondra repens*

**ROSEA ICE PLANT**
*Drosanthemum hispidum*

**INDIAN STRAWBERRY**
*Duchesnea indica*

## DICHONDRA
*D. repens,* also called *D. carolinensis* (dichondra)

Well-grown dichondra lawns in Southern California and Arizona are the envy of gardeners around the world. Although the plant is not a grass, it makes the smooth turf expected of a true lawn. Its glossy round dark evergreen leaves, ¼ to ½ inch across, resemble tiny lily pads and overlap one another like shingles on a roof. Dichondra spreads as surface runners develop roots, as well as by reseeding itself; a beautiful lawn can be established from seeds within six to eight weeks of planting. In soil that is compacted by foot traffic the plants grow very small, often less than 1 inch tall, with tiny leaves. But in loose, fertile soil, especially in light shade, plants may become 6 inches high. Usually dichondra grows about 1½ to 2 inches tall and may be kept at that height by mowing.

USES. Dichondra is grown in Zones 9-10 for lawns, in small decorative beds, and as a crack filler between stones in terraces and paths. It can stand a moderate amount of trampling, but it recovers more slowly than do grasses and, like clover, it will stain light-colored shoes or clothing if crushed. It tolerates temperatures as low as 25° without damage, but it should never be walked on when frosted, or the foliage will be killed.

HOW TO GROW. Plant any time from March through mid-October, preferably in April or May. Prepare soil thoroughly as for a grass lawn *(Chapter 3).* Dichondra can be started by setting plugs of sod 6 to 12 inches apart or by sowing seeds at the rate of 1 to 2 pounds per 1,000 square feet. For a healthy lawn, the soil must be kept moist, not only until the seedlings or plugs are growing well but also thereafter. To maintain a rich dark green color, feed regularly with a low-strength fertilizer.

## DROSANTHEMUM
*D. hispidum* (rosea ice plant)

The rosea ice plant is a South African species that makes a soft, dense, fine-textured mat of hairy gray-green foliage about 6 to 8 inches deep, spreading and rooting rapidly to form a thick covering. The soft hairs on the small fat leaves glisten in the sun except in late spring or early summer, when the foliage is hidden by daisylike rosy purple flowers about an inch in diameter.

USES. This plant grows on the West Coast in Zones 9-10 and will do particularly well near the sea. It is useful for erosion control on steep banks and can be used to drape over rocky outcroppings. It will thrive in almost any well-drained soil in full sun.

HOW TO GROW. Plant any time there is no likelihood of frost, setting plants 8 to 12 inches apart. Pieces of stems root so readily that old stems can simply be shredded, scattered on soft prepared soil, rolled lightly and watered.

## DUCHESNEA
*D. indica,* also called *Fragaria indica*
(Indian strawberry, mock strawberry)

The mock strawberry has three-leaflet 1- to 3-inch leaves like those of wild strawberries, but the ¾-inch flowers, borne from early spring to summer, are yellow instead of white. The bright red ½-inch berries are decorative because they are held above the foliage; they are edible but not very flavorful. Plants spread quickly by runners, producing a thick matting 2 to 3 inches high. The foliage is not completely evergreen but retains its color into winter.

USES. The foliage, flowers and berries of mock strawberry make a handsome cover in large areas that can accommodate its rapid growth. It is a hardy species and will thrive in almost any soil in Zones 2-10, in sun or partial shade; light to medium shade is desirable in desert or sea-shore locations.

HOW TO GROW. Plant in spring, setting the plants 12 to 18 inches apart for quick coverage. New plants can be propagated from seeds, or by dividing old plants in early spring while they are dormant or in early fall after the season's growth is mature.

# E

## EPIMEDIUM

*E. grandiflorum,* also called *E. macranthum*
(long-spurred epimedium, bishop's hat)

Epimedium's delicate-looking but leathery leaves, which are composed of shiny heart-shaped leaflets 2 to 3 inches long, have a reddish tinge in spring and a bronze hue in fall, remaining colorful until late in the year. In late spring delicate sprays of rose, pale yellow, white or violet flowers, which resemble tiny bishop's hats, appear on wiry stalks. The 9- to 12-inch-high plants eventually become large clumps, but increase in size slowly.

USES. Epimediums thrive in light to deep shade in Zones 3-8 and make decorative coverings along paths and beneath trees, in small areas where the texture of the foliage can be appreciated. Cut sprays of the unusual flowers will last two to three weeks indoors. Plants grow best in light, moist, well-drained and organically rich soil.

HOW TO GROW. Plant in spring or fall from divisions, setting plants 8 to 10 inches apart. Mulch to conserve moisture and discourage weeds. Cut the plants close to the ground with hedge or pruning shears in very early spring so that new foliage will not be mixed with leftover leaves.

## ERICA

*E. carnea* (spring heath)

Spring heath is a ground-hugging evergreen shrub whose branches spread 2 to 3 feet across, sending up numerous 6- to 12-inch stems covered with tiny evergreen needles. One of the earliest-blooming garden plants, it bears a profusion of ¼-inch bell-shaped flowers that are white, pink, red or purple, depending on the variety. In Zones 5-7 the flowers open very early in the spring; in Zones 8-10, where winters are mild, spring heaths may begin to blossom as early as December or January and last for four or five months.

USES. Spring heath provides a colorful, informal cover in Zones 5-10; on banks its tangled roots hold the soil to prevent erosion. It will grow in a variety of soils, including slightly alkaline ones, but does best in acid soil with a pH between 4.5 and 5.5. Plants require full sun in Zones 5-8, but light shade is preferable in the hot areas of Zones 9-10. Thorough drainage is essential. Spring heath will tolerate wind and salt spray.

HOW TO GROW. Plant in early spring, setting new plants 2 to 3 feet apart, and water throughout the year. New plants are most easily started by division of clumps in spring, but may also be propagated by layering or from cuttings taken in midsummer and given a protected location until the following spring. To prolong life and promote compact growth, shear off old flower stalks after the blossoms have faded.

## EUONYMUS

*E. fortunei coloratus* (purple winter creeper)

One of the finest of the many varieties of winter creeper, this evergreen vine trails across the ground, rooting as it goes, to form a dense carpet rarely more than 6 inches high. Its small oval leaves, deep green in summer, take on a handsome purplish red hue in fall and winter; this variety does not produce flowers or fruit.

**EPIMEDIUM**
*Epimedium grandiflorum*

**SPRING HEATH**
*Erica carnea*

**PURPLE WINTER CREEPER**
*Euonymus fortunei coloratus*

*For growing zones, see map on page 151.*

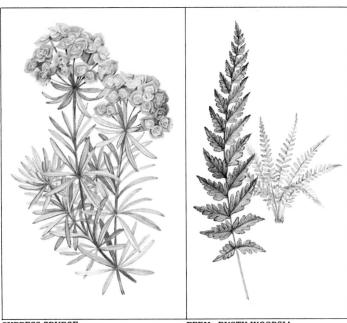

CYPRESS SPURGE
*Euphorbia cyparissias*

FERN: RUSTY WOODSIA
*Woodsia ilvensis*

BLUE FESCUE
*Festuca ovina glauca*

USES. Purple winter creeper is widely used in Zones 5-10 because of its distinctive winter color, and the fact that it requires little care. It will tolerate full sun or light shade and can be used to control erosion on steep banks, or to ramble over tree stumps or barren rocky spots.

HOW TO GROW. Plant in spring or fall in ground enriched with organic matter, setting plants 1 to 2 feet apart; mulch heavily with ground bark or wood chips. New plants are easily started from cuttings, by layering, or by division in spring or early fall.

## EUPHORBIA
*E. cyparissias* (cypress spurge)

The foot-high stems of cypress spurge, densely clothed with needlelike leaves 1 to 2 inches long, resemble gray-green foxes' tails; in spring they bear tiny yellowish flowers set in clusters of bright ½-inch floral bracts that change from yellow to orange as the blossoms mature. The species spreads rapidly by underground stems, forming a thick covering; the foliage dies down to the ground in fall, reappearing in spring.

USES. Cypress spurge will grow in full sun and almost any well-drained soil in Zones 3-9, and is ideal for dry sunny banks where few other plants will thrive. If it is planted in rich, moist soil, it becomes unusually rampant and difficult to contain.

HOW TO GROW. Plant in spring, setting plants 18 to 24 inches apart. New plants may be started by division in the spring or fall, or by stem cuttings taken at any time.

## EVERGREEN CANDYTUFT See *Iberis*

## F
## FERNS

Ferns, primitive plants dating back millions of years, are found growing all over the world. There are thousands of species, ranging from tiny mosslike growths to tree ferns 10 feet or more tall, but the species generally used as ground covers range from 6 inches to 3 feet in height. Nearly all do best in light shade in moist, highly organic, slightly acid soil (pH 5.5 to 6.5); a few kinds will thrive in full sun if given sufficient moisture.

USES. Ferns make lovely ground covers in woodland areas, in shady strips between walks and houses and beneath the filtered shade of trees. *Woodsia ilvensis* (rusty woodsia), which forms a dense deciduous matting 3 to 6 inches high, is well suited to dry, rocky locations in the eastern parts of Zones 3-7.

HOW TO GROW. Plant in spring or fall, setting plants 6 to 18 inches apart according to the size of the species; keep them fairly moist.

## FESTUCA
*F. ovina glauca* (blue fescue)

Unlike other fescues, blue fescue is not a good lawn grass because of its tufted growth habit, but its compact mounds of foliage, 4 to 10 inches high, make a handsome, unusual ground cover. Plants grow rapidly to form a good year-round covering.

USES. Blue fescue is often set in formal geometric patterns in small areas and as an edging for flower beds. It will thrive in almost any soil in full sun or very light shade in Zones 3-9, but its growth will stay more uniform and its color will be more vivid in full sun and poor, fairly dry soil. It will survive exposure to wind-blown sand and salt spray and is suitable for seashore planting.

HOW TO GROW. Plant in spring or fall, setting plants 6 to 12 inches apart, depending on whether an open or tight pattern of clumps is desired, and mulch lightly between clumps to deter weeds. New plants are easily started by division of clumps in spring or fall.

**FIRE THORN, SANTA CRUZ** See *Pyracantha*
**FIVE-LEAF AKEBIA** See *Akebia*
**FORGET-ME-NOT** See *Myosotis*

## FORSYTHIA
*F.* 'Arnold Dwarf' (Arnold Dwarf forsythia)

The low-arching branches of this deciduous shrub root wherever they touch moist soil, spreading outward in an ever-widening circle to form a dense mantle of dark green foliage 18 to 36 inches high. In early spring it bears a scattering of ¾-inch pale yellow flowers.

USES. This dwarf hybrid is a good soil binder on steep banks and is handsome when planted at the top of a wall where its trailing canes can cascade over the edge. Its height and tangled habit of growth make it useful as a barrier planting. It is easily grown in Zones 5-10 in almost any well-drained soil in full sun or light shade.

HOW TO GROW. Plant in spring or fall, setting plants 18 to 24 inches apart. New plants may be propagated in spring from stem cuttings or by layering.

## FRAGARIA
*F. chiloensis* (sand strawberry, wild strawberry)

One of the original species used to develop our cultivated varieties, the sand strawberry grows as a wild flower all the way from Alaska to the southern tip of South America. Plants grow 6 to 12 inches tall, spreading rapidly by runners to make a thick, glistening cover of 2- to 3-inch dark evergreen leaves. In spring plants bear a profusion of 1-inch white flowers, followed by red fruit, which is neither as large nor as tasty as cultivated strawberries.

USES. Sand strawberry, a highly decorative ground cover for beds, banks or borders, grows easily in a variety of soils along the West Coast in Zones 8-10, provided it has full sun or light shade and adequate moisture. It is well suited for planting in sand dunes by the ocean and is not harmed by exposure to salt spray.

HOW TO GROW. Planting can be done at any time of the year, but early spring or late fall is preferable. Set plants 12 to 18 inches apart. New plants are started by cutting off and planting runners. To encourage fresh foliage, mow to a height of 2 inches before new growth starts in spring and feed with a complete fertilizer.

## G
## GALAX
*G. aphylla* (galax)

Galax, a wild flower in the forests of the southeastern United States, forms a dense carpet about 6 inches high composed of shiny heart-shaped evergreen leaves, which vary from ½ inch to as much as 5 inches across and turn a bronzy hue in the fall, except in deep shade. In midsummer the plants send up slender 2-foot-high flower stalks bearing tiny white flowers less than ¼ inch in diameter. Plants spread moderately rapidly by underground stems.

USES. Galax is one of the finest evergreen ground covers for planting under rhododendrons and azaleas, where it is often found growing in the wild. It may be grown in Zones 3-8, provided it has a cool, moist, highly organic acid soil (pH 4.5 to 5.5) and medium to full shade. Its decorative leaves are particularly long lasting when cut.

HOW TO GROW. Plant in spring or fall, setting plants about 12 inches apart. Divide old plants in early spring when they are dormant, or in early fall when the season's growth has matured.

ARNOLD DWARF FORSYTHIA
*Forsythia* 'Arnold Dwarf'

SAND STRAWBERRY
*Fragaria chiloensis*

GALAX
*Galax aphylla*

*For growing zones, see map on page 151.*

## GAZANIA

*G. uniflora,* also called *G. leucolaena* (trailing gazania)

A creeping deciduous plant with slender silvery gray leaves 3 to 6 inches long, trailing gazania is studded with daisylike white, yellow, orange or bronzy red flowers 1½ to 2½ inches across, mainly in spring, with intermittent blossoms throughout the year. The flowers close at night and on dark days. The plants' trailing stems send out runners that root quickly to provide a fairly thick cover.

USES. Trailing gazanias are equally suitable on banks, in level flower beds or cascading over walls, wherever their silvery foliage and bright flowers can be appreciated. They thrive primarily on the West Coast and in the Southwest in Zones 8-10, and will grow in a variety of soils provided there is good drainage and full sun. Trailing gazanias are fairly drought resistant, though they benefit from occasional watering during hot spells.

HOW TO GROW. Plant in spring, setting plants 18 to 24 inches apart; propagate by dividing plants in spring. For best results dig up gazanias every three to four years; discard old woody stems and replant.

GOUTWEED  See *Aegopodium*
GROUND MORNING GLORY  See *Convolvulus*
GROUND PINK  See *Phlox*

# H

## HEDERA

*H. canariensis* (Algerian ivy, Canary Island ivy),
*H. helix* (English ivy)

These two species, among the most popular ivies, are vines that form handsome ground covers, especially when allowed to ramble over rocky areas or when planted as an evergreen carpeting at the base of trees.

Algerian ivy *(H. canariensis),* among the most widely used ground covers in southern California, has large shiny three- to five-lobed leaves as much as 5 to 8 inches across, although most of the foliage is about half that size; a variety, *H. canariensis variegata,* has green and white leaves. Plants trail along the ground, rooting as they go, slowly forming a thick covering 12 to 18 inches high and climbing trees, fences and other obstacles in their path. Their many roots penetrate deeply into the soil, making for excellent erosion control. Algerian ivy grows best in Zones 9-10 in moist, highly organic soil in full sun to deep shade.

English ivy *(H. helix)* has somewhat smaller leaves than Algerian ivy, generally 2 to 4 inches long; *H. helix baltica* (Baltic ivy), one of the hardiest varieties, has leaves only 1 to 2 inches long. Plants trail and root as they spread, taking two to three years to cover the ground completely with an impressive carpet of dark green foliage 6 to 8 inches high. English ivy will thrive in Zones 5-10 in full sun to deep shade provided it has a rich, moist soil.

HOW TO GROW. Plant in spring, preparing the soil 6 to 8 inches deep with an abundance of peat moss or leaf mold. Set young English ivy plants 12 inches apart, Algerian ivy 18 inches apart; a mulch will keep weeds under control until coverage is complete. Fertilize in early spring and midsummer to maintain healthy growth. If growth becomes straggly, shear plants close to the ground in early spring; new growth will quickly reclothe the area. Water deeply during hot spells. Propagate by stem cuttings, which can be taken at any time.

## HELIANTHEMUM

*H. nummularium* (sun rose)

Sun roses, of which there are many hybrid forms generally sold under the name *H. nummularium,* are spread-

**TRAILING GAZANIA**
*Gazania uniflora*

**ALGERIAN IVY**
*Hedera canariensis*

**ENGLISH IVY**
*Hedera helix*

ing evergreen or semievergreen shrubs that rarely grow over 12 inches tall, but often cover an area of 3 feet. Their narrow ½- to 1-inch leaves are glossy green to dullish gray green, depending on the variety. During the spring and intermittently throughout the summer, sun roses bear 1-inch flowers in various shades of pink, red and yellow as well as white. Each flower seems to be made from silky crinkled tissue paper, and though each lasts only a day, developing buds continue to open over several months. The trailing branches of sun roses root as they spread, slowly intertwining to form a dense mat.

USES. The decorative foliage and long blooming period of sun roses enhance beds and rock gardens. They do best in Zones 5-10 in full sun and very well drained alkaline soil (pH 7.5 to 8.5).

HOW TO GROW. Plant in early spring, setting plants 12 to 18 inches apart. Named varieties must be grown from nursery-grown plants, but others are easily propagated from seeds, or from plant divisions or stem cuttings taken in spring after new growth has occurred. Add lime to neutralize an acid soil and fertilize only lightly. In Zones 5-6 it is advisable to protect sun roses over the winter with a layer of evergreen boughs or straw. After flowering, shear off the old blossoms to maintain a neat cover and promote development of fresh blooms.

## HELXINE
*H. soleirolii* (baby's tears, angel's tears)

Baby's tears, a fine, fast-growing ground cover, spreads by creeping runners to form a dense, soft cushion of shiny greenery 2 to 4 inches high composed of tiny (⅛ to ¼ inch) smooth rounded leaves. Tiny, inconspicuous white flowers bloom during the summer.

USES. In most areas baby's tears is grown as a house plant, but in Zone 10 and areas of Zone 9 it makes a good outdoor ground cover, especially for small areas in light or even deep shade. Its delicate foliage creates a lovely effect when planted at the base of trees. Plants do best in moist, organically rich soil.

HOW TO GROW. Plant any time of year, setting plants 6 to 12 inches apart. Unless soil is extremely rich, condition it with well-rotted leaf mold, compost or peat moss; water regularly until the plants are well established. New plants can be propagated by division in spring or by cuttings, which may be taken at any time.

## HEMEROCALLIS
*H. fulva* 'Kwanso' (Kwanso tawny day lily)

The gracefully arching foliage and brilliant lilylike flowers of this species make a lovely summer display in informal beds or along roadsides. The straplike leaves, 2 feet long, fountain from the center of each plant in a bright green mass from spring to early fall but die to the ground during the winter months. The orange-red flowers, up to 5 inches long, burst into bloom in early summer, and unlike the blooms of most day lilies they last up to two or three days. There are sometimes a dozen flowers on a single stalk, and new ones often keep blossoming on the plants through midsummer.

USES. Kwanso tawny day lilies will grow without care in almost any soil, dry or wet, in Zones 3-10 as long as they have full sun or light shade; a rich soil brings more luxuriant foliage and more abundant blooms. They are suitable for seashore planting as they will survive exposure to windblown sand and salt spray.

HOW TO GROW. Plant in spring or fall, spacing plants about 2 feet apart. Propagate by dividing plants after they have finished flowering.

SUN ROSE
*Helianthemum nummularium*

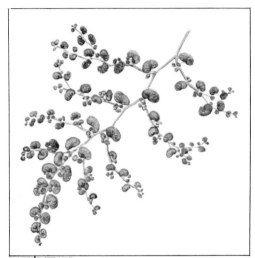
BABY'S TEARS
*Helxine soleirolii*

KWANSO TAWNY DAY LILY
*Hemerocallis fulva* 'Kwanso'

*For growing zones, see map on page 151.*

AARONSBEARD ST.-JOHN'S-WORT
*Hypericum calycinum*

EVERGREEN CANDYTUFT
*Iberis sempervirens*

HOTTENTOT FIG See *Carpobrotus*

## HYPERICUM
### *H. calycinum* (Aaronsbeard St.-John's-wort)

A small shrub that forms an irregular ground cover up to 12 inches high, this species has dark green 2- to 4-inch leaves that are semievergreen in Zones 6-8 but remain evergreen in Zones 9-10. It spreads by creeping runners and roots easily, sending up new plants that cover the ground rapidly. During July and August the plants bear innumerable attractive bright yellow flowers that have five petals and are about 3 inches across.

USES. Aaronsbeard St.-John's-wort is valued for its long summer bloom and is often used as a low border for taller shrubs. It is also a good choice for steep slopes, as its roots effectively bind the soil against erosion. A superb garden plant that will thrive in either sun or light shade, it is most successful in sandy, well-drained sites in Zones 6 and 7 but in the milder climate of Zones 8-10 it will do well in almost any kind of soil.

HOW TO GROW. Plant in spring, setting plants 18 inches apart. New plants may be started from stem cuttings, divisions or seeds; divide old plants in early spring when they are dormant or early fall when the season's growth has matured. In Zone 6 cover plants with evergreen boughs or salt marsh hay in winter. Beds of Aaronsbeard St.-John's-wort look best if they are mowed to the ground early each spring to stimulate fresh foliage.

# I
## IBERIS
### *I. sempervirens* (evergreen candytuft)

This flowering evergreen, familiar in rock gardens, grows in compact mounds 6 to 12 inches high that look like glistening dark green cushions. Its woody stems reach out as much as 2 feet, rooting where they touch moist soil and spreading slowly to form a dense carpet. In spring, and intermittently through the growing season in some varieties, plants are covered with tiny snow-white flowers in clusters up to 2 inches across.

USES. Candytuft is a handsome low-maintenance ground cover that provides year-round interest; it can be used as an edging for walks as well as a border for taller plants; it grows best in Zones 3-10 in fertile, well-drained soil and full sun and is suitable for seashore planting.

HOW TO GROW. Plant in late spring or early fall, setting plants 12 to 18 inches apart. New plants can be easily started from seeds, which take about two weeks to germinate, or from cuttings or divisions after the first flowering. Shear plants part way back after the flowers fade to encourage the growth of fresh foliage.

ICE PLANT  See *Drosanthemum* and *Lampranthus*
INDIAN STRAWBERRY  See *Duchesnea*
IVY, ALGERIAN  See *Hedera*
IVY, AMERICAN  See *Parthenocissus*
IVY, CANARY ISLAND  See *Hedera*
IVY, ENGLISH  See *Hedera*
IVY, PERSIAN GROUND  See *Nepeta*
IVY GERANIUM  See *Pelargonium*

# J
JAPANESE SPURGE  See *Pachysandra*

## JUNIPERUS
### *J. horizontalis wiltonii* (Wilton carpet juniper)

This hardy creeping juniper rarely grows over 4 inches tall but its trailing stems spread, rooting as they go, to a distance of 8 to 10 feet, slowly forming a dense covering. Its shapely pointed evergreen foliage retains its rich blue color throughout the year.

USES. Wilton carpet juniper will grow in most well-drained soils in Zones 2-10, but the blue color of the foliage is intensified when it is planted in rather sandy soil with a lean diet. It requires full sun, but will tolerate light shade in Zones 9-10, and withstands seaside conditions as well as heat and drought.

HOW TO GROW. Spring planting is preferable but container-grown plants can be set out any time the soil can be worked; set plants about 3 feet apart. New plants may be started from cuttings, which should be taken in late summer or early fall. Mulch the soil with ground bark or wood chips to inhibit the growth of weeds.

# K

KEW BROOM  See *Cytisus*
KINNIKINNICK  See *Arctostaphylos*

# L

## LAMPRANTHUS
*L. spectabilis* (trailing ice plant)

This species grows in a sprawling irregular manner 10 to 12 inches tall. The thick, juice-filled gray-green leaves are three-sided and 2 to 3 inches long. The plants spread and root rapidly by trailing stems, continuing to spread by dropping their own seeds. Masses of 2- to 3-inch daisylike flowers in shades of pink and red cover the foliage in spring.

USES. These plants grow primarily on the West Coast in Zones 9-10, thrive in almost any well-drained soil in full sun. They make a fine display on slopes or level ground, but the faded flowers are not attractive and are difficult to remove in wide beds without trampling the delicate, succulent stems of the foliage.

HOW TO GROW. Planting may be started at any time of year. Set plants about 18 inches apart. New plants can be propagated from cuttings; these do not have to be rooted beforehand but can simply be planted in the ground.

## LANTANA
*L. selloviana,* also called *L. montevidensis*
(trailing lantana)

In most parts of the country trailing lantana is grown as a summer annual or a house plant, but in areas where freezing weather rarely occurs this evergreen shrub makes a spectacular ground blanket, covered virtually year round with ¾- to 1-inch clusters of tiny lavender flowers. The arching canes, lined with dark green 1-inch leaves, may trail to 4 to 6 feet but will not not become more than 18 to 24 inches tall; they spread and root rapidly to provide a thick mass of foliage.

USES. Trailing lantana is an excellent choice for sunny slopes and may be used as a low hedge. It will do well in almost any well-drained soil in Zones 9-10; it will stand considerable drought but will grow more satisfactorily if it is watered from time to time.

HOW TO GROW. Plant any time, setting plants about 18 inches apart. New plants can be started from cuttings taken in early fall and set out the following spring. It is advisable to cut back plants hard in spring, before new growth starts, to eliminate old, less vigorous woody stems and force thick branching.

LAVENDER COTTON  See *Santolina*
LEADWORT  See *Ceratostigma*
LEATHER BERGENIA  See *Bergenia*
LILY OF THE VALLEY  See *Convallaria*

WILTON CARPET JUNIPER
*Juniperus horizontalis wiltonii*

TRAILING ICE PLANT
*Lampranthus spectabilis*

TRAILING LANTANA
*Lantana selloviana*

*For growing zones, see map on page 151.*

**CREEPING LILY-TURF**
*Liriope spicata*

**PARROT'S BEAK**
*Lotus bertholetii*

**BIRD'S-FOOT TREFOIL**
*Lotus corniculatus*

## LIRIOPE

*L. spicata* (creeping lily-turf)

Creeping lily-turf forms mounds of grassy foliage that grow 6 to 12 inches tall, spreading moderately rapidly by underground stems. The leaves, long and narrow (about ¼ inch across), are evergreen; in extreme cold weather in Zones 4-7 they turn pale yellowish green but remain to cover the ground. In summer, flower stalks bear elongated clusters of ¼-inch lavender-white blossoms followed by ¼-inch blue-black berries.

USES. This species provides a turflike cover with the added attraction of flowers and ornamental berries; it cannot be walked on without damage but is well suited to beds and borders. It will grow in almost any soil in Zones 4-10 in light conditions that vary from full sun to deep shade, and will tolerate drought.

HOW TO GROW. Plant in spring or fall, setting plants about 12 inches apart. Mow or clip off old leaves as the new ones are emerging in spring to assure attractive foliage. New plants can be started by dividing old ones in spring or fall.

## LOTUS

Although of the same genus, the following species are so unlike in their foliage, flowers and other characteristics that they are best discussed as separate entries.

*L. bertholetii* (parrot's beak, coral gem)

This trailing evergreen shrub, which grows 3 to 4 inches high, has gray-green leaves that are divided into hairlike segments, giving it a fluffy appearance; the vinelike branches spread rapidly, rooting as they go. The flowers, about an inch long, appear in profusion during early summer; shaped much like sweet-pea blossoms, with petals hooked like birds' beaks, they are a brilliant red that gradually fades to coral in the sun.

USES. An unusually decorative ground cover, coral gem is suitable for many uses, and is especially attractive tumbling gracefully down sunny banks. It will do well in any well-drained soil in Zones 9-10, particularly in hot, dry locations, but will not tolerate shade or excessive moisture.

HOW TO GROW. Plant in late summer or early fall, spacing plants 18 to 24 inches apart. New plants may be started from seeds sown in the spring, from cuttings or layers made in the summer, or by division in the fall or very early spring. Shear old plants early in spring before new growth starts to encourage branching.

*L. corniculatus* (bird's-foot trefoil)

This species spreads rapidly by shallow roots to form a closely matted carpet of foliage only 1 or 2 inches high. The three prominent ¼-inch leaflets on each leaf stem account for the name trefoil; the leaves are evergreen in warm climates but drop in winter in cooler zones. During summer and fall, the plants bear a profusion of flowers less than an inch across resembling bright yellow sweet peas; the seed pods that follow open in a clawlike shape that resembles a bird's foot.

USES. Bird's-foot trefoil is an easily cultivated ground cover that will grow in almost any well-drained soil in Zones 3-10, provided the location is sunny; it is especially useful on dry banks. In rich garden soil, however, the species tends to become weedy. A double-flowered form, *L. corniculatus flore peno,* is a rock-garden favorite.

HOW TO GROW. Plant in spring or summer, setting young plants about 6 inches apart or sowing seed at the rate of 2 pounds per 1,000 square feet. New plants are started from cuttings in spring. Plants can be mowed like a lawn to keep growth compact.

## LYSIMACHIA

*L. nummularia* (moneywort, creeping Jenny)

Moneywort, named for its penny-shaped bright green leaves, spreads rapidly by rooting runners to form a ruffled mat about 1 inch deep. The foliage is nearly evergreen, maintaining its color into December in northern zones. During most of the summer the foliage is covered by bright yellow blossoms an inch or less in size.

USES. A troublesome weed in lawns, moneywort is a useful ground cover when planted by itself; it will flourish in shady, moist and even wet ground where other plants will not grow. It can stand occasional trampling when planted around steppingstones in a path or terrace. It will do well almost anywhere in Zones 2-10.

HOW TO GROW. Plant at any time the ground can be worked, setting plants 12 to 18 inches apart. New plants may be had easily by digging up rooted stems, which spread in all directions from established plants.

# M
## MAHONIA

*M. repens* (dwarf holly grape, creeping mahonia)

Dwarf holly grape, an evergreen shrub that customarily grows less than 1 foot tall, has bluish green holly-like leaves; each 3- to 6-inch leaf is composed of from three to seven 1½- to 2½-inch spiny-edged leaflets. In early spring the tip of each cane carries a 1- to 3-inch cluster of bright yellow ¼-inch blossoms, which are followed by black grapelike ¼-inch fruit that makes a tart but tasty jelly. In cooler areas the leaves turn bronze in fall. The species spreads rapidly by underground stems.

USES. Dwarf holly grape is a handsome ground-cover shrub for borders and beds. It will grow in Zones 5-10 in a variety of soils, but does best in those that are reasonably moist and well supplied with organic matter. It may be planted in full sun to deep shade.

HOW TO GROW. Plant in spring, or in early fall at least eight weeks before the first expected frost, setting plants 12 inches apart. A 2- to 3-inch mulch of bark or wood chips will help hold moisture and make weeding practically unnecessary. New plants may be started from divisions in spring or from root cuttings in fall.

**MAIDEN PINK** See *Dianthus*
**MAX GRAF ROSE** See *Rosa*

## MAZUS

*M. reptans* (creeping mazus)

Creeping mazus rarely grows more than 2 inches tall, but spreads across the ground, rooting as it goes, to make a lovely bright green carpet tough enough to withstand occasional traffic. In spring the 1-inch leaves are a foil for numerous ¾-inch purplish blue flowers; the broad liplike petal of each flower is spotted with yellow and white. In Zones 9 and 10 the foliage stays green throughout the year, but in the rest of the country it dies down to the ground during the winter.

USES. This species, suitable in Zones 5-10, can be used in beds or in crevices in flagstone paths or terraces. It grows best in rich, moist soil in sun or light shade.

HOW TO GROW. Plant in early spring, setting plants about 12 inches apart for good coverage. Mazus may be increased easily by division, which should be done in the spring. In exposed locations in Zone 5, it is advisable to protect the plants during the winter with a light covering of salt marsh hay or evergreen boughs.

**MEMORIAL ROSE** See *Rosa*

MONEYWORT
*Lysimachia nummularia*

DWARF HOLLY GRAPE
*Mahonia repens*

CREEPING MAZUS
*Mazus reptans*

*For growing zones, see map on page 151.*

**CORSICAN MINT**
*Mentha requienii*

**YERBA BUENA**
*Micromeria chamissonis*

**MOSS SANDWORT**
*Minuartia verna caespitosa*

## MENTHA
*M. requienii* (Corsican mint, creeping mint)

Corsican mint, a tiny plant, grows only 2 to 3 inches high, sometimes less than an inch, but spreads rapidly by shallow underground stems to form a delicate cushion of greenery. Its round leaves, only $\frac{1}{8}$ inch across, release a strong peppermint fragrance when bruised. In late spring and early summer the leaves are dotted with tiny pale lavender blossoms. Corsican mint is evergreen in warmer climates but when subjected to freezing temperatures it seems to disappear completely, returning in spring.

USES. This is a jewel of a ground cover, one to be set in a special bed by itself where it can be admired at close range. It is well suited for growing among stones in a path, patio or entrance garden, since it can stand some traffic and its delightful fragrance rises whenever it is stepped upon. It will grow in Zones 6-10 and does best in full sun or light shade in soil enriched with leaf mold or peat moss. Being a diminutive plant with a shallow root system, it needs a constantly moist soil.

HOW TO GROW. Plant in early spring, setting plants about 6 inches apart. New plants can be started by dividing older plants in spring.

## MESEMBRYANTHEMUM  See *Carpobrotus, Drosanthemum* and *Lampranthus*

## MICROMERIA
*M. chamissonis*, also called *Satureja douglasii*
(yerba buena)

San Francisco was originally named Yerba Buena—literally, "good herb"—by early Spanish explorers who found this fragrant, mint-scented plant growing in profusion on the shores and islands of its bay *(page 90)*. It spreads rapidly up to 3 feet across, its stems rooting as they go, to form a mass of foliage 3 to 6 inches tall. Its oval, scalloped evergreen leaves are about 1 inch long; tiny lavender-white flowers about $\frac{1}{4}$ inch across are borne in summer.

USES. Yerba buena is grown primarily on the West Coast in Zones 8-10. It can be planted in rock gardens or on the tops of walls and is sometimes used in patios or paths, where its minty fragrance is released when stepped on. Plants do best in loose, moist, organically rich soil; they need full sun near the ocean and partial shade inland.

HOW TO GROW. Plants may be started from seeds or cuttings in spring. Set cuttings about 2 feet apart, using a mulch such as leaf mold to hold moisture and keep down weeds until the covering is established.

## MINT, CORSICAN  See *Mentha*
## MINT, CREEPING  See *Mentha*

## MINUARTIA
*M. verna caespitosa*, also called *Arenaria verna caespitosa*
(moss sandwort)

Moss sandwort is well named, for its low needlelike foliage could easily be mistaken for moss except in spring, when $\frac{1}{8}$-inch white flowers dot the surface like little stars. It spreads quickly by creeping runners to form an undulating carpet about 2 inches high.

USES. This plant makes a delightful ground cover for gentle slopes or small areas where its height is in scale with surrounding plants; it is often used around stones in a path or terrace. It will grow anywhere in Zones 2-10 in full sun or light shade; light shade is preferable in hot locations. It has a shallow root system that requires a moist, well-drained, slightly acid soil (pH 5.5 to 6.5). Moss sandwort will withstand sub-zero temperatures, but extreme cold weather changes its evergreen foliage to a silvery hue.

HOW TO GROW. Plant in spring, setting plants about 6 inches apart. New plants may be grown from seeds in spring or from stem cuttings in early summer, but are usually started from divisions in spring.

MOCK STRAWBERRY  See *Duchesnea*
MONDO GRASS  See *Ophiopogon*
MONEYWORT  See *Lysimachia*
MOSS SANDWORT  See *Minuartia*
MOTHER-OF-THYME  See *Thymus*

## MYOSOTIS

*M. scorpioides semperflorens* (forget-me-not)

This plant, sometimes called the true forget-me-not, forms uneven masses of foliage 6 to 18 inches high; through most of the spring and summer, its smooth 1- to 2-inch leaves are partially hidden by ¼-inch pale blue flowers with yellow, pink or white centers. Plants spread rapidly by creeping stems to provide a dense cover and drop their own seeds freely when established. The foliage dies to the ground each winter, reappearing in early spring.

USES. Forget-me-nots are plants for moist spots in light shade and make a charming covering in woods by a pond or stream. They will grow almost anywhere in Zones 5-10, provided the soil is rich in organic matter, and will flourish for years without care.

HOW TO GROW. Plant in early spring, setting plants about 12 inches apart. New plants may be started from divisions or seeds in spring.

MYRTLE, CREEPING  See *Vinca*

# N

NATAL PLUM  See *Carissa*

## NEPETA

*N. mussinii* (mauve catmint, Persian ground ivy)

A ground cover of mauve catmint is a fairly dense, irregular growth of grayish green foliage, 12 to 18 inches tall. Its 1-inch leaves have a strong minty fragrance very attractive to cats, which like to lie among its leafy stems. During early summer and again in fall it bears clusters of ¼-inch lavender blossoms on slender flower stalks. Plants spread fairly rapidly to provide good cover but lose their leaves over winter.

USES. An area planted with mauve catmint has a soft hazy quality that adds a welcome change of texture to a garden. It makes a nice edging for perennial borders and is lovely when planted on the top of a stone wall. It will grow in a variety of soils in Zones 4-10, provided it has full sun and adequate drainage. Established plants tolerate considerable drought and for this reason will do well in desert locations.

HOW TO GROW. Plant in spring, spacing plants 12 to 18 inches apart. New plants may be started from cuttings rooted in late spring or early summer. Shear the plants to the ground in late fall or early spring so that fresh growth will be encouraged.

NEW ZEALAND BRASS BUTTONS  See *Cotula*

# O

## OPHIOPOGON

*O. japonicus* (dwarf lily-turf, mondo grass)

From a distance, a covering of mondo grass might be mistaken for a true grass, as it forms mounds of grasslike foliage about 6 inches high. Its arching leaves are 8 to 12

FORGET-ME-NOT
*Myosotis scorpioides semperflorens*

MAUVE CATMINT
*Nepeta mussinii*

DWARF LILY-TURF
*Ophiopogon japonicus*

*For growing zones, see map on page 151.*

**TRAILING AFRICAN DAISY**
*Osteospermum fruticosum*

**CANBY PACHISTIMA**
*Pachistima canbyi*

**JAPANESE PACHYSANDRA**
*Pachysandra terminalis*

inches long and may remain evergreen in Zones 8-10. In early summer mondo grass bears lavender flowers less than 1/4 inch across on short spikes, followed by tight clusters of 1/4-inch blue berries. Plants spread slowly when first planted, by means of fleshy rootlike stems beneath the surface of the soil, but are faster growing when established.

USES. Mondo grass makes an interesting ground cover that requires little care and is especially useful as a carpeting under trees. It will thrive in sun or shade in Zones 8-10, but from Zone 7 north its hardier relative, *Liriope spicata* (creeping lily-turf), is a better choice *(page 138)*. Mondo grass grows best in rich, moist soil.

HOW TO GROW. Plant in spring, setting plants 6 to 12 inches apart. Start new plants by division in early spring.

## OSTEOSPERMUM
*O. fruticosum,* also called *Dimorphotheca fruticosa*
(trailing African daisy)

This free-flowering evergreen plant makes an attractive covering about 18 inches high, with gray-green leaves 1 to 2 inches long and handsome daisylike flowers about 3 inches across that are lavender with purple centers. Most of the blossoms appear from November through March, with a scattering of flowers through the rest of the year; they open only in sunshine. Plants spread rapidly by long runners that root as they go.

USES. Trailing African daisy, used primarily on the West Coast in Zones 9 and 10, is suitable for covering large areas of level or sloping ground. It does best in rich soil and full sun.

HOW TO GROW. Plant any time, setting plants about 2 feet apart. Established plants usually stand considerable drought but do best when watered occasionally; since plants tend to become straggly, pinch back young stems to encourage branching and cut back old plants from time to time to keep them within bounds.

# P
## PACHISTIMA
*P. canbyi,* also called *Paxistima canbyi*
(Canby pachistima, ratstripper)

A shrub that grows about a foot high, Canby pachistima spreads across the ground to make a shining carpet of 1/2- to 1-inch leaves that are a rich green in summer and take on a handsome bronze hue in winter. Its reddish spring flowers are so small they are rarely noticed. Plants spread slowly by trailing, rooting branches.

USES. Canby pachistima is one of the finest evergreen ground covers and is particularly attractive when planted in front of rhododendrons. It will grow in Zones 5-8 in full sun or partial shade and in partial shade in the hotter sections of Zone 9; it does best in rich, moist, well-drained acid soil (pH 4.5 to 5.5).

HOW TO GROW. Plant in spring, setting plants about 12 inches apart in soil enriched with peat moss or leaf mold, and mulch with ground bark or wood chips to conserve moisture and inhibit weed growth. New plants can be easily started from divisions in spring, from cuttings in summer or by layering in spring.

## PACHYSANDRA
*P. terminalis* (Japanese pachysandra, Japanese spurge)

This species is one of the best and most widely grown evergreen ground covers in North America. Its clustered, saw-toothed leaves, 1 to 3 inches long, form a lush carpeting 8 to 10 inches high. Three- to 4-inch spikes of small white flowers appear above the leaves in spring; infrequently these are followed by inconspicuous white berries. Plants spread slowly by underground stems but gradually grow together to form a handsome covering.

USES. Pachysandra can be grown virtually anywhere in Zones 4-9, on slopes or level ground, and is especially valued for beds and borders in light to deep shade where other plants will not grow; it thrives even in the dense shade of Norway maple trees and competes successfully with their shallow roots for nourishment, particularly if helped by occasional feeding. It needs a rich, moist, slightly acid soil (pH 5.5 to 6.5) but requires no other care.

HOW TO GROW. Plant in spring or early summer, enriching soil with well-rotted leaf mold or peat moss and setting new plants 6 to 12 inches apart. Mulch the soil with ground bark or wood chips to conserve moisture. New plants may be started from divisions or rooted stem cuttings in spring or early summer.

**PARROT'S BEAK** See *Lotus*

## PARTHENOCISSUS

*P. quinquefolia*

(Virgina creeper, American ivy, woodbine)

A fast-growing deciduous vine, Virginia creeper forms a blanket of foliage 10 to 12 inches high. Each leaf is made up of five coarse-toothed leaflets, 2 to 4 and even 6 inches long, which are a rich green color during summer and turn brilliant red before falling in autumn. Those vines spread rapidly, rooting as they go. Inconspicuous greenish flowers in spring are followed by clusters of ¼-inch berries that are bluish black.

USES. Virginia creeper should be used in a naturalistic setting where it can be allowed to ramble at will. It is excellent on slopes or rocky ground, but will climb any tree or bush it encounters. The variety *P. quinquefolia engelmannii* has smaller leaves. Virginia creeper will grow in most areas in Zones 3-10 with little or no care, provided it has rich, moist soil and has been planted in a location that is sunny or lightly shaded.

HOW TO GROW. Plant in early spring or fall, setting plants 3 to 4 feet apart. New plants may be started from seeds in very early spring or by layering in spring.

## PELARGONIUM

*P. peltatum* (ivy geranium)

Ivy geraniums take their name from their five-lobed leaves, which are similar in shape to those of English ivy. Clusters of 2- to 4-inch pink, red, lavender or white flowers bloom mostly during summer in inland areas of the West Coast and year round in coastal areas where frosts and freezes rarely occur. Their trailing stems spread rapidly, covering the ground with dense, shrubby mounds of foliage 3 to 5 feet across.

USES. Ivy geraniums, charming in pots and hanging baskets, make a truly stunning display massed on open ground. They will grow in Zones 9 and 10 in sun or light shade and are not particular as to soil, although ideally they should have a light, well-drained soil with some organic matter, on the dry side to stimulate flower production.

HOW TO GROW. Plant any time, spacing plants 12 to 18 inches apart. New plants may be started from cuttings at any time. The tips of new growth on young plants should be pinched out to encourage the development of as many branches as possible.

## PHLOX

*P. subulata* (moss phlox, moss pink, ground pink)

Moss phlox, the ubiquitous flower of rock gardens, often appears in harsh magenta shades, but there are varieties

VIRGINIA CREEPER
*Parthenocissus quinquefolia*

IVY GERANIUM
*Pelargonium peltatum*

MOSS PHLOX
*Phlox subulata*

*For growing zones, see map on page 151.*

**SANTA CRUZ FIRE THORN**
*Pyracantha koidzumi* 'Santa Cruz Prostrata'

**MAX GRAF ROSE**
*Rosa* 'Max Graf'

**MEMORIAL ROSE**
*Rosa wichuraiana*

that provide many other colors, ranging from snowy white through soft pinks and violets to deep red. In the spring a flush of ½- to 1-inch blossoms completely covers the plants. The evergreen foliage is made up of sharp scalelike leaves ¼ to ½ inch long; individual plants rarely grow more than 4 or 5 inches tall but may spread to a diameter of 2 feet or more, sending out trailing stems that create a thick, tufted carpet of foliage.

USES. Besides making a colorful display in rock gardens, moss phlox can be used in front of perennial borders or cascading over retaining walls. It will grow in almost any well-drained soil in Zones 3-9, provided the site is sunny.

HOW TO GROW. Plant in spring, setting plants 12 to 18 inches apart. New plants are started from divisions or cuttings made after the plants have flowered. After flowering, it is advisable to shear the stems back halfway to stimulate fresh new foliage.

**PURPLE WINTER CREEPER** See *Euonymus*

## PYRACANTHA
*P. koidzumi* 'Santa Cruz Prostrata' (Santa Cruz fire thorn)

Fire thorns are evergreen shrubs widely grown for their abundant crops of ¼-inch bright red or orange berries, which stay on the branches most of the winter. Most types are tall growing, but the red-berried Santa Cruz fire thorn is spreading in habit, usually remaining under 3 feet in height. It bears shiny deep green leaves 1½ to 2½ inches long and masses of tiny ¼-inch white flowers in spring. The thorny branches can be expected to spread quickly, forming a dense mat of foliage.

USES. The decorative berries of Santa Cruz fire thorns make a fine winter display almost anywhere in Zones 7-10, on rocky slopes or in beds, borders or low ornamental hedges. Plants will grow in most soils provided there is full sun and adequate moisture.

HOW TO GROW. Plant container-grown plants in spring, setting plants 2 feet apart. New plants can be started from cuttings taken in fall and rooted over winter in a protected bed. They should be watered thoroughly when they are first planted but once established, fire thorns should be grown with a minimum of moisture to encourage longevity and the production of berries.

# R
## ROSA
*R.* 'Max Graf' (Max Graf rose),
*R. wichuraiana* (memorial rose)

Some gardeners think of roses only as fragile, aristocratic shrubs, to be raised and pampered in formal beds and cut for delicate flower arrangements. Several species, however, make surprisingly rugged, fast-spreading ground covers, ideally suited for rough terrain, for holding soil on problem slopes or for creating thick, thorny barriers that will discourage traffic where it is not wanted. One outstanding species is *R.* 'Max Graf,' a deciduous shrub whose long trailing canes sprout wiry, brierlike stems 2 to 4 feet high; it has glossy leaves and in June is covered with fragrant five-petaled, 3-inch flowers, bright pink with golden centers. A lower and even stronger-growing species is the memorial rose, *R. wichuraiana,* a native of Japan and a parent of the Max Graf and other modern rambler roses. It trails along the ground, rooting as it goes, seldom growing over a foot high; in early summer it produces very fragrant white flowers, 2 inches across, with five petals each. Its clusters of lustrous 1-inch leaflets are evergreen in warm climates but drop in winter in cooler regions.

USES. Both species can be used in Zones 5-10 for planting on banks or other terrain where smaller, less vigorous ground covers might not thrive; they also make decorative low hedges. *R. wichuraiana* has a lower, somewhat neater profile than its offspring, but both are better used in a naturalistic setting than a formal one, and both are best seen at a slight distance, particularly since it is almost impossible to keep weeds from growing among their canes. They grow best in full sun (*R. wichuraiana* can take partial shade) and flourish in enriched soil with good drainage.

HOW TO GROW. Plant in spring, setting plants 2 to 4 feet apart. New plants may be produced by digging up natural layers that occur where the trailing canes touch the ground, or from cuttings.

## ROSMARINUS
*R. officinalis prostratus* (creeping rosemary)

Creeping rosemary is a small spreading evergreen shrub that rarely exceeds 2 feet in height and develops a gnarled, picturesque habit of growth when grown slowly under dry conditions. The ½- to 2-inch needlelike leaves have a pleasant, pungent aroma; tiny clusters of ½-inch pale lavender-blue flowers bloom in winter and spring and occasionally in fall. Individual plants spread slowly by rooting along their creeping stems and may reach a diameter of 5 to 6 feet, but initial growth is slow and good coverage may take several years.

USES. Creeping rosemary is an especially useful ground cover in hot, dry areas. It prevents soil erosion on slopes and tolerates seaside conditions. It thrives in Zones 8-10 in full sun and well-drained soil.

HOW TO GROW. Plant in spring, spacing plants 18 to 24 inches apart. Keep moderately moist until established, but avoid excessive watering thereafter. New plants can be started from stem cuttings, which may be taken any time during the growing season and replanted when they have established roots, or from seeds.

## RUSTY WOODSIA See *Ferns*

# S
## SAGINA
*S. subulata* (Corsican pearlwort)

This species, sometimes called Irish moss, forms a mossy evergreen matting about 4 inches high, composed of spiky ¼-inch leaves surmounted by ½- to ¾-inch white flowers in midsummer. The plants have slender creeping stems that hug the soil, rooting as they spread rapidly to form a dense mass of foliage.

USES. Corsican pearlwort makes a unique ground cover and is well suited to rock gardens and for filling in crevices around steppingstones. It does well in a variety of locations in Zones 4-10, thriving in moist, well-drained, organically rich soil and light shade.

HOW TO GROW. Plant in spring, setting plants about 6 inches apart. New plants can be propagated by division after the first flowering in spring.

## ST.-JOHN'S-WORT See *Hypericum*

## SANTOLINA
*S. chamaecyparissus* (lavender cotton)

Lavender cotton, a woody evergreen herb with fragrant, finely cut gray foliage, is widely used as an annual in cold areas, but in milder climates it makes a beautiful ground cover because of the striking color and texture of its foliage. Untrimmed plants become 2 feet tall, but they are more attractive when kept sheared to 1 foot or less. Flowers, less than an inch across and resembling yellow but-

CREEPING ROSEMARY
*Rosmarinus officinalis prostratus*

CORSICAN PEARLWORT
*Sagina subulata*

LAVENDER COTTON
*Santolina chamaecyparissus*

*For growing zones, see map on page 151.*

**STRAWBERRY GERANIUM**
*Saxifraga stolonifera*

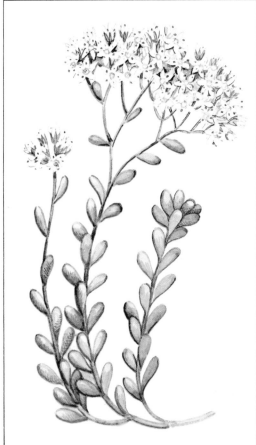

**WHITE STONECROP**
*Sedum album*

tons, bloom in summer. Individual plants spread rapidly by creeping stems and may reach 3 feet across.

USES. A favorite among desert gardeners, lavender cotton makes an attractive bedding or low hedge. It is drought resistant and will grow in most well-drained garden soils in full sun in Zones 7-10.

HOW TO GROW. Plant in spring, setting plants 18 to 24 inches apart. New plants can be started from cuttings taken in spring and held over in protected beds for planting the following spring.

## SAXIFRAGA
*S. stolonifera,* also called *S. sarmentosa*
(strawberry geranium)

This species, a favorite house plant in most of the country, makes a fine evergreen ground cover wherever winters are mild. A tufted plant about 4 inches high, it has round, hairy geraniumlike leaves with white veins and reddish undersides; in midsummer it sends up slender 2-foot flower stalks with dainty 1-inch white blossoms. It spreads rapidly by reddish runners, which root as they go, forming colonies of young plants around each mother plant.

USES. Strawberry geraniums are frequently used in Zones 8-10 as decorative ground covers for small areas. They do best in rich, moist soil in light shade.

HOW TO GROW. Plant in spring, setting plants 8 to 10 inches apart. New plants that develop on the runners may be detached and replanted at any time to help attain complete coverage.

## SCOTCH HEATHER  See *Calluna*
## SEA FIG  See *Carpobrotus*
## SEA PINK  See *Armeria*

## SEDUM
*Sedum* species and varieties (sedum, stonecrop)

Most of the 300 known species of sedums, or stonecrops, are very low-growing succulent plants, often no more than 2 to 3 inches tall, with thick juicy evergreen or semi-evergreen leaves that vary in size, shape and color. *Sedum album,* one of the most popular species, forms a dense mat of ¼-inch-long evergreen leaves whose tips turn reddish in winter. It bears ¼-inch white flowers in late summer; the variety *S. album murale* has pale pink flowers and purple foliage. The creeping runners of stonecrops spread rapidly, sending up foliage as they go.

USES. Many species, including *Sedum album,* are suitable for planting in Zones 3-10; they will grow in almost any well-drained soil in full sun or light shade, and will thrive in the poorest soil and driest locations, in rock gardens and the borders of flower beds.

HOW TO GROW. Plant at any time of the year when the soil can be worked, setting plants 9 to 12 inches apart. New plants can be started at any time from divisions or by taking cuttings.

## SILVER MOUND  See *Artemisia*
## SNOW-IN-SUMMER  See *Cerastium*
## SPRENGER ASPARAGUS  See *Asparagus*
## SPRING HEATH  See *Erica*

## STACHYS
*S. olympica,* also called *S. lanata*
(lamb's ears, woolly betony)

The name lamb's ears is very descriptive of the silvery, woolly 4- to 6-inch leaves of this species, which spreads rapidly by underground roots to make a solid mat of foliage 12 to 18 inches tall. In summer, whorls of small blossoms appear on 12-inch flower spikes. The foliage dies to the ground during the winter.

USES. Lamb's ears is an excellent choice for hot, sunny spots, and its foliage and flowers add an unusual note to borders or flowering beds. It will grow in most well-drained soils in Zones 3-10, provided it has full sunshine.

HOW TO GROW. Plant in spring, setting plants 12 to 18 inches apart. In spring, rake the plants over to remove old foliage and apply a light feeding of all-purpose fertilizer to enhance new growth. Watering should be limited, as plants do better when the soil is somewhat dry. New plants can be started by division in spring, or from seeds.

STAR JASMINE  See *Trachelospermum*
STONECROP  See *Sedum*
STRAWBERRY, INDIAN  See *Duchesnea*
STRAWBERRY, MOCK  See *Duchesnea*
STRAWBERRY, SAND  See *Fragaria*
STRAWBERRY, WILD  See *Fragaria*
STRAWBERRY GERANIUM  See *Saxifraga*
SUN ROSE  See *Helianthemum*
SWEET FERN  See *Comptonia*
SWEET WOODRUFF  See *Asperula*

# T

## TAXUS

*T. baccata repandens* (spreading English yew)

This low, slow-growing variety of English yew forms tangled mounds of needlelike evergreen foliage only 2 to 3 inches high, with new stems trailing slowly out from the base of each plant. The variety is female, and if male yews are nearby will bear ½-inch red berries that add to its ornamental value.

USES. Spreading English yews will grow in Zones 5-10 in full sun, or in deep shade beneath trees where many other plants cannot survive. They require practically no maintenance when planted in moist, highly organic soil that has good drainage.

HOW TO GROW. Plant in spring, setting plants 3 to 4 feet apart in soil enriched with peat moss or well-rotted leaf mold. A mulch of ground bark or wood chips will conserve moisture and keep down weeds. New plants can be started from cuttings taken in fall and held over in protected beds until the following spring.

## TEUCRIUM

*T. chamaedrys* (germander, chamaedrys germander)

Germander is a shrub that grows up to 18 inches tall but makes a neater, thicker ground cover if sheared to a height of 10 to 12 inches. Its saw-toothed hairy leaves, ¾ inch long, remain evergreen in milder zones but fall off in winter in cooler regions. Germander's underground rootstalks spread quickly. During late summer ¾-inch rosy lavender blossoms are borne on small upright stalks set among the leaves. The variety *T. chamaedrys prostratum* grows only to a height of 4 to 6 inches.

USES. Germanders are so responsive to shearing they are often grown as low, formal hedges or edgings for walks as well as covers for larger areas of ground. They do well in Zones 5-10 in full sun and well-drained soil.

HOW TO GROW. Plant in spring, setting plants about 12 inches apart. New plants can be easily started from divisions in spring, stem cuttings in late spring or early summer. In Zone 5 and the colder areas of Zone 6, branches sometimes suffer from winterkill but if dead tips are removed in spring the plants make a fast recovery.

THYME, CREEPING  See *Thymus*

LAMB'S EARS
*Stachys olympica*

SPREADING ENGLISH YEW
*Taxus baccata repandens*

GERMANDER
*Teucrium chamaedrys*

*For growing zones, see map on page 151.*

WILD THYME
*Thymus serpyllum*

STAR JASMINE
*Trachelospermum jasminoides*

WHITE CLOVER
*Trifolium repens*

## THYMUS

*T. serpyllum* (wild thyme, mother-of-thyme, creeping thyme)

Wild thyme, a trailing evergreen herb, forms a flat close-napped carpet that grows 1 to 6 inches high depending on the moisture and nutrients available. Its tiny round leaves, $\frac{1}{4}$ inch or less in size, are highly aromatic. In summer, flower stalks bear clusters of miniscule rosy purple, white, pink, lavender or red blossoms that are particularly attractive to bees. One variety, *T. serpyllum lanuginosus,* has hairy gray-green foliage. Plants spread rapidly by means of long trailing stems that hug the soil, rooting as they go to form a dense ground cover.

USES. Wild thyme is a favorite in rock gardens, but its rapid growth is often too aggressive for such locations; it is better suited to growing as a ground cover or among steppingstones (it will stand mowing and occasional trampling). It will do well in Zones 3-10 in full sun and rather dry, well-drained soil; in rich soil its stems become tall and weak and the plant loses its character.

HOW TO GROW. Plant in spring, setting plants 6 to 12 inches apart. New plants may be had easily by dividing old plants in spring.

## TRACHELOSPERMUM

*T. jasminoides* (star jasmine, Confederate jasmine)

This species may be grown as a vine or a densely foliaged ground cover ranging from 8 inches to 2 feet high. It has glossy evergreen leaves $1\frac{1}{2}$ to 3 inches long and from late winter through early summer, depending on the area, bears a profusion of exceedingly fragrant 1-inch white flowers. Because the woody shoots of this climber spread rather slowly it may take several growing seasons to achieve full coverage.

USES. Star jasmine is one of the most common ground covers in the South and West. It may be grown in Zones 8-10 in full sun to deep shade and does best in cool, moist, highly organic soil.

HOW TO GROW. Plant container-grown plants any time, setting plants 2 to 3 feet apart. New plants may be started from rooted stem cuttings in spring. Plants benefit from two feedings a year, in early spring and late summer, and will branch more fully if stem tips are pinched back.

## TRIFOLIUM

*T. repens* (white clover)

White clover makes a dense, irregular carpet about 3 inches high; the leaves, divided into three $\frac{1}{2}$-inch leaflets, die to the ground in winter in Zones 2-9 but flourish year round in Zone 10. The stems creep rapidly across the ground, rooting as they go. In summer the plants bear $\frac{3}{4}$-inch clusters of tiny white flowers that bees favor.

USES. At one time, every good lawn-grass mixture contained some white clover seeds, but clover in lawns has largely gone out of fashion. It is vulnerable to broad-leaf weed killers and is best used alone as a low ground cover. It may be mowed or not as desired, and will stand a reasonable amount of traffic, although it is not as tough as grass and is notorious for staining clothes. It will grow in Zones 2-10 in any moist, rich soil with full sun.

HOW TO GROW. Plant in spring, sowing seeds at a rate of 3 pounds per 1,000 square feet in soil prepared with organic matter and fertilizer.

## V

## VERONICA

*V. repens* (creeping speedwell)

Creeping speedwell forms a low, neat mat about 4 inches high composed of shiny dark green $\frac{1}{2}$- to $\frac{3}{4}$-inch leaves, topped in spring by clusters of ¼-inch blue, white or pink flowers. The foliage dies down in winter except in Zone 10 and warmer areas of Zone 9. The shallow roots spread rapidly to assure a good cover.

USES. Creeping speedwell makes a fine bed in which to plant a scattering of low-growing spring bulbs such as crocuses or miniature daffodils. It requires full sun in Zones 5-8, but will do best in very light shade in Zones 9-10. A rich, moist soil is advisable; since the plants have shallow roots they may have to be watered regularly.

HOW TO GROW. Plant in early spring, setting plants 6 to 12 inches apart. New plants may be had easily by dividing old ones in spring or fall.

## VINCA
*V. minor* (common periwinkle, creeping myrtle)

One of the finest evergreen ground covers, this species forms a trailing carpet of shiny ½- to ¾-inch leaves that grow up to 6 inches high and are dotted in early spring with lavender, blue or white flowers about an inch across. *V. major,* a larger-leaved species, grows to a height of 2 feet but thrives only in Zones 8-10. Plants spread rapidly, rooting as they trail.

USES. Periwinkle can be used on slopes or level land, in beds by itself or as a backdrop for higher flowering bulbs, beside paths or in plantings around the base of trees. Although it will grow virtually anywhere in Zones 4-10 it does best in light to deep shade, taking full sun only in Zones 4-7, and grows faster and more attractively in deep moist soil enriched with organic matter. Once established it needs little care.

HOW TO GROW. Plant in spring or early fall, setting plants 12 to 18 inches apart. Mix peat moss or well-rotted leaf mold into the soil about 6 inches deep. New plants may be had easily by dividing old ones in spring or by taking cuttings at any time.

## W
WALL ROCKCRESS  See *Arabis*
WHITE CLOVER  See *Trifolium*
WILD GINGER  See *Asarum*
WILTON CARPET JUNIPER  See *Juniperus*
WOOLLY BETONY  See *Stachys*
WOOLLY YARROW  See *Achillea*

## X
### XANTHORHIZA
*X. simplicissima* (yellowroot)

A deciduous shrub that grows about 2 feet tall, yellowroot has branchless yellow stems of nearly uniform height, topped with crowns of dark green celerylike foliage that turns a lovely golden orange in fall before dying to the ground. In early spring, plants bear sprays of tiny brownish purple flowers. Yellowroot spreads rapidly by creeping underground stems.

USES. This species is especially suitable for wild or naturalistic gardens, particularly in low, wettish spots where few other plants will thrive. Soil enriched with peat moss is ideal, but plants will do well in most soils in Zones 4-10 if they have moisture and sun or light shade.

HOW TO GROW. Plant in spring or fall, setting plants 18 to 24 inches apart. New plants are most easily started by dividing old ones in early spring before growth starts.

## Y
YELLOWROOT  See *Xanthorhiza*
YERBA BUENA  See *Micromeria*
YEW, ENGLISH  See *Taxus*

*For growing zones, see map on page 151.*

**CREEPING SPEEDWELL**
*Veronica repens*

**COMMON PERIWINKLE**
*Vinca minor*

**YELLOWROOT**
*Xanthorhiza simplicissima*

# Appendix

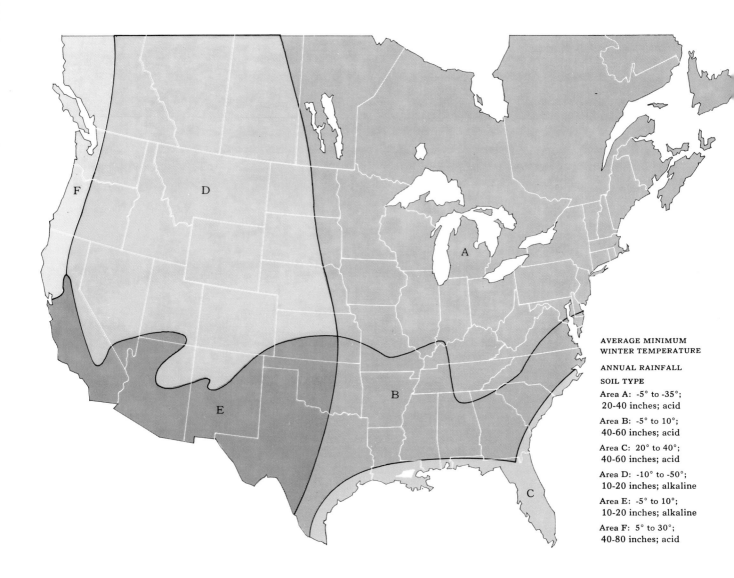

AVERAGE MINIMUM
WINTER TEMPERATURE

ANNUAL RAINFALL

SOIL TYPE

Area A: -5° to -35°;
20-40 inches; acid

Area B: -5° to 10°;
40-60 inches; acid

Area C: 20° to 40°;
40-60 inches; acid

Area D: -10° to -50°;
10-20 inches; alkaline

Area E: -5° to 10°;
10-20 inches; alkaline

Area F: 5° to 30°;
40-80 inches; acid

## Where the grass is greener

Choosing the right grass for the right area can make the difference between having a smooth green carpet or a scruffy patch that will never become a healthy lawn *(Chapter 1)*. The map above divides North America into six areas, each hospitable to different grasses. These divisions are based on three factors: minimum winter temperatures, rainfall and the acidity or alkalinity of the soil. Each grass described in the encyclopedia is given a letter or letters corresponding to those on the map, to indicate the recommended areas for planting.

In general, hardy grasses (blues, bents and fescues) thrive in the three cool northern areas (A, D and F). But they need plenty of water, so they should be irrigated in Area D, where native gramas and buffalo grass do well with what nature offers. Such grasses as Bermuda and Zoysia are suited to Areas B, C and E. But St. Augustine grass, which does well in C, should be planted only in the southern sectors of B and E. In southern California a strip of coast and the Imperial Valley near Arizona are as warm as southern Florida (Zone 10 on the temperature map on the facing page).

Soil is mostly acid in the East and alkaline in the West. But in Area F alkalinity extends only as far as the Cascade Range. Most grasses prefer slightly acid soil, although gramas and buffalo grass do well in alkaline soil *(Chapters 2 and 5)*.

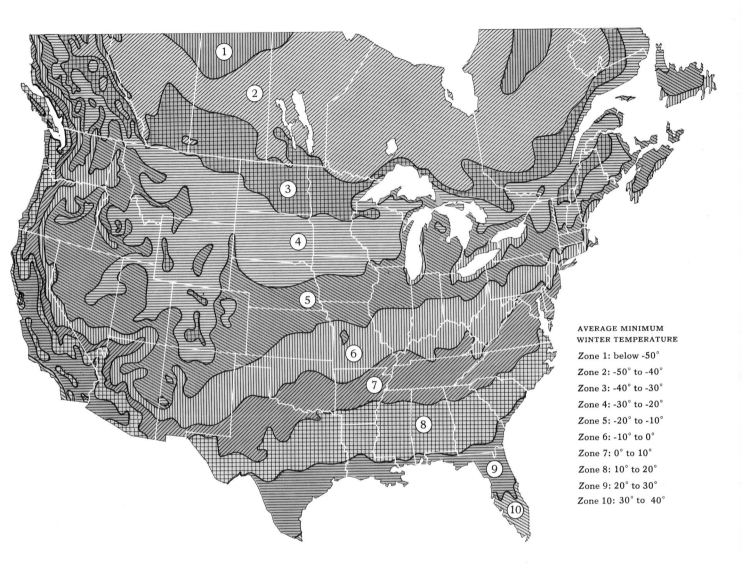

AVERAGE MINIMUM
WINTER TEMPERATURE

Zone 1: below -50°

Zone 2: -50° to -40°

Zone 3: -40° to -30°

Zone 4: -30° to -20°

Zone 5: -20° to -10°

Zone 6: -10° to 0°

Zone 7: 0° to 10°

Zone 8: 10° to 20°

Zone 9: 20° to 30°

Zone 10: 30° to 40°

# Where the ground covers will survive

Winter hardiness is the essential consideration in selecting a ground cover. A ground cover can be saved by feeding if the soil is poor, or by watering if the ground is too dry, but nothing can save it if it is too delicate for the low temperatures that prevail in the area where it has been planted.

The map above, based on official United States and Canadian weather data, divides North America into numbered zones according to average minimum winter temperatures. The ground covers described in this book are given zone numbers corresponding to those on the map, to indicate where each ground cover will survive. In Zone 2, for instance, where the thermometer hits −40° to

−50° F., moss sandwort flourishes; but tawny day lilies or stonecrop should not be planted north of Zone 3. Since most ground covers do well in areas to the south of their northernmost range—though a few have southern limits, too—the variety of choices increases as the zone numbers rise to the semitropical Zone 10, where ground can be covered with a carpet of Crimson Jewel bougainvillea.

More than the latitude affects the climate. Mountains contribute to the southward bulges of Zones 4 and 6; seashores benefit from the ocean's slower cooling. And everywhere there are exposed or sheltered climate islands, which are harsher or milder than the surrounding zones.

# Characteristics of 88 ground covers

| | HEIGHT | | | | LIGHT AND SOIL REQUIREMENTS | | | | | TYPE OF FOLIAGE | | | FOLIAGE COLOR | | | | USES | | | | | | OTHER | |
|---|---|---|---|---|---|---|---|---|---|---|---|---|---|---|---|---|---|---|---|---|---|---|---|---|
| | Less than 6" | 6" to 12" | 12" to 18" | More than 18" | Sun | Shade | Acid Soil | Moist Soil | Dry Soil | Evergreen | Semievergreen | Deciduous | Green | Dark green | Blue green | Gray green | Slopes | Under trees and shrubs | Accents | Rock pockets | Flowers | Fruits | Rapid Growth | Easy Maintenance |
| ACHILLEA TOMENTOSA (woolly yarrow) | ● | | | | ● | | | ● | ● | ● | | | | | | ● | | | ● | ● | | | ● | ● |
| AEGOPODIUM PODAGRARIA VARIEGATUM (silveredge goutweed) | | ● | | | ● | ● | | | | | ● | | | | | ● | | ● | ● | ● | | | ● | ● |
| AJUGA REPTANS (bugleweed) | ● | | | | ● | ● | ● | | | ● | | | | ● | | | | | ● | | ● | | | ● |
| AKEBIA QUINATA (five-leaf akebia) | | ● | | | ● | | | | | ● | | ● | | | | ● | ● | | | | | | ● | ● |
| ANTHEMIS NOBILIS (chamomile) | ● | ● | | | ● | | | | ● | | | | ● | | | | | | ● | | ● | | ● | ● |
| ARABIS ALBIDA (wall rockcress) | ● | | | | ● | | | | ● | | | | | ● | | | | | ● | ● | ● | | | ● |
| ARCTOSTAPHYLOS UVA-URSI (bearberry) | | ● | | | ● | | | | | ● | | | | ● | | ● | | | | ● | ● | ● | | |
| ARMERIA MARITIMA (common thrift) | ● | ● | | | ● | | | | | | | | | ● | | | | | ● | ● | ● | | | |
| ARTEMISIA SCHMIDTIANA 'SILVER MOUND' (Silver Mound artemisia) | | | ● | | ● | | | | | | ● | | | | | ● | | | ● | | | | ● | ● |
| ASARUM CAUDATUM (British Columbia wild ginger) | | ● | | | | ● | ● | ● | | ● | | | ● | | | | | ● | | | | | | ● |
| ASPARAGUS SPRENGERII (Sprenger asparagus) | | ● | ● | ● | | | | | ● | | | | ● | | | | | | | | ● | | ● | ● |
| ASPERULA ODORATA (woodruff) | | ● | | | | ● | ● | ● | | | | ● | ● | | | | | ● | | | ● | | ● | ● |
| BACCHARIS PILULARIS (coyote bush) | | ● | ● | ● | ● | | | | ● | ● | | | ● | | | | ● | | | | | | ● | ● |
| BERGENIA CRASSIFOLIA (leather bergenia) | | ● | | | | ● | ● | | | ● | | | | ● | | | | | ● | | ● | | | |
| BOUGAINVILLEA 'CRIMSON JEWEL' (Crimson Jewel bougainvillea) | | | ● | ● | ● | | | | | ● | ● | | | | | ● | | | ● | | ● | | | |
| CALLUNA VULGARIS (Scotch heather) | ● | ● | ● | ● | ● | | ● | | | ● | | | | ● | | ● | | | ● | | ● | | | ● |
| CAMPANULA POSCHARSKYANA (Poscharsky bellflower) | | ● | ● | | ● | ● | | ● | | ● | | | ● | | | | | | ● | | ● | | ● | |
| CARISSA MACROCARPA 'GREEN CARPET' (Green Carpet Natal plum) | | | ● | | ● | | | | | ● | | | | | ● | | | | ● | | | ● | | |
| CARPOBROTUS EDULIS (Hottentot fig) | ● | | | | ● | | | | ● | ● | | | | | ● | ● | | | ● | | ● | | ● | ● |
| CEANOTHUS GRISEUS HORIZONTALIS (Carmel creeper) | | | ● | ● | ● | | | | ● | ● | | | | | ● | | ● | | | | | | ● | |
| CERASTIUM TOMENTOSUM (snow-in-summer) | ● | | | | ● | | | | ● | | | | | | | ● | | | ● | | ● | | ● | ● |
| CERATOSTIGMA PLUMBAGINOIDES (leadwort) | | ● | | | ● | | | | ● | | | ● | ● | | | | | | ● | | ● | | | ● |
| COMPTONIA PEREGRINA (sweet fern) | | | ● | ● | ● | | ● | | ● | | | ● | ● | | | ● | | | | | | | ● | ● |
| CONVALLARIA MAJALIS (lily of the valley) | | ● | | | | ● | | ● | | | | ● | ● | | | | | ● | | | ● | | | ● |
| CONVOLVULUS MAURITANICUS (ground morning glory) | | ● | ● | ● | ● | | | ● | ● | | | | | | ● | ● | | | ● | | ● | | ● | |
| CORONILLA VARIA (crown vetch) | | ● | ● | | ● | | | | ● | | | ● | ● | | | | ● | | | | ● | | ● | |
| COTONEASTER DAMMERI (bearberry cotoneaster) | | ● | | | ● | | | | ● | | | | ● | | | ● | | | ● | | ● | ● | ● | |
| COTULA SQUALIDA (New Zealand brass buttons) | ● | | | | ● | | ● | | ● | | | ● | ● | | | | | | | | ● | | ● | ● |
| CYTISUS KEWENSIS (Kew broom) | ● | | | | ● | | | | | ● | ● | | ● | | | | ● | | | | ● | | ● | |
| DIANTHUS DELTOIDES (maiden pink) | | ● | | | ● | | | | ● | | | | | ● | | | | | ● | ● | ● | | | ● |
| DICHONDRA REPENS (dichondra) | ● | | | | ● | ● | | ● | | | | | | ● | | | ● | ● | ● | | | | | ● |
| DROSANTHEMUM HISPIDUM (rosea ice plant) | | ● | | | ● | | | | ● | | | | | | ● | ● | | | ● | | ● | | ● | ● |
| DUCHESNEA INDICA (Indian strawberry) | ● | | | | ● | | | ● | | | | ● | ● | | | | | ● | | | ● | ● | ● | ● |
| EPIMEDIUM GRANDIFLORUM (epimedium) | | ● | | | | ● | ● | | | | ● | | ● | | | | | ● | ● | | ● | | | ● |
| ERICA CARNEA (spring heath) | | ● | | | ● | ● | ● | | | ● | | | ● | | | ● | | | ● | | ● | | | ● |
| EUONYMUS FORTUNEI COLORATUS (purple winter creeper) | ● | | | | ● | | | | | ● | | | ● | | | ● | ● | | | | | | ● | ● |
| EUPHORBIA CYPARISSIAS (cypress spurge) | ● | ● | ● | | ● | | | | ● | | | ● | | | ● | ● | | | | | ● | | ● | ● |
| FERN: WOODSIA ILVENSIS (rusty woodsia) | ● | | | | | ● | ● | | ● | | | ● | ● | | | | | | | ● | | | | ● |
| FESTUCA OVINA GLAUCA (blue fescue) | ● | ● | | | ● | | | ● | | | | | | | ● | | | | ● | | | | ● | |
| FORSYTHIA 'ARNOLD DWARF' (Arnold Dwarf forsythia) | | | ● | ● | ● | | | | | | | ● | ● | | | | ● | | | | ● | | ● | |
| FRAGARIA CHILOENSIS (sand strawberry) | | ● | | | ● | | | | ● | ● | | | ● | | | | | ● | | | ● | ● | ● | ● |
| GALAX APHYLLA (galax) | ● | ● | | | | ● | ● | ● | | ● | | | ● | | | | | ● | | | ● | | | ● |
| GAZANIA UNIFLORA (trailing gazania) | ● | | | | ● | | | | ● | | ● | ● | ● | | | ● | | | ● | | ● | | ● | ● |
| HEDERA CANARIENSIS (Algerian ivy) | | ● | | | ● | ● | ● | | ● | ● | | | ● | | | | ● | ● | ● | | | | ● | ● |

152

Plant characteristics reference chart.

| | HEIGHT | | | | LIGHT AND SOIL REQUIREMENTS | | | | | TYPE OF FOLIAGE | | | FOLIAGE COLOR | | | | USES | | | | | | OTHER | |
|---|---|---|---|---|---|---|---|---|---|---|---|---|---|---|---|---|---|---|---|---|---|---|---|---|
| | Less than 6″ | 6″ to 12″ | 12″ to 18″ | More than 18″ | Sun | Shade | Acid Soil | Moist Soil | Dry Soil | Evergreen | Semievergreen | Deciduous | Green | Dark green | Blue green | Gray green | Slopes | Under trees and shrubs | Accents | Rock pockets | Flowers | Fruits | Rapid Growth | Easy Maintenance |
| HEDERA HELIX (English ivy) | | • | | | • | • | | • | | • | | | | • | | | • | | • | | | | • | • |
| HELIANTHEMUM NUMMULARIUM (sun rose) | | • | | | • | | | | • | | • | | | • | | | | | • | • | | | | • |
| HELXINE SOLEIROLII (baby's tears) | • | | | | | • | | • | | • | | • | | • | | | | • | • | | | | • | • |
| HEMEROCALLIS FULVA 'KWANSO' (Kwanso tawny day lily) | | | | • | | • | • | | | | • | • | • | | | | | | • | | • | | • | • |
| HYPERICUM CALYCINUM (Aaronsbeard St.-John's-wort) | | • | | | • | | | | • | | | • | | • | | • | | | • | | • | | | • |
| IBERIS SEMPERVIRENS (evergreen candytuft) | | • | | | • | | | • | | • | | | | • | | | | | • | | • | | | • |
| JUNIPERUS HORIZONTALIS WILTONII (Wilton carpet juniper) | • | | | | • | | | | • | | | | | | • | | • | | • | | | | | • |
| LAMPRANTHUS SPECTABILIS (trailing ice plant) | | • | | | • | | | | • | | | | | • | • | | | | • | | • | | • | • |
| LANTANA SELLOVIANA (trailing lantana) | | | • | • | • | | | | • | | | | | • | | • | | | | • | | • | | |
| LIRIOPE SPICATA (creeping lily-turf) | | • | | | • | • | | | | • | | | | • | | | | | • | | • | • | | • |
| LOTUS BERTHOLETII (parrot's beak) | • | | | | • | | | • | • | | | | | • | • | | | | • | | • | | • | • |
| LOTUS CORNICULATUS (bird's-foot trefoil) | • | | | | • | | | | • | • | • | | | • | | | | | • | | • | | | • |
| LYSIMACHIA NUMMULARIA (moneywort) | • | | | | | • | | • | | • | | | | • | | | | | • | | • | | | • |
| MAHONIA REPENS (dwarf holly grape) | | • | | | • | • | | • | | • | | | | • | | • | | | • | | • | • | • | • |
| MAZUS REPTANS (creeping mazus) | • | | | | • | | | • | | | • | | | • | | | | | • | • | • | | | • |
| MENTHA REQUIENII (Corsican mint) | • | | | | • | | | • | | | • | | • | | | | | • | • | • | | | | • |
| MICROMERIA CHAMISSONIS (yerba buena) | • | | | | • | | | • | • | | | | | • | | | | • | • | | • | | | • |
| MINUARTIA VERNA CAESPITOSA (moss sandwort) | • | | | | • | | • | • | | | • | | • | | | | • | • | | | • | | | • |
| MYOSOTIS SCORPIOIDES SEMPERFLORENS (forget-me-not) | | • | • | | | • | • | | | • | • | | | • | | | | • | | | • | | • | • |
| NEPETA MUSSINII (mauve catmint) | | • | | | • | | | | | • | | | | • | | • | | | • | | • | | • | • |
| OPHIOPOGON JAPONICUS (dwarf lily-turf) | • | • | | | • | • | | • | | • | | • | | • | | | • | | | • | | | • |
| OSTEOSPERMUM FRUTICOSUM (trailing African daisy) | | • | • | • | • | | | | • | | | | | • | | • | | | • | | • | | • | |
| PACHISTIMA CANBYI (Canby pachistima) | | • | • | | • | • | • | • | | | • | | | • | | | | • | | | • | | | • |
| PACHYSANDRA TERMINALIS (Japanese pachysandra) | | • | | | | • | • | • | | • | | | | • | | | • | • | • | | | | | • |
| PARTHENOCISSUS QUINQUEFOLIA (Virginia creeper) | | | | • | • | • | | | • | | • | • | | | | • | | | • | | | • | • | |
| PELARGONIUM PELTATUM (ivy geranium) | | | | • | • | | | • | • | | | | | • | | | | | • | | • | | • | |
| PHLOX SUBULATA (moss phlox) | • | | | | • | | | | • | • | | | | • | | | | | • | • | • | | | • |
| PYRACANTHA KOIDZUMI 'SANTA CRUZ PROSTRATA' (Santa Cruz fire thorn) | | | • | • | • | | | | • | • | | | | • | | | • | | • | | • | • | | • |
| ROSA 'MAX GRAF' (Max Graf rose) | | | • | • | • | | | | | | • | | | • | | • | | | • | | • | | | • |
| ROSA WICHURAIANA (memorial rose) | | • | | | • | | | | | • | | | | • | | • | | | • | | • | | • | • |
| ROSMARINUS OFFICINALIS PROSTRATUS (creeping rosemary) | | | • | • | • | | | | • | • | | | | • | | • | | | • | | • | | • | • |
| SAGINA SUBULATA (Corsican pearlwort) | • | | | | • | • | | • | | | | | | • | | | | | • | • | • | | | • |
| SANTOLINA CHAMAECYPARISSUS (lavender cotton) | | | • | • | • | | | | • | | | | | • | | | | • | | | • | | | • |
| SAXIFRAGA STOLONIFERA (strawberry geranium) | • | | | | | • | | • | | • | | | | • | | | | | • | | • | | | • |
| SEDUM ALBUM (white stonecrop) | • | | | | • | | | • | • | • | | | • | | | | | • | • | | • | | | • |
| STACHYS OLYMPICA (lamb's ears) | | • | | | • | | | | • | | • | | | | • | • | | | • | | | | | • |
| TAXUS BACCATA REPANDENS (spreading English yew) | • | | | | • | • | • | | • | • | | | | • | | | • | | | • | | | | • |
| TEUCRIUM CHAMAEDRYS (germander) | | • | | | • | | | | • | • | | | | • | | | | | • | | • | | | • |
| THYMUS SERPYLLUM (wild thyme) | • | | | | • | | | | • | | • | | | • | | | | | • | | • | | • | • |
| TRACHELOSPERMUM JASMINOIDES (star jasmine) | | • | • | • | • | • | | • | | • | | | | • | | | • | | • | | • | | • | • |
| TRIFOLIUM REPENS (white clover) | • | | | | • | | | • | | | • | • | | • | | | | | • | | • | | • | • |
| VERONICA REPENS (creeping speedwell) | • | | | | • | | | | • | | | | | • | | | | | • | | • | | • | • |
| VINCA MINOR (common periwinkle) | • | | | • | | • | | • | | • | | | | • | | • | | • | • | | • | | • | • |
| XANTHORHIZA SIMPLICISSIMA (yellowroot) | | | • | • | | • | | • | | | | • | • | | | | • | | • | | • | | • | • |

153

# Picture Credits

The sources for the illustrations that appear in this book are listed below. Credits for the pictures from left to right are separated by semicolons, from top to bottom by dashes. Cover—Ralph Crane. 4—Keith Martin courtesy James Underwood Crockett; Leonard Wolfe. 6—Dean Brown. 11 through 14—Copied by Paulus Leeser from *The Gardeners' Chronicle and Agricultural Gazette,* courtesy Brooklyn Botanic Garden Library. 18—Drawing by Vincent Lewis. 23 —George Kido. 24,25—Nicholas Foster. 26,27—Ralph Crane. 28,29—Dean Brown. 30,31,32—Nicholas Foster. 33 —Marcia Kay Keegan. 34,35—Robert Walch. 36—Dean Brown. 37—Robert Walch; Humphrey Sutton. 38—Dean Brown; Nicholas Foster. 39—Nicholas Foster; Dean Brown. 40,41—Robert Walch. 42—Douglas Faulkner. 45,51,52,54, 55,58,60,61,62—Drawings by Vincent Lewis. 66—Drawings by Davis Meltzer. 70 through 73—Illustrations by Allianora Rosse. 75—Ken Kay. 76—Chevron Chemical Co.—Ken Kay (2). 77,78—Ken Kay. 79—Chevron Chemical Co.—Ken Kay (2). 80—Dr. Henry Indyk. 81,82—Ken Kay. 83— Photo Service, Cornell University, Ithaca, N.Y., except center left U.S. Department of Agriculture. 84—Ryan Equipment Co. 86,88,89,93,97,98,99,101,106,108,111—Drawings by Vincent Lewis. 102—Nicolas de Larmessin, Prints Division, The New York Public Library, Astor, Lenox and Tilden Foundations. 113 to 149—Illustrations by Allianora Rosse. 150,151—Maps by Adolph E. Brotman.

# Acknowledgments

For their help in the preparation of this book, the editors wish to thank the following: F. Raymond Brush, Executive Secretary, American Association of Nurserymen, Washington, D.C.; Dr. Glenn W. Burton, Agricultural Research Service, U.S. Department of Agriculture, Tifton, Georgia; Prof. John F. Cornman, Department of Ornamental Horticulture, College of Agriculture, Cornell University, Ithaca, N.Y.; Mr. and Mrs. Robert Coryell, Lake San Marcos, Calif.; Mrs. Edith Crockett, Librarian, Horticultural Society of New York, New York City; Mrs. Muriel C. Crossman, Librarian, Massachusetts Horticultural Society, Boston, Mass.; Elmco Distributors, Inc., Parsippany, N.J.; Mr. and Mrs. Edward Fargo Jr., Santa Barbara, Calif.; Mr. and Mrs. Clinton Gerlach, Mr. and Mrs. Lawrence Goodman and Dr. and Mrs. A. Fletcher Hall, Pacific Palisades, Calif.; Miss Elizabeth Hall, Senior Librarian, Horticultural Society of New York, New York City; Allen C. Haskell, New Bedford, Mass.; Mr. and Mrs. John Valle Janes, St. Louis, Mo.; Gordon E. Jones, Planting Fields Arboretum, Oyster Bay, N.Y.; Dr. F. V. Juska, Agricultural Research Service, Plant Industry Station, U.S. Department of Agriculture, Beltsville, Md.; Dr. Howard N. Lafever, Department of Agronomy, Ohio Agricultural Research and Development Center, Wooster, Ohio; Mark Marko, Advertising Manager, Monrovia Nursery Co., Azusa, Calif.; Millburn Grinding Shop, Inc., Short Hills, N.J.; James Ousley Sr., Ousley Sod Co., Pompano Beach, Fla.; Pierson's Mill Co., Maplewood, N.J.; Mr. and Mrs. Alfred Saxdel, Shaw Gardens, St. Louis, Mo.; Dr. Robert Schery, Director, The Lawn Institute, Marysville, Ohio; George H. Spalding, Botanical Information Consultant, Los Angeles State and County Arboretum, Los Angeles, Calif.; Mr. and Mrs. J. H. Thompson, Bel Air, Calif.; Robert Titus, Planting Fields Arboretum, Oyster Bay, N.Y.; Dr. and Mrs. John Torrens, Albuquerque, N.M.; David S. Verity, Botanist, UCLA Botanical Garden, UCLA, Westwood, Calif.; Dr. Donald V. Waddington, Department of Agronomy, Penn State University, University Park, Pa.; Mrs. Sonia Wedge, Reference Librarian, New York Botanical Garden Library, N.Y.

# Bibliography

### LAWNS

Brooklyn Botanic Garden Handbook, *Lawns.* Brooklyn Botanic Garden, 1963.

Dawson, R. B., *Practical Lawn Craft.* Crosby Lockwood and Son, Ltd., 1968.

Dittmer, Howard J., *Lawn Problems of the Southwest.* The University of New Mexico Press, 1950.

Gould, Dr. Frank W., *Grass Systematics.* McGraw-Hill, 1968.

Hanson, A. and F. V. Juska, eds., *Turfgrass Science.* The American Society of Agronomy, Inc., 1969.

Lemmon, Kenneth, *The Covered Garden.* Dufour Editions, 1963.

Montgomery, F. H., *Weeds of the Northern United States and Canada.* Frederick Warne and Co., Inc., 1964.

Musser, H. Burton, *Turf Management.* McGraw-Hill, 1962.

Rockwell, F. F. and Esther C. Grayson, *The Complete Book of Lawns.* The American Garden Guild and Doubleday & Company, Inc., 1956.

Schery, Robert W., *The Lawn Book.* The Macmillan Company, 1961.

Sprague, Howard B., *Turfgrass Management Handbook.* The Interstate Publishing Co., 1970.

Sunset Books, *Lawns and Ground Covers.* Lane Books, 1964.

Voykin, Paul, *A Perfect Lawn the Easy Way.* Rand McNally and Co., 1969.

### GROUND COVERS

Atkinson, Robert E., *A Complete Book of Ground Covers.* David McKay Co., Inc., 1970.

Brooklyn Botanic Garden Handbook, *Vines and Groundcovers.* Brooklyn Botanic Garden, 1954.

Fish, Margery, *Ground Cover Plants.* David and Charles (Publishers) Ltd., 1970.

Foley, Daniel J., *Ground Covers for Easier Gardening.* The Chilton Co., 1961.

Wyman, Donald, *Ground Cover Plants.* The Macmillan Company, 1970.

# Index

*Numerals in italics indicate an illustration of the subject mentioned*

PRINTED IN U.S.A.